# China in Transformation

# China in Transformation

Edited by Tu Wei-ming

Harvard University Press
Cambridge, Massachusetts
London, England
1994

First Harvard University Press paperback edition, 1994

*Library of Congress Cataloging-in-Publication Data*

China in transformation / edited by Tu Wei-ming.
  p.  cm.
  ISBN 0-674-11754-9 (alk. paper) (pbk.)
  1. China—Civilization—1976–  I. Tu, Wei-ming.
DS779.23.C4595  1994         93-42866
951.05'7—dc20             CIP

# Contents

China in Transformation

# Preface

I F 1989 HAS TAUGHT THE WORLD ANYTHING, it is the hazard of prophecy. 1992 did not turn out to be the year individuals in Brussels or Washington expected it to be at the time of its fair beginnings. 1993 will bring yet other surprises, perhaps more agreeable ones, but almost certainly striking new evidences of the difficulties of making predictions. An issue of *Dædalus* entitled "China in Transformation" must therefore not be read as one more exercise in that hazardous game called "futures." There is no suggestion in this volume that we know how China will develop in the years immediately ahead, that we are prepared to guess what it will look like in the year 2000.

Our enterprise is in fact a more modest one. It is based on the simple proposition that China, like much of the rest of the world, is today being looked at in quite new ways. Inquiry that would have been impossible during much of the period after World War II, particularly in societies dominated by regimes hostile to every sort of close scrutiny, is today at last conceivable. This is not to say that everything can now be studied, that archives of every kind are available for scholarly investigation. Still, there is a freedom of inquiry today that has not existed for a very long time.

Because of what has happened in the Soviet Union, because of what has happened to Marxism more generally in the world, it is not too much to say that "tectonic forces" are indeed at work, that yesterday's seeming stability has been very largely lost, and not only because of Tiananmen Square.

In the case of China, this encourages scholarship that dwells in all sorts of novel ways on conditions—political, social, economic, intellectual, and cultural—that affect Chinese men and women in the People's Republic, but also in those other societies where Chinese-speaking peoples are in a majority.

Not the least of the accomplishments of this issue is to make the reader aware that communism did not simply erase the past. Indeed, the past lives on in China, muted and transformed in certain ways, vital and persistent in others. A study of the Chinese experience may shed light on what is happening in other societies where there has been even more drastic and deliberate political change. It may be the supreme irony of this last decade of the twentieth century that we find ourselves asking questions about the vitality of every kind of tradition in societies where they seemed scarcely relevant only a few years ago, given the *tabula rasa* that Marxism and Communist Party rule had purportedly created.

To suggest that China may provide insights into developments in countries like Russia—which is not to say that the situations are at all analogous—and indeed into the role of custom and belief in the world outside Asia, may seem an exaggerated claim for an issue of *Dædalus* that aims to be modest. Yet, some such possibility may impress those prepared to look at the many faces of China revealed in this issue, who see that modernity takes many forms, that memory, repressed for a time, may reassert itself, that myth, the invention of individuals and collectivities, may be more powerful than prosaic fact. The Chinese experience has much to teach us about that once imagined residue of history called nationalism.

A great debt is owed to the Dialogue of Civilizations Project in the Program for Cultural Studies at the East-West Center, whose help has been invaluable to us. This issue was conceived by Professor Tu Wei-ming. His leadership has been crucial in every phase of its development.

Stephen R. Graubard

# Introduction: Cultural Perspectives

SINCE THE PUBLICATION OF THE special *Dædalus* issue on "The Living Tree: The Changing Meaning of Being Chinese Today" in the spring of 1991, the Union of the Soviet Socialist Republics has disintegrated, Yugoslavia and Czechoslovakia as unified states have disappeared from the map, and the Cold War has abruptly ended. The socialist camp, it appeared, was about to begin the inevitable transition to democratic polity and market economy, assuring the triumph of modern Western and, by implication, American values. Indeed, the jubilation following the collapse of the Berlin Wall in 1989 and the unification of Germany, the euphoria after the seemingly easy military solution to the Gulf War in February 1991, not to mention Russia's nerve-racking August Revolution some months later, evoked hopeful images of an integrated Europe and even sensations of a true age of *Pax Americana*.

Yet, the anticipation of the emergence of a new world order led by the United States and defined in modern Western terms proved unrealistic, if not simpleminded. Instead, the former Soviet states and Moscow's former satellites struggle, with a profound sense of inadequacy and humiliation, to survive economically and redefine themselves politically; primordial ties, having evoked powerful ethnic, linguistic, religious, and territorial sentiments, unleash dark forces of genocidal conflicts in South Asia, East Africa, and Eastern Europe, and governments in leading democracies (e.g., Canada, France, Germany, Italy, and Japan) suffer from major public distrust.

XI

Totally unexpected, however, despite Japan's economic recession, is the "Sinic world's"[1] unprecedented dynamism in democratization and marketization. Singapore, South Korea, and Taiwan all successfully conducted national elections in 1992, clearly indicating that democracy in Confucian societies is not only possible but also practicable. The most surprising story is perhaps the economic vibrancy of the coastal areas of mainland China. Already the balance of payments in Sino-American trade was more than 18 billion dollars in China's favor in 1992. If we also consider China's trade with the European Economic Community and other Asian markets (including Taiwan), in economic terms, the sleeping giant is wide awake. As the Four Mini-Dragons (South Korea, Taiwan, Hong Kong, and Singapore) continue to lead the world in growth and development and prompt the upsurge of economic vitality in the Association of Southeast Asian Nations (ASEAN) countries (notably Malaysia, Thailand, and Indonesia) and Vietnam, the Asia-Pacific region is challenging the supremacy of North America and Western Europe in global economic strength. Will the People's Republic of China (PRC) emerge as an unabashed mercantilist nation?[2] Moreover, if the "many Chinas" (an expression none of the political entities in Beijing, Hong Kong, Taipei, or Singapore would embrace) become a new economic superpower, what are the political and cultural implications for the Asia-Pacific region as a whole, for the United States, and for the rest of the world?

The volatile economic situation renders political and cultural perspectives on China shifting and indeterminate. We can no longer assume that agriculture defines the nature of the Chinese economy, that authoritarianism defines the Chinese polity, and that family-centered hierarchy defines Chinese society. The economic dynamism energized by the village, cooperative, and individual enterprises throughout mainland China (which is now estimated to provide roughly 30 percent of the gross domestic product of the entire country)[3] compels us to rethink not only the distinction between private and public spheres, which has always been problematical in the Chinese case, but also the interaction between state and society. Similarly, the nature of Chinese politics is so amorphous that the term authoritarianism or "soft" authoritarianism is simply too restrictive to accommodate the full range of its ideological underpinnings and its modus operandi. The Chinese state can be totalitarian in exercising its military control, as in the case of the Tiananmen tragedy; yet, it can also be anarchistic in dealing with local initiatives, fundamentally challenging, in theory and practice, the authority at the center. Indeed, Chinese society may be hierarchically stratified, but it is also enormously fluid, allowing information, ideas, values, and goods to flow incessantly from one stratum to another.

This volume, the result of a joint venture involving a variety of disciplines in Chinese studies—philosophy, history, literature, law, sociology, anthropology, political science, and religion—intends to offer complementary cultural perspectives on China in transformation. The purpose is neither to judge nor to predict, but to *understand*. Our essays, preliminary and tentative but informed by our professional callings, are engaged and often agonized reflections. We try to understand not as detached outside observers but as deeply concerned students of China, wishing to enlarge the discourse through our personal but open-minded approaches. While we do not subscribe to the naïve belief that there are immutable objective truths about China, we cherish the hope that our quest for a better appreciation of the many faces of China will deepen our own cultural sensitivities and bring some understanding to China, not only as an economic presence or a political reality, but also as a cultural universe.

We have chosen, based on our competence and dictated by our limitations, a few salient features of the seemingly restless landscape of the Sinic world. All of them, we believe, have long-term relevance and far-reaching implications for the People's Republic of China as a modernizing state and for the world.

China is at an ideological crossroads, confronting a profound identity crisis which will fundamentally restructure her national character. The meaning of being Chinese is forever changing and China as a civilization-state has been undergoing an unprecedented transmutation in recent decades. The current situation, however, will have a lasting impact far beyond her own borders. Since the Opium War in the mid-nineteenth century and the subsequent political upheavals, economic collapses, social disintegration, and intellectual effervescence in China, every Chinese has been engulfed in an ocean of suffering, but this has had only limited effects on the outside world. To the industrialized societies, China's failure to become an inexhaustible market might have been a disappointment, but, as far as their forms of life are concerned, China was totally irrelevant, at most a sleeping lion or, to use an indigenous Chinese expression, a "hidden dragon."

China is now roaring for recognition. Communism, the national glue for more than forty years, is gradually losing its grip. Among dissident intellectuals as well as government officials, the fear of social disintegration, with disastrous consequences for China's neighbors including Russia, Japan, India, Vietnam, and the Asia-Pacific region, has greatly intensified. The government's deliberate effort to promote and use patriotism to unify and hold the nation together, often done in bad faith simply to protect the vested interests of the gerontocracy, may not effectively inspire the commitment and sacrifice of the people. On the other hand, an upsurge in Han nationalist sentiments might provoke ethnic conflicts among the minorities. The Chinese state,

> stretching from Buddhist Tibet to Korean enclaves in Manchuria, from Muslim Xinjiang near Pakistan to Cantonese-speaking Guangdong next to Hong Kong—is arguably the last great multi-ethnic trans-continental empire left in the world. And while its grasp is enormous, its reach is even greater: Chinese claims stretch across seas to encompass Taiwan and the Spratly islands near the Philippines and Malaysia.[4]

The "socialist market economy," an apparent oxymoron, implies the awkward combination of economic promise and political despair. There is no easy way out of the dilemma: xenophobic chauvinism or contentious separatism.

The market economy throughout the country, especially in the coastal area from Guangzhou (Canton), via Shanghai, to Dalian, is reminiscent of Hong Kong and Taiwan two decades ago, giving some credibility to the idea of an East Asian economic developmental model.[5] We should defer technical issues to the economic historian: for instance, is this a new network capitalism modeled after Japan and the Four Mini-Dragons or a variation of Western capitalism?[6] Yet, our superficial impression warns us against any facile application of familiar analogies. We need to develop a new conceptual framework, significantly different from those readily available in English, to make sense of what we observe. Lest we prematurely celebrate the supremacy of classical liberalism and the universal applicability of Adam Smith's "invisible hand," we must note that the dynamism of the Chinese market economy appears to be predicated on tacit acceptance, if not deliberate promotion, of the state as an engine of development. Surely the leadership in Beijing may be either insensitive or even irrelevant to the economic vibrancy in Zhuhai, Shenzhen, Wenzhou, or Tianjin, but the coastal areas would have difficulty sustaining their unprecedented growth without its implicit approval.

The immediate cause of economic dynamism may be due to individual and collective entrepreneurial initiatives. The peculiar economic strength lies in the intricate relationship between state and economy, involving the continuous negotiation and collusion of central, provincial, and local governments. The interdependence of economy and polity is such that the state plays a vitally important role at all levels in removing "structural impediments" to development and building necessary infrastructures for manufacturing industry, commerce, and trade. The mixed pattern is certainly not a socialist planned economy, nor is it a Western capitalist system. The so-called township village enterprise is a new animal, a species in economic development that has yet to be properly defined.[7]

The rise of regional autonomy, as a result of the development of an integrated economic system in the Guangdong-Hong Kong nexus, presents a major challenge to Beijing's leadership, the nationally integrated Communist state, and even China's sovereignty. While we fully recognize regional diversity as a truism in the Chinese polity, we are impressed by the willingness, power, and ingenuity of local leadership, especially in Guangdong province, to assert its independent mindedness. Whether or not the spheres of influence in China have irreversibly shifted from the yellow northwest (central plain) to the blue southeast (coastal areas), the special economic zones along the southern coast have set China's economic development in motion since 1980. The attempted integration of Hong Kong into China's economy may lead to the unintended consequence of transforming China's "one-nation/two-system" into a de facto federation of semi-autonomous economic regions. It is unlikely that Hong Kong will be melted into a monolithic China; on the contrary, in light of the Guangdong-Hong Kong experience, the newly emerging "natural economic territories"—Taiwan/Fujian, Shanghai/Japan, Shandong/South Korea, and, with a stretch of the imagination, Dalian/Vladivostok—may add vibrant color to the future Chinese economic scene.[8]

For China's polity to become sufficiently decentralized to accommodate the centrifugal forces generated by its powerful regions requires a kind of political wisdom and ideological flexibility that the current regime in Beijing apparently lacks. The regions themselves have clearly benefited from the accommodating policies of the center. They seem to know well how to exploit Beijing's lack of self-confidence and the ambiguity of the central directives, without totally undermining the system and thus risking the danger of anarchism or, perhaps worse, warlordism. The scenario of autonomy without disintegration and unity without dictatorship may only be wishful thinking, but Chinese intellectuals of divergent ideological persuasions have been working together to bring forth a rhetoric of assent, despite fierce argumentation and seemingly irreconcilable conflicts of interpretation of China's state of affairs and her best future course of action.

A dominant theme of this new rhetoric is the rejection of the revolutionary ideology characteristic of much of Chinese political culture for the last century. Instead of revolution, the key term is reform. Deeply rooted in Chinese historical consciousness, reform evokes ideas of pragmatism, realism, and gradualism. Above all, it recognizes the constraint of embedded conditions. The unbridled romantic assertion about the fundamental restructuring of Chinese society through violent continuous class struggle is, even to the leftist Maoists, no more than sound and fury. Mao's parable of the Foolish Old Man, who was determined to move the mountain in front of his house (instead of relocating his house), appears silly in the reformist ethos. The revolutionary spirit, as revealed in self-sacrifice and commitment to the infallibility of the Party, has been rejected as a form of unreflected first loyalty: passionate, naïve, and dangerous. A second loyalty, or a higher loyalty, involving a much more sophisticated view of the public good, is not incompatible with local pride and self-interest.[9]

The consensus that the radicalization of twentieth-century Chinese political culture may have been the single most important factor in destabilizing any reform effort and in marginalizing the Chinese intelligentsia, an unprecedented departure from the Chinese political tradition which, though punctuated by dramatic ruptures, exhibits remarkable resiliency and continuity. If the radical revolutionary ideology, in the panoramic view of Chinese political history, was an aberration, why did the Chinese intellectuals persist in its creation and implementation with such indefatigable determination for so long? It is beyond dispute that their active participation enabled radicalism as a national ideology to prevail. As Chinese intellectuals, fueled by nationalist sentiments, voluntarily provided the symbolic power to radicalize polity to such an extent that compromise was condemned as a betrayal in bad faith, they fundamentally undermined their own role and function as political critics.

Mao Zedong may have been a beneficiary of this process but his subversive scheme in the narrative reconstruction of reality since the Yan'an period (1936–1947) precipitated the totalistic iconoclasm of this radicalization which eventually also wrecked the basis of his own authority. The "inversionary ideology" that Mao initiated through the creation of a discourse community and the fastidious praxis of "exegetical bonding"—a deliberate effort to create a set of core texts as "dogmas" for the socialist revolution—more than forty years ago remained a recurring theme in the first reform decade (1978–1988). Often as distant echoes but sometimes as volcanic explosions, Mao's revolutionary radicalism occasionally erupted, reducing years of collaborative effort at reform to debris. The Tiananmen tragedy is a constant reminder that although the central state may not possess the infrastructure to interfere with local governance on a regular basis, its capacity as an engine of destruction, armed with military force and symbolic power, must not be underestimated.

The ubiquitous presence of the state, through mechanisms of control such as the "work-unit" system, may give the impression that the authority of Beijing is felt and feared throughout the country. However, we have found that this newest version of "oriental despotism" is more myth than reality. Surely, the intent of the regime, specifically the Party, to be in full control of the behavior, attitudes, and beliefs of the entire populace is clear. Indeed, repeated attempts have been made to insure the Party's authority at every level of governance. If we refer only to the propaganda machine, politics is in command and the will of the Party leadership is enforced everywhere. In practice, however, the overall administrative structure is porous: the room for deviation, manipulation, and deceit is quite spacious. The discretionary rights that local authorities earn or simply presume are extensive. The looseness of the vertical network, which is supposed to integrate the entire political system, gives saliency to the old Chinese proverb, "the sky is high and the emperor is distant." Besides, recent sociological surveys in China also indicate that the government's role in the daily lives of ordinary people is not at all prominent.

The implications of this seemingly omnipresent state, which paradoxically does not feature prominently in the social and cultural life of the masses, are profound for China's democratic prospects. As the state's role in the economy diminishes, symbolic resources—a sort of social and cultural capital—are being generated by nongovernmental (but not necessarily private) structures such as clan associations, religious organizations, and secret societies. Even when the Party enjoyed high prestige and the official ideology was unrivaled, traditional patterns of networking based on primordial ties with deep roots in kinship, religion, and history played a significant role in urban as well as rural China. The retreat of the state from active involvement in shaping the economic life of the country, either by strategic withdrawal or by forced retirement, opens up an ever-extending space for "civil society."

Admittedly, the concept of civil society which presupposes not only a substantial middle class but also a full-fledged public sphere directly challenging the authority of the political center is not applicable to the Chinese situation today. Yet, since the emerging economism and regionalism have made pluralism possible, the conditions for different voices and alternative structures of power are already present. We may suggest that, as a result, liberalization (bourgeois or socialist) in speech, publication, religion, assembly, and association is inevitable. The voice of the people, cacophonous but loud, must be heard. The government and intelligentsia are ill-advised not to pay special attention to the demands and aspirations of the overwhelming majority of the Chinese population who, primarily farmers rather than peasants, are increasingly vocal in actively defining the Chinese national character.

The heroic deaths of student martyrs in front of the Goddess of Democracy in June 1989, deeply ingrained in our mind's eye, have sparked an enduring hope for China's eventual democratization. Whether or not the Chinese government will fully embrace the United Nations' Declaration of Human Rights, it cannot avoid human rights issues in dealing with both domestic affairs and international politics. The current regime in Beijing may be either woefully insensitive or cynically manipulative in reference to charges of human rights violations, but it can no longer afford (in pure economic terms) to ignore them. The very fact that Beijing is compelled to respond, often awkwardly, to international pressure clearly shows that they have reluctantly acknowledged the rules of the game, even if the intention is simply to criticize them. While the Communist regime in Beijing has vowed never to "redress" the brutally handled Tiananmen case, the calculated policy to tone down the aftermath, far from satisfactory to the participants of the Democracy Movement, has actually embarked on a gradual path of reconciliation. In this light, Deng Xiaoping's southward journey to drum up support for reform in January of 1992, which was credited by the official press as instrumental in reinvigorating the economy, was no more than an official recognition and endorsement of what had been developing informally for years. There is no reason not to entertain the possibility that China is on her way to democracy, via economism and regionalism.

We may wistfully surmise that since the industrial East Asian states—notably Japan, South Korea, Taiwan, and Singapore—have all, in principle, accepted the "democratic method" defined in terms of fair and open elections, no intrinsic cultural factors inhibit mainland China, North Korea, or Vietnam from becoming democratic. As Samuel Huntington notes, "Confucian democracy may be a contradiction in terms, but democracy in a Confucian society need not be."[10] The central question is: What elements in China today are favorable to democracy, and how and under what circumstances can these supersede the undemocratic "habits of the heart" in the cultural tradition?[11]

Nevertheless, the overall assessment of the well-being of the Chinese people and the prospects for China's sustained peace and prosperity is not optimistic but extremely cautionary, if not outright pessimistic. Although demographic and environmental issues loom large in our minds as we focus our attention on the negative side of China's pragmatic strategies for economic growth, we do not undermine China's ability to benefit from the competitive market so that she can become an economic giant. Nor do we doubt her determination to overcome inhibiting factors in development and even her ability to blunt the hard edges of authoritarianism so that she may evolve into a democratic country. Nevertheless, one other issue, not strictly in the domain of political economy, may turn out to be equally challenging. The phenomenon, variously characterized by Chinese intellectuals as well as China watchers overseas as the erosion of the moral fabric of society, a loss of faith in the socialist course, flagging conscience, anomie, or meaninglessness, is widely discussed in the mass media. The point in question deeply worries politicians and intellectuals, but for different reasons. To the Beijing regime, it is primarily a matter of law and order, but to intellectuals, especially those in exile, who are overwhelmed by the depth and magnitude of this crisis, it involves the collapse of social solidarity and the absence of a sense of direction.

Certainly it is not new for the Chinese intelligentsia to engage itself in a frantic search for cultural bearings in the turbulent sea of changes in modern times. The intellectual struggle, charged with strong emotions and fortified by a fierce determination to find a way out of China's backwardness, has been going on for more than a century. Since the founding of the People's Republic, however, the coercive ideology—a Sinicized Marxism in the form of "Mao Zedong Thought"—has for forty years provided a path, an orientation. In retrospect, Mao's proposed approach to China's modernization, with an overdose of cultural self-assertiveness, was no more than nativistic revolutionary romanticism. For at least a generation, however, it was embraced by the best minds in the People's Republic of China as the most thoughtful and practicable strategy to destroy the three mountains—imperialism, feudalism, and bureaucratic capitalism—blocking China's way to socialism. The reform, aiming at releasing the economic vitality of both the rural and urban sectors through the mechanism of the market, exposed not only the naïveté of the Maoist economic strategy but also the vulnerability of the political system. The Party, undermined by the Cultural Revolution, reemerged as a wounded beast anxious about its own survival and exclusively concerned with its own self-interest.

This was the context in which the Chinese intelligentsia, alienated from the Party, rediscovered its own soul for the first time since 1949. The painful, and often agonizing, experience of the Chinese intellectuals, old and young, to retrieve the meaning of their existence as reflective minds of the cultural tradition, critical observers of politics, conscientious voices of the people, and transmitters of social values has been unfolding through the written word as poetry, prose, and essays, in newspapers and journals, and on radio and television. It seems that Chinese intellectuals have already constructed an international forum and some of their works have been acclaimed as the new Chinese conscience by sympathetic critics from North America to Australia.

Prior to the Tiananmen tragedy, the passion of the Chinese intellectuals had been focused on political liberalization. An overwhelming majority of university professors and students as well as educated scholar-officials voluntarily and openly allied themselves with the political leadership committed to reform: Hu Yaobang before January 1987 and Zhao Ziyang afterwards. For two years (1987–1989), the most popular international political figure on Chinese university campuses was Gorbachev. Many college students took Gorbachev's perestroika to be the ideal course of action for the Chinese Communist Party. Nowadays, worries about excessive inflation, rising levels of corruption, and increasing inequality (ironically, similar concerns initially ignited Tiananmen in 1989) seem to outweigh concerns about political lethargy or oppression, let alone demands for liberties and human rights.

The need for political stability, a precondition for steady economic growth, has become an overriding mission of the Beijing leadership. This provides an expedient pretext for the government to relegate political liberalization to the background. Under the banner of patriotism, the Chinese Communist Party is making an all-out effort to rally support for the status quo. The politics of accommodation, with ample precedents in traditional Chinese political culture, has replaced revolutionary mobilization as the modus operandi of the government. Paradoxically, the resources of two of the three aforementioned mountains, Confucian feudalism and bourgeois capitalism, are being tapped to prop up flagging socialism. Traditional symbols are widely exploited to inspire nationalist sentiments. Western methods, such as market mechanisms, advertising, international loans, and commercial taxation, are fully employed to stimulate economic activities. While the possibility of a fruitful interaction among Confucian ethics, liberal democratic ideas, and Marxist humanism is there, it is painfully difficult to put it into practice. Rather, the vicious circle caused by nepotistic networking, conspicuous consumption, and bureaucratic corruption dominates the social landscape, rendering any serious cultural discussion seemingly vacuous and even irrelevant.

Still, the "intellectual effervescence in China"[12] enables us to probe the interior landscape of the life of the mind in the People's Republic of China with a kind of lived concreteness and spiritual immediacy unimaginable a decade ago. The willingness of the most articulate and reflective minds in China to express their deep feelings of guilt and grave doubts about China's future may have been the natural consequence of what Wang Ruoshui identified as "alienation in socialism" in 1980,[13] but the series of intellectual movements in subsequent years clearly show the independent-mindedness of Chinese scholars, students, journalists, and reform-minded officials. This unfolding of a communal critical self-consciousness of the Chinese intelligentsia may be chronicled in a few significant cultural events: the "wounded literature," the discussion of the criteria of truth, the humanist discourse, and the debate on tradition and modernity. They symbolize a cultural vitality unparalleled since the May Fourth Movement in 1919. Beijing's desperate attempts to overcome or to channel the tidal waves of protest against ideological closure were ineffective. The antispiritual pollution of 1983 and the antibourgeois liberalization campaigns of 1986, launched to preserve some measure of ideological purity, were nipped in the bud for lack of popular support. The authentic Chinese intellectual voices have become audible and can no longer be silenced. Nevertheless, and not without a touch of irony, the anxiety of total ideological confusion and the concern over the paucity of cultural resources rather than the excitement over a profusion of spiritual creativity characterize the intellectual ethos.

The perceived vacuum of thought, suggesting a spiritual crisis as well as an ideological crisis, provides fertile ground for the upsurge of folk religious practices, secret societies (notably the *Yiguandao* or "Way of Basic Unity"), Buddhist monastic life, Daoist alchemy, Christian evangelism, and *qigong* (a generic term for a variety of indigenous psychosomatic exercises intended for enhancing one's "vital energy"). It also impels sensitive and conscientious intellectuals to redefine themselves as individuals who are participating members of an evolving, and not merely imagined, community. They are no longer the "knowledgeable elements" of a socialist collectivity; nor can they presume to be the respected scholar-officials of bygone days. They must find their niche in a reconstituted political environment, defining their role and function in reference not only to the workers, farmers, and soldiers but to party functionaries, government officials, entrepreneurs, and merchants. A profound sense of alienation from the political center coupled with a vibrant economy may have empowered some of the intellectuals to search for their own identity independent of wealth and power. A more likely scenario is the commercialization as well as the politicization of the intellectual-scholarly community as a whole.

It is, therefore, most uplifting to witness the emergence of a highly publicized dissenting voice among a small but vocal coterie of intellectuals. Their inner strength, acquired through sacrifice and commitment, exhibits remarkable resiliency. Their reflectiveness, as the result of long and tortuous quests for integrity and authenticity, shows a depth of self-understanding and a sympathetic grasp of the dehumanizing realities around them. They survived the holocaust of the Cultural Revolution with its pain, suffering, and documented cannibalism.[14] Despite innumerable personal hardships and trage-dies, their spirit was not broken and their sense of duty not lost. It is awe-inspiring to observe how they managed to use law as a double-edged sword to challenge the legitimacy of the political regime.

On April 25, 1956, during the golden days of the Chinese Communist regime, Mao Zedong summarized the deliberations of the Politburo on the overall situation of the country in terms of "ten great relationships," which specifically meant the major contradic-tions in Chinese economic and political life:

1. The relationship between industry and agriculture, and be-tween heavy industry and light industry.

2. The relationship between industry in the coastal regions and industry in the interior.

3. The relationship between economic construction and defense construction.

4. The relationship between the state, the units of production, and the individual producers.

5. The relationship between the Center and the regions.

6. The relationship between the Han nationality and the national minorities.

7. The relationship between Party and non-Party.

8. The relationship between revolutionary and counter-revolutionary.

9. The relationship between right and wrong.

10. The relationship between China and other countries.[15]

Mao's grandiose design "to mobilize all positive elements and all available forces in order to build socialism more, faster, better and more economically"[16] collapsed with the Great Leap Forward two years later. Mao's ominous note that "The Communist Party was produced by history, and for that reason the day will inevitably come when it will be destroyed"[17] rings singularly true in light of the "breakdown of communist regimes"[18] since 1989.

Thirty-seven years have elapsed. The ten contradictions, which have all become much more intensified, must now be augmented by a host of other equally, if not more, serious threats: an annual population increase of twenty million, depletion of natural resources, environmental deterioration, a massive rural-urban migration (which may reach a staggering three hundred million by the turn of the century), the delegitimation crisis, political disorder, and social chaos. Nevertheless, predictions abound that China will become an economic giant. Dwight Perkins observed in 1986 that "a fundamental change in Chinese society is underway affecting how people live and, of comparable importance, how they think"[19] and that "the momentum toward reform will be difficult to derail." He concluded with a most encouraging note:

> If this change does take place, one-quarter of the world's population will have moved in the latter half of the twentieth century from a closed, poor, rural, peasant society to a society where living standards are rising rapidly, where the dominant share of the population is increasingly urban and industrial, and where the nations of the region are fully integrated into the international economic system. Few if any events in the last half of the twentieth century are of comparable significance either to the people of East Asia or to the rest of us.[20]

Even in the aftermath of 1989, this prophetic statement remains thought-provoking.

Has China embarked on a path of modernization that is uniquely Chinese? Will China definitely help to transform the Asia-Pacific region into the most powerful economic zone in the world, and, as a civilization-state, endure well into the twentieth-first century as the longest continuous unified "Middle Kingdom" in human history? Since "a strong central government in China is a greater evil for the Chinese peoples than a multiplicity of more or less autonomous 'little Chinas,'"[21] is it not more desirable to see the demise of a monolithic Chinese Communist Party and the disintegration of the central government in Beijing? Indeed, is it not likely that, despite fears attendant on regionalism, the wishful thinking of many Chinas will eventually be realized? On the other hand, since economic growth depends on political stability, will the collapse of the center necessarily bring about disorder and chaos? And, as a result, will a disintegrated China inevitably lead to internecine warfare making a federated Chinese commonwealth totally infeasible? Or, is it conceivable that the weakening of the political center which compels Beijing to exercise her authority with utmost caution will actually enhance the dynamism of economic China and engender more vitality, creativity, and originality in cultural China? These options as well as other alternatives are likely to unfold in the near future. Beyond a doubt, China in transformation is a human drama on the global stage.

Tu Wei-ming

ACKNOWLEDGMENTS

I am grateful to the eleven authors in this issue who in various ways are pivotal in shaping my approach to and feel for China, to the other friends and teachers, David Xiaokang Chu, Ken Lieberthal, Robert Neville, Robert Smith, and Benjamin Schwartz, who helped to make the authors' conference in September of 1992 a memorable intellectual event, and to Rosanne Hall and Nancy Hearst for searching criticisms of early versions of the Introduction. I am also indebted to Geoff White of the Cultural Studies Program at the East-West Center for his generous support and to Iris Rulan Pian and Loh Waifong, cofounders of the Kangqiaoxinyu (New Discourse in Cambridge), for providing a continuous forum on cultural China for more than a decade.

ENDNOTES

[1]Edwin O. Reischauer, "The Sinic World in Perspective," *Foreign Affairs* 52 (2) (January 1974): 341–48.

[2]A set of statistics, directly resulted from the post-Cultural Revolution reform, is worth mentioning: Real GNP grew at an average annual rate of 10.4 percent from 1980 to 1988 compared with only 6.4 percent during 1965–1980; total GNP grew more than twofold between 1978 and 1988. During 1978–1988, per capita GNP doubled in real terms. See Kang Chen, Gary Jefferson, and Inderzet Singh, "Lessons form China's Economic Reform," *Journal of Comparative Economics* 16 (June 1992): 210–25.

[3]For a general discussion of Chinese industry, see Robert Michael Field, "China's Industrial Performance since 1978," *China Quarterly* 131 (September 1992): 577–609.

[4]Nicholas D. Kristof, "China, the Conglomerate, Seeks a New Unifying Principle," *The New York Times,* 21 February 1993.

[5]See Peter Berger and Hsin-Huang Michael Hsiao, eds., *In Search of an East Asian Development Model* (New Brunswick, N.J.: Transaction Publishers, 1988).

[6]Gary G. Hamilton, ed., *Business Networks and Economic Development in East and Southeast Asia* (Hong Kong: Centre of Asian Studies, University of Hong Kong, 1991).

[7]Two recent articles are suggestive in conceptualizing the "township village enterprise" as a new economic force in China. See Yia-ling Liu, "Reform from Below: The Private Economy and Local Politics in the Rural Industrialization of Wenzhou," *China Quarterly* 130 (June 1992): 293–316 and Jean C. Oi, "Fiscal Reform and the Economic Foundations of Local-State Corporation in China," *World Politics* 45 (2) (October 1992): 99–126.

[8]Robert A. Scalapino, "The U.S. and Asia: Future Prospects," *Foreign Affairs* 70 (5) (Winter 1991–1992): 20–21.

[9]Liu Binyan, *A Higher Kind of Loyalty: A Memoir by China's Foremost Journalist,* trans. Zhu Hong (New York: Pantheon Books, 1990).

[10]Samuel P. Huntington, *The Third Wave: Democratization in the Late Twentieth Century* (Norman, Okla.: University of Oklahoma Press, 1991), 310.

[11]Ibid.

[12]Tu Wei-ming, "Intellectual Effervescence in China," *Dædalus* 121 (2) (Spring 1992): 250–92.

[13]Wang Ruoshui, "Tantan yihua wenti" ("Let's Talk about the Problem of Alienation"), *Wei rendaozhuyi bianfu (In Defense of Humanism)* (Beijing: Sanlian Publications, 1980), 186–99.

[14]The horrifying report on politically and ideologically motivated cannibalism in the Guangxi province during the Cultural Revolution by the famous writer and dissident, Cheng Yi, was first published in Chinese-language magazines in June 1992. Since his dramatic escape from the mainland in November 1992, his

findings have been widely circulated through the mass media. See his interview with *Kaifang* (*Open Magazine*) (Hong Kong) 73 (January 1993): 62–68.

[15]Stuart Schram, ed., *Chairman Mao Talks to the People: Talks and Letters: 1956–1971* (New York: Pantheon Books, 1974), 61–62.

[16]Ibid., 61.

[17]Ibid., 75.

[18]S. N. Eisenstadt, "The Breakdown of Communist Regimes," *Dædalus* 121 (2) (Spring 1992): 21–41.

[19]Dwight H. Perkins, *China: Asia's Next Economic Giant?* (Seattle, Wash.: University of Washington Press, 1986), 83.

[20]Ibid., 85. For some recent observations on the Chinese economic scene, see Nicholas R. Lardy, "Chinese Foreign Trade," *China Quarterly* 131 (September 1992): 691–720; and Joseph C. H. Chai, "Consumption and Living Standards in China," Ibid., 721–49.

[21]Henry Rosemont, Jr., *A China Mirror: Moral Reflections on Political Economy and Society* (La Salle, Ill.: Open Court, 1991), 99.

## Provinces of China

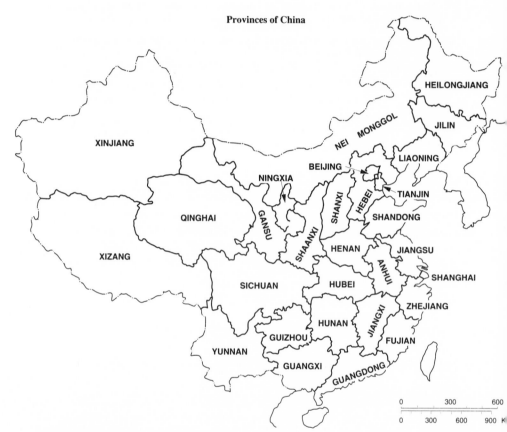

Originally published in "Environmental Change as a Source of Conflict and Economic Losses in China" by Václav Smil, University of Manitoba. Occasional Paper Series, American Academy of Arts and Sciences.

*Edward Friedman*

# A Failed Chinese Modernity

A S ALL FORMER LENINIST DICTATORSHIPS, rulers in Beijing also confront a crisis of legitimation.[1] Surface tranquillity in China hides moving tectonic forces that are reshaping China's national project. The most politically conscious Chinese already have dismissed the Leninist system with its claim to embody the interests of all Chinese in an anti-imperialist nationalism as a betrayal of the nation. The millions of democracy demonstrators in the spring of 1989 dubbed their movement "patriotic," in contrast to a regime which they found had wasted the people's hard-earned wealth on imported luxury items such as Mercedes-Benzes for a parasitic ruling caste.[2] Increasingly in the post-Mao era, reformers in the Government are abandoning the Capitol of Beijing in the North to work in the South or in coastal regions or at local levels with entrepreneurs who have brought China some of the world's most rapid economic growth, a high level of both foreign confidence and investment, and an extraordinary record of export success.[3]

Slighting this delegitimation crisis, ruling groups hope that mass money-making will absorb the energies of China's people. Their hopes for political stability seem to be realized, but only on the surface. This political quiet is premised on a merely momentary consensus in which party conservatives, lacking economic alternatives, accept economic reform, and in which reformers, lacking political alternatives and believing the reform project irreversible, accept a temporary bracketing of political change to avoid the chaos and decline of post-Leninist Europe and to escape the vengeful wrath of China's ruthless senior troglodytes.

Meanwhile, those shifting tectonic plates are remaking China. Strong shoots of a new nationalism are breaking up out of the old

---

*Edward Friedman is Professor of Political Science at the University of Wisconsin.*

1

discredited debris, producing a new identity holding the promise of a better future for all Chinese, though not necessarily a democratic future. The anti-imperialist nationalism embodied in Maoism that once won Chinese hearts has been discarded.

Nationalism, at one time, seemed to be the essence of the legitimation of Mao Zedong's popular, anti-imperialist revolution. It seemed presuppositional to the identity of proud Chinese responding to the Communist Party's proclaimed mission of helping the people "stand up" to foreign exploiters, domestic traitors, and imperialism in any form. Almost no one realized that this patriotism was actually a very recent and fragile construction, and not the essence of some imagined, eternal China. What appeared as permanent national truth was merely passing national mythos. Increasingly, educated Chinese are aware that the once presuppositional Leninist notion of a Chinese nation uniting behind and sacrificing for a Communist-led movement of paradigmatic, poor, hinterland peasants who suffer and even die to keep out foreign invaders, especially the Japanese, in order to maintain Chinese independence was merely a creation of the mythologized Yan'an era[4] (1936–1947) when Mao's guerrilla headquarters were situated among the poorest of North China's peasants.

This extraordinary myth, where the Yan'an era North China peasants sacrificed to save China, is a story that trivializes the tremendous regional variety in China where many Chinese, including peasants, actually opposed Mao's movement as being anti-Chinese. In the pre-Yan'an era, for example, remnant Communist armed forces in South China, fleeing for their lives, tended to ally with the Hakka people in the hill regions. And they were opposed by indigenous southerners, tenants, and owner-tillers as well as landlords. Mao embraced a minority to survive.[5] The partiality and particularity of the Communists are coming again to consciousness in the post-Mao era. The myth of an intrinsic and indivisible nation of the poor supporting the Communists is increasingly challenged by a very different nationalist identity for China.

Bubbling up from beneath a superficially tranquil political surface, new nationalisms have arisen, as already have surfaced and spread in other Leninist and formerly Leninist nations where anti-imperialist patriotisms have disappeared in an instant, leaving the Soviet Union, Yugoslavia, Czechoslovakia, and Ethiopia split, with others teetering on the brink of stability.[6] It is worth exploring similar forces in

China. It is remarkable how swiftly an artificial Leninist nationalism can disappear.[7]

Knowledge of China illuminates central features of conflicting notions of national identity that discredit the previous Maoist anti-imperialist patriotism. Some researchers point to the growth of the idea that a progressive China has historically always been tied to areas other than the isolated and insulated northern Chinese mountainous hinterland, that China's dynamism is tied rather to the South, the coasts and oceans, or to the West for international trade along the ancient silkroad towards the Middle East and the Mediterranean.[8] These revisions of national identity transform the northern hinterland peasants from paradigmatic patriots, Mao's Yan'an era hope of an armed, struggling Chinese people pushing foreigners out, into backward xenophobes who bound the nation to a backward concept of isolationist patriotism that kept China painfully apart from the dynamic and progressive scientific, technological, and commercial forces of the world. Increasingly, Yan'an era anti-imperialism seems as self-defeating as fifteenth-century Ming dynasty nativism that burned ship blueprints and executed astronomers. Maoist nationalists are reexperienced as know-nothings, keeping China backward.[9]

One set of works, revealing the unjust politics behind the purported Leninist embrace of the rural backward as China's pure patriots, investigates the historic conflict in China's major metropolis of Shanghai between the Subei people and the Jiangnan people, a conflict between invaders from the poorest countryside who failed to subsist on the soil and who brought stagnation and decline into the People's Republic after seizing power in Shanghai from longtime, dynamic, educated, market-oriented dwellers from the riverine plains of both the Jiangsu and Zhejiang provinces.[10] In promoting Subei over Jiangnan, Mao's anti-imperialism is felt to have privileged the incompetent. Politicized nationalism is totally devoid of legitimacy in a world seeking the economically competent.

Another illuminating approach to the rapid deconstruction of this Maoist-great-Han-nationalism, that turned into traitors all not at one with suffering—subsistence farmers—studies the recent renaissance of numerous primary identifications in China that are cultural, regional, linguistic, and/or religious—for example, the Muslim, Buddhist, Maoist, Christian, or non-Confucian; the Cantonese, Fukienese or Wu speaking; the Yueh, Chu or Ba ancestry in Jiangsu, Hunan, and Sichuan; the Manchu, Mongol, Turkic, Tibetans, and Hakka. The prior national chauvinism that celebrated the Han people is reexperienced as a fraud. No Chinese asserts intrinsically, "I am a Han." None![11] So who is Chinese? What, in the post-Mao era, makes for a legitimate patriotism?

It is important to focus on alternative sources of identity because when the Maoist, anti-imperialist notion of Leninism implodes, a conflict over a new nation or nations is likely to emerge from these other, still somewhat subterranean forces. Not all of what is now sprouting, however, is open or tolerant, let alone liberal or democratic.[12]

The conflictful potentials in the new national identities are revealed in the popularity of the heavy-metal band, the Tang Dynasty.[13] On the one hand, it borrows Western music as well as Chinese minority music and lionizes the Tang era capital, an open, global cosmopolis. On the other hand, it celebrates a great Chinese empire and imagines a glorious Chinese future including a war to destroy Japan. Aspects of the new nationalism often include bitter chauvinism.[14] My own conversations in 1992 with working-class Chinese found an expansive, nativistic, and militaristic identity within the delegitimated old nationalism as is portrayed in the following dialogue:

> Beijing worker: "We Chinese are not patriotic or powerful like you Americans. We're tremendously impressed by what you did in 1991 to Saddam Hussein's force in Kuwait."
>
> Friedman: "America's power is in relative decline. It is most important for America to revive the forces of long-term economic growth."
>
> Beijing worker: "Our nation should be able to do what you did. We should be able to sell weapons and make money so we can buy modern weapons and get strong. But mainly we need a government that is at one with the people, as yours was in the Los Angeles riots."
>
> Friedman: "The Los Angeles riots?"
>
> Beijing worker: "Your government stood with the people against the forces of crime and disorder. Here, [African] blacks gang rape a Chinese woman and the government does nothing. We too need a strong government on the people's side."

As elsewhere in the post-Leninist world, the experience of ruling Communists as hypocritical, corrupt criminals and greedy parasites produces an openness to politics redefined by purist, tough notions that could, as elsewhere, respond positively and strongly to virtually Fascist, militarist appeals of demagoguery. In China, as in other post-Leninist systems, reactionary leaders appeal to patriarchal notions in which women are kept in their place and evils, such as prostitution, AIDS, drugs, divorce, and juvenile delinquency, are blamed on outsiders who would corrupt a pure people.[15]

In noting that national identity is contested in China, one is not claiming that good replaces bad, but that a failed anti-imperialist, nativist project has opened up a Pandora's box of possibilities in which democracy is not necessarily the most popular alternative, a situation where nativistic chauvinisms grow in strength, feeding on the hateful, poisoned seeds sewn in the anti-imperialist era.

Two ideas have almost become presuppositional in Leninist-China as in other transforming Leninist and post-Leninist states in discrediting anti-imperialist, nationalist identity. First, people speak as if no progress had occurred under Leninism, as if time had been wasted.[16] In China, this means rethinking history so that Leninist rule, instead of being a rupture away from a benighted past, is identified as one of a number of similar failures, such as the crushers of the 1898 Reform to modernize the monarchy or the defeaters of the 1911 Revolution to establish a republic or the rejecters of the May Fourth Movement's message to build a popular, democratic, and scientific culture. There is a popular feeling in China of lost time, of having "returned to square one," as Wang Gungwu has characterized it. In fact, by attacking *feng, yang,* and *xiu* (feudalism, the nonnative, and revisionism), the Leninists are understood to have attacked or annihilated, as Ying-shih Yü says, the proven good of the Chinese essence. Hence, there is a popular desire to return to what is authentically Chinese, which often is patriarchal, nativistic, and authoritarian. Democracy, in this historical reemergence, is discredited, as is Leninism, as just another foreign imposition. Reborn jingoists oppose both Leninist despotism and liberal democracy for imposing on China unsuitable foreign ideas, models, and projects picked up in Japan, Bolshevik Russia, and the West. People instead embrace Wang Shuo's stories in the local argot and flock to the traditionally restorative breathing regimens such as *qigong,*[17] in which masters save disciples. Exclusive, authoritarian localism is ever more potent as a source of identity.

The second popular view that Chinese share with others who have discarded a Leninist national identity is the conclusion that violent political revolution, the essence of Leninism, only brings evil. What is desired is a peaceful transformation based on presumed real national essences, instead of hateful, splintering political struggles premised on violence. In this popular understanding, revolution can achieve no unifying national good, for it merely turns Chinese against Chinese. The apologists for the June 4, 1989 Beijing massacre unconsciously appeal to these presuppositions which actually delegitimate Mao's violent Leninist revolution that pit group against group, portraying innocent prodemocracy victims as violent hooligans from Hong Kong or Taiwan. A violent project in post-Leninist China is an antinational project.

Because peaceful and open political challenges are illegal, the new, hopeful national agenda must come from inherited social identities. An equation of reform progress with a peaceful continuity leads people to identify true Chineseness with one or another ongoing communalism, an emotional imperative strengthening and enhancing many ultimate communities that elsewhere have splintered post-Leninist nations to disintegration, chaos or civil war. This ideational process receives tremendous impetus from the logic of economic reforms that necessarily transfer economic initiative away from the center of the stagnant command economy to the rapidly advancing regions. In a hidden struggle, each region tries to build locally and to keep its funds from going to the center. A powerful process with divisive tendencies is underway.

To free ourselves from seeing the future of China as an endless, large unity built on now discredited, yet previously quintessentially Chinese, Maoist nationalism, it is worth remembering just how recent is the construction of the Maoist myth history. This narrative creates an identity of a Han people arising millennia ago in the inland Yellow River valley, defending against steppe barbarians, and spreading out to unify all of China by transforming all people in the territory, such as the Manchu, into the superior civilization of the Han. In fact, opponents of that last dynasty of the foreign Manchus found them to be a group who did not become Han, who, in fact, would not assimilate. At the outset of the twentieth century, Chinese patriots often identified the hated, conquering Manchus with an alien North and a backward Czarist Russia, while identifying patriotic Chinese (not Han) with the South and modernizing Japan. As Helen Siu finds in her work on South China, the South cheered for Japan in the 1904–1905 Russo-Japanese war. The Southern Study Society appealed "for physical education to create a new martial *chün-tzu* robustly modeled on the Japanese samurai. . . . "[18]

Southern patriots embraced southern languages, or even Esperanto, as superior to the North's Mandarin Chinese, the tongue of the traitorous, foreign court. The patriotic heroes of the last dynasty, such as Tan Sitong or Sun Yat-sen, tended to come from the South, identifying with the nativistic Ming dynasty, and experiencing the North as a traitor that had allied with British imperialism to survive against the people's popular patriotism. These northern traitors were seen as heirs of other northern groups over the millennia who had been made over by aliens.[19]

Southerners in the late Qing dynasty opposed British imperialism plundering China from the colony of Hong Kong and foreign concession areas of Canton (Guangzhou) and Shanghai. In the racist nationalism of the late nineteenth century, the patriots identified with Japanese success, interpreted in the hegemonic discourse of the then dominant racism such that China and Japan were joined in a struggle of yellow races to throw out Europeans from Asia.[20] Chinese went into Japan for exile, inspiration, and aid, hoping to achieve what Meiji Japan had achieved—national vigor sufficient to defeat the white race from European Russia as Japan did in a 1904–1905 war, a victory that thrilled and attracted even West Asians in Persia.

No Chinese at this time imagined China's future in terms of hinterland North China peasant courage. At the end of the nineteenth century, the influential nationalist popularizer, Zhang Binglin, synthesized China's plight,[21] using globally hegemonic categories, to conclude that,

> yellow people who achieved a higher level of social integration and organization.˙. . fared better than the black, the brown, and the red; and. . . were being trampled under by white people, who were better organized. . . . [22]

By the first decade of the twentieth century, Zhang championed a violent and vengeful liberation struggle of all peoples against expansionists. He imagined a Han people who rose in an area to the West of what was now China and who, based on cultural heroes such as the Yellow Emperor and Minister of Agriculture (Shen-nung), were being oppressed by a Manchu Government.[23] Zhang imagined Han

Chinese, in contrast to Japanese, as especially egalitarian and non-feudal. He sought to comprehend China's unique cultural essence. He privileged idealistic Mahayana Buddhist analogues such as Wang Yangming's spiritual teachings which "played an important part in the success of the Meiji Revolution in Japan."[24] Whether as a yellow race or a Han nation, Chinese and Japanese shared a moral cause of national liberation to Zhang, who was born in Zhejiang in South China.

In a similar manner, another leading patriotic publicist, Liu Shipei, from the Yangzhou prefecture in the Jiangsu Province in South China, identified anti-Manchu, Chinese independence with a long history of struggle against barbarian invaders.[25] For Liu, the formalistic particularism of Confucianism blocked this national project. That ideology of an effete literary served the ruling Manchu family at the expense of the Chinese people.[26]

By 1915, when Japan imposed Twenty-One Demands on China's independence, the final demand being the right to proselytize Japanese religion in China as Europeans did with Christianity, Chinese national sentiment began to be focused in an anti-Japanese direction. China, which previously imagined itself a superior culture that was borrowed by the Japanese more than a millennia earlier in the Tang dynasty, seemed in need of a new culture that could stand up to the Japanese who were using the Great War in Europe to take over German concessions in China. As Chinese fought among themselves, both as selfish parliamentary politicians and greedy, regional warlords, it increasingly seemed that what China needed to be free and independent was a mobilization of all China's people in a unified effort to push Japan out of China and back across the Yalu River that separated China's northeast from Korea. The invading Japanese military crossed the Yalu River and turned the northeast into a Japanese puppet state called Manzhouguo (Manchukuo) and then invaded deep into China's heartland, massacring, raping, and pillaging as they came. The pro-Japanese, anti-British, yellow race nationalism of the pre-World War I South needed to be discredited if everyone (even Europeans) were to be mobilized to save the Chinese nation.

After 1935, Mao Zedong's guerrilla force in the northern hinterland of Yan'an became a national salvation movement of liberation that met the imperatives of the new circumstances. Modern China was reimagined as a victim of imperialist invaders since the Opium War of 1839–1842. The lesson from that war was:

> to defend the open ocean is not as good as to defend the seaports, and to defend the seaports is not as good as to defend the inland rivers. . . . The phrase "enticing the enemy to enter the inland rivers" means that soldiers, guns and mines are sown. . . as if making a pit to wait for tigers. . . . [27]

This guerrilla strategy, a narrative of national defense, was read in the lessons of the Ming dynasty which threw out the foreign Mongols and built the Great Wall while smashing seaborne commerce.[28] This heroic Chinese tale of defense against invaders was identified with human liberation in general by linking it to the national resistance of the motherland of socialism which defeated Fascist invaders on Socialist soil after Stalin's Red Army fell back to the Ural Mountains. This militaristic nationalism harmonized with a universal Leninist-Jacobin tradition of human liberation through Spartan virtue in which citizen soldiers sacrificed everything to save the nation. The poor, young, courageous boys from China's villages who joined Mao's revolutionary army, faced every hardship, and sacrificed life itself to defend the nation and save the people from Japan's imperialistic invasion became modal personalities, idealized, worthy of emulation. Chinese history was reimagined in terms of a Han race from the northern plains whose virtue had time and again unified and defended China against savage invaders as represented in the sacrifice to build the Great Wall of China. The people's army in Yan'an, under Mao, came singularly to embody this new narrative project, a historical Chinese nationalist essence, a unified and indivisible force which alone knew how to save China's people from imperialist domination. In 1949, Mao proclaimed that the Chinese people had stood up and asserted themselves. It seemed obvious that it was a new chapter in the continuous history of Chinese struggle and sacrifice that won the Chinese people their independence in the People's Republic of China.

By the 1990s, however, this nationalistic narrative is discredited. Maoism, in the post-Mao era, is seen as having kept China poor and backward, as having made the military weak, as proved by its costly 1979 venture into northern Vietnam. Southern China, peripheralized in the Maoist-mythos, has been reprivileged, once again made the central focus of imagination and yearning for a better Chinese future. In the view of Mao's Yan'an era nativistic nationalism, the South was the home of weak gentry and foreign-facing merchants who made China vulnerable to foreign invasion and subversion. Former guerrilla soldiers sent down from the conquering North after the establishment of Mao's People's Republic had been ruling the South in state-imposed collectives of virtual serf (or slave) labor since 1949. The South's liberation has recently been locally reimagined as some date, usually in the 1980s, when these northern outsiders passed on and local people, at last, rose. Whereas the northerners were scandalized by southern mourning rituals, preferred a different diet (e.g., black tea, not green, or flour, not rice) and spoke differently, now, in the post-Mao era, empathetic, capable local people are taking over. China is again winning glory as in ancient times. The great economic gains of the post-Mao era are credited to southerners whose inventiveness skirted around northern bureaucrats, envisioned as useless, corrupt parasites. Contrary to popular newspaper reports, southerners do not credit China's recent, extraordinary growth to the policies of the rulers in the North.[29]

In the South, the anti-imperialist capital of Beijing is ridiculed as a backward town of mere talkers who live off the people's wealth and contribute nothing to wealth expansion. Northerners are mocked as people who would not even recognize money lying in a street. The new doers and shakers ridicule northerners who spout propaganda saying, "in Beijing, people say anything, while in Canton people do anything." In Canton, China's fastest growing metropolis, southerners sarcastically repeat the northern canard that "northerners love the country, (*ai guo*) [are patriots], while southerners sell the country, (*mai guo*) [are traitors]," knowing that people interpret the phrase to mean that while northerners talk, southerners did the business that earned China the foreign exchange that raised the people's standard of living. To survive, the regime in Beijing needs a stronger, new nationalism to compete with the open, market-orientation of the South.

Northern proponents of Fascist chauvinism, the natural heir to Leninist-Fascist-socialism[30] in Beijing as well as in Serbia or anti-Semitic Pamyat in Russia, responded to successful southern commerce,

Shysters, the lot of them—buying cheap down south and selling dear up north things nobody with good sense needed anyway. The bums ought to be turned up and spruced up and signed up. In no time the army would turn them into real men.[31]

However strong the invective, changed consciousness puts northern chauvinists on the defensive. Beijing residents nervously joke about a new encirclement of China's cities. Mao's revolution had been presented as the pure rural patriotic soldiers liberating weak, corrupt urban centers whose passive people previously welcomed capitalism and then were polluted by foreign imperialist germs. But, by the 1990s, Beijing was full of economic actors from the outside who were not allowed to reside legally in Beijing. These money-makers established residence by illegally buying household registration permits in the villages that surrounded Beijing and other similar cities. The problem for northern tyrants in Beijing is that even Beijing residents welcome the southern project that promises to raise China's standing in the world as well as raising the standard of living of the Chinese people.

Inside Beijing, people paid a premium price for Cantonese food. New restaurants in Beijing featuring various regional cuisines high-lighted regional virtues. Beijing and northern hinterland soldiers were no longer considered central to the Chinese future. Even in Beijing, people understood that the future was coming into China from the commercialized South and the trading coasts. Cantonese language and culture spread. Even farther north, traders hired Catonese tutors. In the northern hinterland, future-minded rural officials displayed their merit by drumming two left fingers on the table when tea was poured, a Cantonese custom of humble gratitude previously mocked in the North as crude. Northerners are popularly adapting to a new consciousness that imagines China's future in the economically open South; they flood to the South seeking jobs. Even though the North controls the media and the secret police, northern chauvinists feel encircled and endangered.

In China's capital, Beijing, there is an elite response to the attraction of a new national identity equated with southern virtues, insisting that the South has nothing to offer. In this northern perspective, the South, at best, is a cultural desert with nothing of value to offer. In fact, the South, as in Mao's nationalist defense against an imperialist culture of Christian missionaries and commercial markets, is seen by supporters of the old anti-imperialism as the opening through which AIDS, drugs, venereal diseases, prostitution, juvenile delinquency, disrespect for elders, consumerism, and other supposed foreign capitalist inhumanities flow. In contrast, Beijing is imagined and presented by such anti-imperialists as virtue incarnate, the capital of a Confucianism that has supposedly provided the economic basis and the moral glue for the miraculous development of Pacific Asia, of which Confucian[32] China is to be an ever more crucial element, a joining of a coercive hierarchical authoritarianism with a state-managed economy, a Fascist socialism.

Northerners who identify with this world view of wanting to join the successful worlds of Japan, South Korea, among others, will declare themselves to have felt more at home in Tokyo than in Canton. The ancient North is reimagined as China's Confucian essence, the core of the rise of Pacific Asia. China's southern national project is consequently stigmatized by such people in a discourse of romantic nostalgia as the antithesis of a warm, caring community. China's good Confucian heartland is felt to be home to an ethical people opposed to money-making, materialistic and selfish greed. A communitarian North is presented as the antithesis of alienating individualism, and, instead, favors cultural mutualities bonding people across gender and generation into a purportedly caring patriarchy. The South, in contrast, stigmatizes these northern claims as old-fashioned and sellouts to exploitative Japan, while southerners appear as both individually free and communally rooted with humane openness to all the world, and at one with individualistic Taoism.[33] This southern project could, but need not, be compatible with democracy and liberalism. It certainly is stigmatized by old-fashioned anti-imperialists as liberal.

To the extent that any northern nationalist vision is disbelieved and discredited as a mere, self-serving rationale of parasitic tyrants to block needed reform toward democracy or human rights, then even the apolitical are predisposed to reinterpret the regime's frantic, recent appeals in ways that actually subvert the regime. The regime's propaganda line defending its dictatorship and opposing peaceful evolution into democracy is taken to mean only that one should not hurry toward democracy and inadvertently fall into chaos, as in the former Soviet Union; evolution toward democracy is good. The northern message of opposition to peaceful evolution is in fact popularly interpreted as a rationale for peaceful evolution, for patience, for gradual change, that, as throughout Confucian East Asia, will, in a not too distant future, win a better world of democracy peacefully for all Chinese. When the northern regime points out that it took four decades before the perpetrators of the February 28, 1947 massacre in Taiwan were openly recognized and the victims rehabilitated, Chinese interpret that to mean that China too will democratize. Given the prior deconstruction of the northern national narrative, even northern chauvinist propaganda is interpreted to legitimate the inevitability and the desirability of the southern national project, a vision not of a separate South, but of a new Chinese nation enlivened by the southern ethos.

Having lost any robust promise for a happy future, northern anti-imperialist nationalists are left appealing unconvincingly to worst case anxieties, hates, and fears. China's media plays up violence in the former Soviet empire and plays down the gains from democracy, human rights, and initiatives from society. Rulers in Beijing fear losing control. Yet, they have already lost command of the categories and narratives that give meaning to a desirable future. The legitimating discourse has been reconstructed.

At the level of cultural magnetism, for the new generation of young northerners, the conservative northern Confucian appeal for patience is wholly unpersuasive. They want a better life now. They already buy goods with southern brand names, prefer beauty parlors promising Cantonese style, and identify the open and rapidly prospering South with better-paying job opportunities and a happier future for China.

There seems no way for the anti-imperialist old guard to relegitimate their nationalistic project. In the post-Mao era, they have tried to modernize the military to make China respected (feared?) in Asia and influential in the world through arms buildups and arms sales. But rather than feel pridefully uplifted, what ordinary Chinese see are corrupt rulers allowing their children to enrich themselves illegally in arms sales, and not caring about China's suffering people.

The old guard rulers do not even win credit for post-Mao economic successes that have swiftly raised standards of living. Instead, people see success in terms of getting around a system imposed from the North in which villagers are ordered to be patriots and grow grain, but then are not paid a living wage for the grain. In the countryside, villagers condemn a corrupt rulership imposing arbitrary taxes that Communist Party bosses are believed to pocket.

This delegitimation of anti-imperialist nationalism does not mean that tomorrow China will change its political direction and choose between the now rising nationalist projects, a racist chauvinism of the old guard, and a democratic constitutionalism of the new forces. Other possibilities could explode. As with the re-Balkanization of the Balkans and the experience of finding the period from 1917–1989 in the former Soviet Union as an era where time was wasted, Leninism's inheritance is a poisoning of communalist forces. In Europe, all the World War I era divisions and problems have reemerged in a more poisoned form. So it could be with China. One must remember what China was before the temporary domination of Mao's artificial anti-imperialist nationalism.

China, at the end of the nineteenth century, experienced power flowing to the regions out from the center. By the early twentieth century, cruel regional warlords ruled. And Leninist economic reforms, all analysts agree, strengthen local tendencies, intensify alienation from the old state center, and worsen intraregional (language, ethnicity, culture, religion, etc.) divisions, as groups struggle over taxes, prices, and monopoly shares while raising economic barriers, with each blaming the other. One should not underestimate the potency of the divisive forces that China's Leninist rulers correctly assert are spreading just beneath the surface.

The longer the old guard delays political reforms, the stronger these angry and divisive political forces grow. Chinese outside of China, in touch with China's diverse explosive angers, aware that there is no longer a binding anti-imperialist Han chauvinism as an easy, unifying glue, suggest the creation of a federation with great autonomous local power that could preserve order and progress, and also hold the allegiance of the Tibetans, Muslim Turkestanis, Cantonese, and Taiwanese. There was a Federalist movement in China in the early part of the twentieth century that even appealed to Mao Zedong. Although there is much wisdom in that wise and humane confederated vision, an analysis of the comparative experience of other post-Leninist transitions suggests that achieving that happy outcome will require great political wisdom and also, perhaps, a bit of good luck.

Meanwhile, the old guard clings tenaciously to power and rejects needed political reform. This political stagnation permits communal identities to grow into frustrated outrages, leaving less room and less hope for new democratic shoots to flower and flourish.

Mao's anti-imperialist nationalism has long since died, but its corpse cannot be buried. A cadaver sits on the Leninist throne of national power. It is not possible to predict when this still fearsome corpse will be permitted a burial. One cannot predict which straw is the last straw.

ENDNOTES

[1] Edward Friedman, *New National Identities in Post-Leninist Transformations: The Implications for China* (Hong Kong: Chinese University of Hong Kong, 1992).

[2] Edward Friedman, "Permanent Technological Revolution and China's Tortuous Path to Democratizing Leninism," in Richard Baum, ed., *Reform and Reaction in Post-Mao China* (New York: Routledge, 1991).

[3] "Guangdong has become a haven for refugees from the former Government of Prime Minister Zhao Ziyang. His loyalists have set themselves up as independent economic consultants in Guangzhou, and in the special economic zones. Some are researching reforms like the legalization of bankruptcy, a quick way of getting state enterprises off the dole. Others advise local governments on such matters as real estate investment and how to tax wage earners rather than making employers carry the whole burden." Jay Gao, "Is Guangdong Asia's Fifth Tiger?" *New Zealand Herald*, 28 January 1992.

[4] See the forthcoming volume by David Apter and Tony Saith on myth construction in Yan'an.

[5] See I. Yuan, *Mao Zedong and the South China Peasantry* (Ph.D. thesis, University of Wisconsin, Department of Political Science, 1993). He finds the Chinese language *World Herald* of 26 February 1993 reporting that Mao's family was itself originally Hakka.

[6] Edward Friedman, "Ethnic Identity and the De-nationalization and Democratization of Leninist States," in M. Crawford Young, ed., *The Rising Tide of Cultural Pluralism: The Nation State at Bay?* (Madison, Wis.: University of Wisconsin Press, 1993).

[7] Lowell Dittmer and Sam Kim have edited a forthcoming volume on this theme to be published by Cornell University Press.

[8] This theme of a China that includes its diaspora versus a China whose core is in the hinterland far from the coast is highlighted in *Dædalus* 120 (2) (Spring 1991).

[9] Edward Friedman, "The Eclipse of Anti-Imperialist Nationalism in China and the Rise of a Southern National Project," (forthcoming). Similarly in Vietnam, people say, "Hanoi has no seaport; it was the capital of the peasantry." Murray Hiebert,

"Vietnam's Dichotomy: North Dominates Politics, But South Drives Economy," *Far Eastern Economic Review* (15 October 1992): 47.

[10]Historian Emily Honig has a forthcoming volume on this topic.

[11]See Dru Gladney, *Muslim Chinese: Ethnic Nationalism in the People's Republic* (Cambridge, Mass.: Harvard University Press, 1991).

[12]Tony Judt, "The Past Is Another Country," *Dædalus* 121 (4) (Fall 1992): 83–118.

[13]Andrew Jones, "Beijing Bastards," *Spin,* October 1992.

[14]See Michael Sullivan's article on Chinese anti-African racism in *China Quarterly* (forthcoming, 1993).

[15]Edward Friedman, "Consolidating Democratic Breakthroughs in Leninist States," in M. L. Nugent, ed., *From Leninism to Freedom* (Boulder, Colo.: Westview Press, 1992).

[16]See Zhang Xianliang, *Getting Used to Dying* (New York: Harper and Collins, 1991).

[17]For an introduction to the reception of Wang Shuo and *qigong,* see Geremie Barmé and Linda Jaivin, eds., *New Ghosts, Old Dreams* (New York: Times Books, 1992).

[18]Frederic Wakeman, Jr., "The Price of Autonomy: Intellectuals in Ming and Ch'ing Politics," *Dædalus* 101 (2) (Spring 1972): 60.

[19]William Stevenson, *The Yellow Wind* (Boston, Mass.: Houghton Mifflin, 1959), 93–94, reminds readers, "The desire for an independent Yunnan state was always known to exist among leaders who regarded the Chinese as intruders. . . . the Mongols. . . drove the Burmese Shans out of this territory and turned it into a part of China. As recently as World War II, the feeling of separation from China was strong. The Governor of Yunnan had even suggested a distinctive Yunnan assistance program to U.S. officials. . . . "

[20]See Frank Dikotter, *The Discourse of Race in Modern China* (Stanford, Calif.: Stanford University Press, 1992).

[21]See Kauko Laitinen, *Chinese Nationalism in the Late Qing Dynasty: Zhang Binglin as an Anti-Manchu Propagandist* (London: Curzon Press, 1990), and Martin Bernal, "Liu Shih-pei and National Essence," in Charlotte Furth, ed., *The Limits of Change* (Cambridge, Mass.: Harvard University Press, 1976), 90–112.

[22]Chang Hao, *Chinese Intellectuals in Crisis* (Berkeley, Calif.: University of California Press, 1987), 110.

[23]Ibid., 112–16.

[24]Ibid., 144.

[25]Ibid., 146–47.

[26]Ibid., 163.

[27]Wei Yuan in 1842 in Sss-yu Teng and John K. Fairbank, *China's Response to the West* (Cambridge, Mass.: Harvard University, 1954), 30, 31.

28 Arthur Waldron, *The Great Wall of China: From History to Myth* (Cambridge: Cambridge University Press, 1990).

29 Guangdong leaders responded to claims that Beijing is responsible for the South's post-Mao growth, "What have they invested here?" "We pay for our railroads, our highways, our power plants." "They have no right to tell us what to do." Jay Gao, "Is Guangdong Province Asia's Fifth Tiger?" *New Zealand Herald,* 25 January 1993.

30 For an introduction to the Chinese democratic analysis of Leninism as a Fascist socialism, see Edward Friedman, "The Societal Obstacle to China's Socialist Transition," in Victor Nee and David Mozingo, eds., *State and Society in Contemporary China* (Ithaca, N.Y.: Cornell University Press, 1983), 148–71.

31 Bette Bao Lord, *Legacies* (New York: Knopf, 1990), 190.

32 Confucius was a northerner.

33 For some in the South, the southern cultural renaissance is a reemergence of the vibrant, open culture of the ancient southern state of Chu that northern Confucians had tried to repress and suppress. The ecstatic poems "came to be 'superseded, discouraged, persecuted and mocked' (though fragments of its mythology survived, particularly in popular Taoism). When. . . Chu was destroyed. . . Confucian-minded scholars. . . seldom deigned to mention them. . . . the world of erotic imagery and. . . beliefs from which. . . shamistic hymns sprang only filled them with repugnance, and they allowed it to pass out of existence or to subsist in corrupted form among the illiterate masses. . . . " Burton Watson, *Early Chinese Literature* (New York: Columbia University Press, 1962), 242–43.

Such a development of civil society will be possible only if the students and intellectuals inside and outside China also do some soul-searching, a process that has already begun among some of the more sober minds. Above all, they must learn to be responsible, to act with a sense of accountability to any entity in whose name they speak to demand sacrifices from themselves and others. They also should learn that freedom and human rights include the right not to participate, to be silent, to be free from what I call the "politics of involvement." They should divest themselves of the modes of thought and political styles (including a paranoid Chinese McCarthyism) that they have subconsciously assimilated from the political system under which they have lived so long.

Perhaps such a reconciliation and reconstruction of the state and society will turn the moral blundering and ideological exhaustion of the regime into moral redemption and political renewal; perhaps the utter political irresponsibility and ineptitude in dealing with the real world shown by some of the students will become transfigured into new concepts of citizenship, loyal opposition, and ultimately responsible leadership. Reconciliation between the party-state and society will in turn foster a reconciliation between China and world opinion.


Tang Tsou


From "The Tiananmen tragedy: the state-society relationship, choices, and mechanisms in historical perspective" in Brantly Womack, ed., *Contemporary Chinese Politics in Historical Perspective*

*Helen F. Siu*

# Cultural Identity and the Politics of Difference in South China

T HE TERM "CHINA" PRESENTS US WITH many faces and meanings. Scholars have been intrigued by the intensity of differentiating experiences beneath the surface of an enduring, naturalizing uniformity, and call for analytical tools that illuminate the paradox at various historical junctures.[1] The basic assumption of this paper is that "Chineseness" is not an immutable set of beliefs and practices, but a process which captures a wide range of emotions and states of being. It is a civilization, a place, a polity, a history, and a people who acquire identities through association with these characteristics.[2] I will highlight crucial moments in the construction of cultural identities in a region loosely termed South China (Huanan), where different meanings of being Chinese are selectively pursued. Instead of presenting reified, objectively identifiable traits and boundaries imposed on a population, I stress their fluid and negotiated qualities as perceived by those asserting them. However circumstantial the contestations, and however duplicitous these identities may have seemed, their emergence is also rooted in particular social, political, and economic relationships.[3]

In view of the deadly ethnic strife in the former Soviet Union and Eastern Europe, one may wonder if the Chinese Communist Party (CCP) loses its mandate or ability to rule, is China going to fall apart as a polity? Will local power groups assert their autonomy based on cultural, religious, and historical differences, and challenge the authority of Beijing? This applies not only to those classified as "national minorities," but also to deep-rooted regional particular-

*Helen F. Siu is Professor of Anthropology at Yale University.*

19

isms among those who consider themselves "Han." The question is not confined to postsocialist regimes. Its general relevance is illustrated by the painful restructuring of local societies following the withdrawal of colonial authorities. One may argue that when a political boundary is imposed upon diverse cultural groups and when connection with the center is largely administrative, disintegration is inevitable in a power vacuum. The question is whether the same logic can be applied to China, where cultural identification with the political center is so diffused in social life that periodic assertion of diversity has often contributed to the enrichment of the imagined community one calls the Chinese state. In other words, can one argue that "being Chinese" is at once an intensely unifying and differentiating experience, and that when a nationalist master narrative erodes under whatever circumstances, a new one replaces it?[4] If that is the case, what are the analytical implications for cultural autonomy and criticism?

To address these issues, I focus on a region within the geopolitical boundary of China which, in the hierarchical territorial map of power holders in Beijing, has always been one of the most distant from the center.[5] For centuries, the inhabitants of this southernmost region were believed to live in rugged mountains and unhealthy swamps. It was where disgraced imperial bureaucrats were exiled. In recent history, it acquired a more "civilized" image but a no less comfortable one for officials. Its population has remained ethnically diverse. Although they speak a distinctive dialect (*yue*), they maintain a range of territorial reference points relative to the political center and among themselves. The cultural loading of these reference points has also shifted over time.[6] In the last few centuries, its regional core, linked by the Pearl River system, has been commercialized and urbanized. It has extensive contacts with the world through trading with Arabs and Europeans as well as through waves of emigration. The local population is distinguished by an enterprising ethos, a life-style, and political thinking unorthodox by Beijing standards. These images were illuminated by the activities of Qing guild merchants whose *hong* (trade monopolies granted by the Qing government) stood majestically at the western edge of Guangzhou (Canton), the region's leading metropolis. At the Peabody and Essex Museum in Salem, Massachusetts, one finds colorful displays of the goods and art work produced in Guangzhou for the Western market in the eighteenth and nineteenth centuries.[7] Today, foreign and Hong Kong enterprises employ nearly three million workers in the region's open economic zones, bringing unprecedented prosperity that challenges the basic tenets of the socialist government. Young entrepreneurs imitate the life-styles presented in Hong Kong television dramas. One expects that South China has the potential to break away.[8] (See the map of the Pearl River Delta on page 43.)

The natural question to pursue is whether the Chinese state has been able to maintain control in this relatively open geopolitical region. The blatantly disrespectful maneuvers of Party cadres illustrate the problem. Although their positions of wealth and power in the post-Mao era continue to rely on connection with the Party hierarchy, heads of the prosperous market towns in the delta would eagerly demote their own administrative status. They feel that ties to the government only mean unnecessary interference.[9] Dressed in Western-style suits tailored in Hong Kong, they ride in chauffeur-driven Mercedes-Benzes and Toyota Crowns, and are brashly in command with their cellular phones.

For those who have sacrificed in the Maoist period but who do not have the personal or political resources to ride the uncertain times today, cynicism prevails.[10] A young generation of workers feels particularly adrift. The alarming rates of drug addiction, gambling, and violent crimes in the booming towns and cities point to the problems of a society in flux where opportunities and frustrating restrictions are equally compelling in everyday life.[11]

It may be premature to conclude that ten years of post-Mao liberalization have spun this southern region out from under Beijing's control. There is definite commitment toward the larger polity, enough for local residents to feel pained and concerned about its future. Reactions from intellectuals, village cadres, farmers, and workers in the wake of June 4, 1989 were frighteningly intense. Tearful and angry in front of their television sets which received Hong Kong stations, many agonized about what should be and could be done. The mood can be captured in a gnawing statement frequently made, "Our country (*guojia*) is in such turmoil, it is so difficult to be Chinese."

These sentiments highlight the tensions between a strong cultural identity, an assumed political commitment toward a government which claims to represent that identity and which aggressively appropriates allegiance, and an unorthodox political-economic environment in this part of China. The tension has historically engendered a multilayered and engaging political narrative in which three elements intertwine but are individually pursued: *minzu,* a cultural definition of being Chinese; *guojia,* the idea of legitimate governance with binding obligations for a population; and *zhengfu,* the apparatus of governance. Myron Cohen makes an eloquent summary in his article in *Dædalus,*

> . . . for much of China's population, being Chinese is culturally much easier today than it ever was in the past, for this identification no longer involves commonly accepted cultural standards. Existentially, however, being Chinese is far more problematic, for now it is as much a quest as it is a condition.[12]

I would like to elaborate on this tension in South China, and argue that in historical circumstances, being Chinese has involved diverse groups in continuous negotiation of their cultural identity and history in order to establish a legitimate position in a volatile but all encompassing state order. When the state was but a cultural idea, the very "pretense" of identifying with the center has been a shrewd strategy for asserting ultimate room for maneuver. Nation-building in the twentieth century has transformed this cultural idea into an organized administrative machinery which increasingly dictates the terms of negotiation. With the recent developments in South China complicating the terms, how is the tension sustained?

## THE HISTORICAL ROOTS OF CULTURE IN SOUTH CHINA

In the early 1950s, the Provincial Committee for National Minorities Affairs in Guangdong conducted a survey on the ethnic compositions in the province. Apart from the farmers who called themselves Han Chinese, there were several major ethnic groups, for example, the Zhuang and the Yao in the mountains and the Dan who lived on boats in the delta. These broad classifications are problematic. Historical evidence of the Ming (1368–1644) and Qing (1644–1911) dynasties shows that those who claimed to be Han Chinese were largely the upwardly mobile part of an indigenous population who became Han as they actively acquired the cultural symbols of the larger polity. The results of the 1950s surveys remained classified. It was said that the authorities were worried that if the local Han population knew about the findings, they might reverse the cultural strategy, trace their historical ethnic roots, and claim the political status of an autonomous region, a status Beijing had granted to other territories where large ethnic minorities lived.[13]

The worries of the central authorities were quite unwarranted. Judging from historical experience, few southern Chinese would eagerly claim the status of an ethnic minority. Non-Han labels were used for centuries by local elites to push the rest of the indigenous population to regional peripheries. From the Song dynasty (960– 1279) onward, the population in Guangdong who claimed to have a common cultural ancestry with those in the North had created myths and regional historiographies, compiled genealogies, and built ornate ancestral halls with literati pretensions. These were shrewd strategies to create an important place in the evolving "Chinese" history and polity for themselves. Those marginalized were heaped upon with demeaning labels. In making a highly stratified local society, local elites helped consolidate an authoritarian imperial state with a distinct cultural-territorial hierarchy.[14]

Actively drawing themselves toward the Chinese imperial center has not led to the eradication of cultural or political differences. In fact, given the geographical distance, South China developed on its own terms and at its own pace into a diverse, rich, open, and vibrant region. In terms of cultural origins, most of the major lineages in the Pearl River delta claim that their ancestors had come from the *zhong yuan* (central plains). They had migrated south when nomads from the North threatened the Han settlements. Many even linked their genealogies with royal families and prominent literati figures who fled south. It is not difficult to detect the blatant fabrications and inconsistencies in these lineage histories.[15] But in the open frontier of the delta during the Ming and Qing periods, where the accumulation of material wealth was almost unlimited due to the intensified reclamation of the river marshes,[16] lineage membership was at once proof of cultural identity and a shrewd strategy for strength in numbers, for social mobility and political legitimacy. As Oxford historian David Faure has noted in his studies of Guangdong, the destitute might not have been a tenant farmer, but a nonvillager or a nonlineage member who had no settlement rights as defined by the dominant cultural norms.[17]

Even if lineage identity is an all encompassing cultural marker used by those who call themselves respectable members of the Confucian order, lineage organizations have varied greatly over time and space. Subject to intense local improvisations, they provide a wide range of meanings and experiences. Scholars have wondered whether lineages based on the genealogical mode, commonly found in North China, are a different social form altogether from those based on the associational mode, found in the South.[18] Within Guangdong, the variations are remarkable. David Faure argues that localized lineages in the Pearl River delta, with their landed estates and ornate ancestral halls and rituals, were products of particular historical junctures of state-making in the Ming and Qing dynasties.[19] Moreover, in the older part of the delta where the late Oxford anthropologist Maurice Freedman based his observations, lineages with limited land for expansion were vastly different operations from the super-lineages built on extensive estates in the sands during late Qing.

Lineage building in the open "frontier" of the delta was intimately tied to the market towns and regional cities which mushroomed at about the same time. In fact, unlimited expansion in the sands and the wealth it brought proceeded with intense specialization in urban places. Merchants owning vast corporate estates in the Pearl River delta extended the trading of local cash crops to the entire country through powerful organizations that were buttressed by the academic titles and official posts they acquired. The Fan Palm Guild (Kuishan *huiguan*) in Xinhui county and the Minglun *tang* of Dongguan county were established examples.[20] They were tied to the regional and ultimately to the central power apparatus through overlapping membership with academies, and, after the mid-nineteenth century, with the self-defense corps. The development of the sands was an agrarian revolution in which a unique rural-urban nexus created its own multilayered, pluralistic cultural spectacle reaching an apical peak at political metropolises. The imperial bureaucracy meandered through complex structures of native place and charitable associations, corporate trusts, guilds, and temples to reach both urban and rural society.

The merchants' practices and their literati pretensions penetrated deeply into the countryside, as villages were linked by an increasingly dense network of river ports, marketing and financial centers.[21] Regional cities such as Shantou (for embroidery), Foshan (for iron products and pottery), and Zhaoqing and Jiangmen (for goods from the upper reaches of the Xi River system) were urban terrains where owners of native industries and banks, pawn shops, brokers, and imperial bureaucracies traversed.[22]

Guangdong's contact with the world had also developed over the centuries, and it was not limited to the trading of luxurious goods. The region started importing foreign rice since mid-Qing because its agriculture was specialized in cash crops, and water transport along the coast was cheaper and easier than over the mountains that separated the province from the North.[23] Many of its crops and handicraft products (tea, silk, ceramics) were sold to foreign traders in Guangzhou. Just as Arab travelers were sinicized in popular religion,[24] silver dollars were used in temple renovations. By the late nineteenth century, the region was exporting labor to Southeast Asia and the Americas.

In the first half of the twentieth century, this unique urban cultural process developed at an accelerated pace. Leading merchants and overseas Chinese industrialists contributed to a new infrastructure in the form of ports, railroads, and modern schools. They introduced technologies and conducted an extensive trade with the world outside of China through a network of county and prefectural capitals (Foshan, Jiangmen, Zhaoqing, Shiqi, Daliang, and Shantou). The focal point of these commercial networks was Guangzhou and eventually Hong Kong. During this golden age of the Chinese bourgeoisie, Guangdong printed its own money, and used it side by side with Hong Kong currency.[25]

Given the unique paths of development in South China, was there a wide and visible North-South divide? Historian Sun Lung-kee, in a recent article, quoted an editorial in *Dongfang zazhi* which points to the numerous arguments and justifications Chinese scholars and politicians have subscribed:

> The dispute between north and south today is an unprecedented disaster... the differences between north and south are transformed into that between Han and Manchu, between those behind the empress and the young emperor. In the realm of foreign relations, it is between supporters for Russia or Japan. And for political programs, it is between the reformers and the conservatives.[26]

Sun also summarizes mutual prejudices in cultural and literary circles. Scholars in Beijing considered themselves legitimate heirs of the May

Fourth tradition while those in the South were irrational romantics and ruffians. Many southern scholars, on the other hand, equated the North with enclosure, chaos, and backwardness.[27]

The issue here is not what had caused the differences in attitudes and temperaments or the nature of mutual prejudices. If the gap was so visible for all concerned, what have been the bases for their commitment to the cultural and political "center" and their continual engagement? The circumstances for South China are not an exception to the general experience of dynastic empires. As Benedict Anderson has noted, diverse populations in these empires were administered by those who were often ethnically and linguistically different.[28] This had not necessarily been a source of conflict between ruler and ruled. Benjamin Schwartz has also marveled at the awesome historical absorptive capacities of "the Chinese civilization," that even conflict seemed highly centripetal (comments made during a conference in September of 1992). In fact, different dynasties centered in Beijing tolerated the region's unorthodox diversity and benefited from the wealth it generated. Local elites did not aggressively advocate political autonomy. In the early twentieth century, China was literally carved by regional warlords. They declared independence from the Manchu empire but they were not interested in maintaining control merely over their territories. They wanted the whole of China.[29] For South China, what worried Beijing was not whether the region wanted to break away, but when local elites took their Chineseness too seriously and competed to control the political center. In the name of revitalizing the Mandate of Heaven for the rulers, or of building a modern nation-state, they had challenged the legitimacy of the Beijing regimes many times.

It is not difficult to see that regimes in Beijing were ambivalent towards South China. They have taken for granted that the region was historically incorporated into the Middle Kingdom and therefore would be a part of the modern nation-state. At the same time, they needed to keep its unorthodox influences at a distance. For the locals, the China complex has been equally strong. It is best for the powers in Beijing to leave them alone, but they have also used all the cultural pretensions of the dynastic order to make their prosperity legitimate. At times, they have even seriously acted on their acquired Chineseness to engage in vigorous political dialogue. With the rising importance of political and economic centers in the South during the late imperial and modern era and the corresponding shifting of cultural reference points, this tension had deepened.

In evaluating these dynamic intellectual and political economic processes, the question is not whether they represented orthodoxy or heterodoxy from the standpoint of regimes in Beijing, but rather, were these processes an integral part of modern China in the making? If Beijing does not occupy the privileged position as the center of Chinese history, that cultural distance from it does not mean marginality or anomaly, then the entire process of becoming Chinese needs to be seen as involving a much wider range of players and voices. Instead of upholding the prevailing image of a reified China enshrouded with primordial sentiments, one may see how advocates on different ends of the spectrum have negotiated their respective positions to generate a complex, open cultural process.[30]

The issue has comparative relevance in contemporary times. It is well known that regimes use their interpretations of national history to legitimize their powerful positions and to claim the allegiance of those associated with that history. But the tensions generated are different between the imperial and modern periods. The Chinese imperial state was more a malleable cultural idea than a tightly organized structural entity. Its administrative presence was remote but its moral authority was pervasive. Under the all encompassing symbolisms of *tianxia* (all under heaven), local improvisations thrived. Modern nation-states, especially Marxist-Leninist regimes, wielded much more organized power. Katherine Verdery's study of Eastern Europe points to this nationalist strategy of socialist regimes by which Marxist-Leninist parties promote the reading of history as inevitable, one directional social movement based on class struggles.[31] Brandishing their assumed vanguard position in the movement, they justify the persecution of those in the way. Among the Chinese Communists, the ideas of building socialism and a strong China are often intertwined. In fact, many peasants and intellectuals who became Communists in the early years were motivated by their anger over the Nationalists' inability to stop foreign aggression. After they came to power in 1949, the Communist regime used the nationalist agenda repeatedly. Those who did not conform to the socialist programs were "traitors," "foreign subversives," "enemies of the people" as well as "counterrevolutionaries." Their voices were systematically purged in political campaigns. The party-state's eagerness to register the population under its administrative control within a marked boundary, coupled with its inability to tolerate internal differences, has created unprecedented tensions among its own true believers, and between center and locality. It is interesting to note that nearly every major political campaign in post-1949 China was triggered by committed intellectuals voicing opinion, and that before the central government launched a major campaign, the commanders of the military regions were often reshuffled.

## THE GUANGZHOU-HONG KONG NEXUS

The emergence of Hong Kong as a significant player in the shaping of the regional complex in South China further complicated the issue of cultural identity and nationality, of the ambiguity of "being Chinese" and "being part of the China polity." It unleashed a historical and cultural dynamics in its own right. Ceded to Britain in 1842 after the Opium War, Hong Kong's social and cultural ties to the mainland had remained strong. Home to some fishing villages, it was first used as a resting place where ships moored for repair. Merchant houses such as Jardine, Matheson & Co., Butterfield and Swire established themselves with warehouses and business networks. A multiracial merchant culture developed with close ties to India, London, and Guangzhou.[32] Agricultural communities, thriving market towns, and large lineages which traced their ancestry to Guangdong were added to the social map when the New Territories were leased to Britain in 1898. But until the first half of the twentieth century, Hong Kong was marginal in the regional political economy.

The population was largely Cantonese-speaking, with family and business ties in both Hong Kong and Guangdong. Relationships between the two places were mobile and fluid: goods, money, and people crossed the political boundary as if Hong Kong were no different from any other foreign concession within China.[33] Large lineages with ornate ancestral halls and estates continued to be built on the plains. Members negotiated with colonial officials as much as they used the cultural symbolisms of Chinese imperial power to maintain dominance and to feud with neighbors. The works of Maurice Freedman, Hugh Baker, James and Rubie Watson, David Faure, and James Hayes on these communities are well-known.[34] In the urban neighborhoods adjacent to the colonial establishment, a burgeoning merchant class became the second government of Hong Kong through their management of temples and charity organizations. The Man Mo (Wenwu) temple, built on Hollywood Road in 1854, was their ritual headquarters as well as a refuge for sojourning traders and laborers.[35]

As late as during World War II, one hundred years after British rule, Hong Kong residents maintained close ties with the mainland. When parts of China were occupied by the Japanese military, many southern Chinese fled to Hong Kong, and when Hong Kong in turn was occupied, many went back to northern Guangdong and the Guangxi province. There are tales of loyal servants who carried food by boat and on foot to feed families in the occupied zones, and of families separated and later reunited. A Chinese cultural identity, however composite it might have seemed, continued to induce political commitment toward China and Guangzhou. This assumed identification was expressed in the sympathy strikes by workers and merchants in Hong Kong against foreign aggression on the Chinese mainland during the turbulent decades of civil war.

A British education and administrative system did gradually exert its naturalizing presence among the Hong Kong population.[36] Until the late 1940s, the major political players constituting public sentiments were an alliance of British and East Indian civil servants, British-trained Chinese and Eurasian professionals, prominent merchant families with their charity organizations, guilds, and temples, and heads of powerful lineages in the rural area which continued to be recorded in unofficial documents as being part of Pao'an county in Guangdong Province.

It would be naïve to judge Hong Kong society as being more or less "authentically Chinese."[37] For over a century and a half, its population was racially and culturally composite. Many took for granted their political place in the British empire. They would solemnly salute the British flag and rise to the tune of "God Save the Queen," but they feel patriotic to the Chinese "motherland" as well. Their political concern with the Chinese mainland is reinforced by their social connectedness with it. Over the decades, generations of native-born Hong Kong residents blended in with waves of emigrants from across the border. The continuous process of disembeddedness and reintegration created a cultural kaleidoscope that resettled into a new pattern after each political turn. Social life might seem transient and momentous, but "Chinese traditions," "colonial legacies," and their accompanying symbolisms have been vital ingredients that are constituting and meaningful in everyday life. The pervasive influence of the colonial experience, for example, can be detected even in the Cantonese dialect. The Guangzhou version (*shengcheng hua*), spoken in the dominant merchant communities of the early twentieth century, has given way to a deeply Anglicized version with Western professional concepts and romanized terms.[38]

From 1949 to the 1990s, the colony underwent drastic transformations. The Communist Revolution in 1949 forced it to assume new economic and political roles. The sudden influx of capital, refugees, and skills helped its painful transition from an entrepôt to a manufacturing and financial hub for East and Southeast Asia. The government embarked on a massive building of a new economic and political infrastructure. By the time China reopened its doors in 1980, Hong Kong had become a prosperous world metropolis with six million people. It has surpassed many cities in the Chinese mainland in its cosmopolitan openness and its irreverence for nationalistic authority.[39]

It will be naïve to assume that Hong Kong has spun off from the China orbit. Its population fluctuated due partly to uneven waves of refugees fleeing from and to China during various political crises. Before the Japanese occupation in 1942, there were 1.5 million residents. By 1945, only a little over half a million remained. But 1949 brought many refugees from various parts of China, particularly Shanghainese entrepreneurs.[40] By 1953, when the revolutionary dust had settled, the population in Hong Kong had swelled to 2.5 million.[41] In the wake of the famine in the early 1960s when an estimated 15 million died of famine-related diseases in China, hundreds of thousands crossed the border. After the reign of the Maoist radicals in the late 1970s, another half a million or more slipped through. By 1980, one out of twelve residents had not been settled in Hong Kong for more than three years.[42]

Scholars and politicians have marveled at the resilience of the immigrants. Some attribute it to the age-old "Chinese" cultural tradition. Others credit the laissez-faire attitudes of the Hong Kong government. Taken in a historical view, however, the issue is complicated. In the early 1950s, the refugees brought with them capital, skills, and urban outlooks, which dovetailed with the needs of postwar transformations in Hong Kong. By the late 1970s, a visibly cosmopolitan Hong Kong with its Western-educated generations were firmly in place. The recent wave of immigrants was largely unskilled youths from rural Guangdong. Leaping desperately from their cellularized existence in the villages, they found the composite cultural sentiments and the fast pace of city life extremely disorientating. Even the Cantonese dialect they share with Hong Kong residents seems to convey vastly different meanings. Their eventual absorption, painful also to the host community, created new cultural currents and social conflicts. To homegrown residents, Hong Kong has also become uncomfortably unfamiliar.[43]

RENEGOTIATING CULTURAL IDENTITY IN THE 1990s

What is the social ethos of Hong Kong (and indirectly South China) in the 1990s, when the fast moving urban society now faces the claims of a power whose authority rests on the assumed rights of an ageless, primordial origin? One observes intensified partisan emotions in the public sphere, a visible mixture of skepticism and panic with reference to political leadership, low moral and self censorship in the arts and media, and a pervasive feeling that the social fabric is rapidly eroding at home, school, and work. The political landmark of 1997 deeply punctuates Hong Kong society. The belief in its inevitable return to China triggers a wide range of interests, hopes, and anxieties. These sentiments are complicated by the fact that in the last few decades, the pulsations of life in Hong Kong have been fueled by its miraculous globalization. The process has resulted in an ever dynamic cultural kaleidoscope—open, unorthodox, brash, and luxurious—of which Beijing is both envious and uncomfortable.[44] The tension has long entered the popular consciousness through a dense media complex.[45]

There are many unexplored questions: how are the images of Hong Kong as a world metropolis and as part of China juxtaposed? What is happening to the cultural identity of its inhabitants and the related political implications? With an ever accelerating influx of refugees from southern China and the exodus of Western-trained professionals, how is cultural identity reconfigured? What is the dynamic interplay between the Chinese tradition, the colonial infrastructure, and the uncertain socialist future in a multiethnic land of immigrants, foreign workers, and emigrants? Would the rapid turn-over of its population and their resources create a global middle class? All these questions require the definition of "culture." Its analytical coherence is made increasingly ambiguous by the acceler-ated movement of people, technologies, images, and commodities across the globe.[46] What Hong Kong is undergoing dramatizes the century-old cultural tension between "center" and "periphery." More importantly, the kaleidoscopic quality of its experiences di-rectly confronts the efforts to define China in terms of a self-contained population, a place, a polity, a shared history or culture.

In the post-Mao era, major political players are reconfigurating another set of public sentiments. Despite the disembedded orienta-tions of Hong Kong's population, leaders in Beijing feel that it can count on the loyalties of the older émigrés toward "their motherland" and their hometowns in South China. The "politics of native roots" works to an extent. The regime plays up the assumed connection between cultural identity and political commitment. "Patriotic" overseas investors are pursued as sources of capital, technology, and market. More importantly, the Chinese leaders estimate that their investments pave the way to eventually integrate Hong Kong and Machau back into the China mainland. The claims are based on primordial sentiments and in the name of national unity, territorial bond, and family pride.

Ironically, the Chinese government can count on the efforts of the recent refugees at the grass-roots level. Although they fled China for various reasons, many have found a profitable niche as brokers for small- and medium-scale entrepreneurs who are relatives and who eagerly invest in the booming market towns of the Pearl River delta. There are no patriotic sentiments or grand political schemes. What drive the feverish energies are quick windfall profits where personal connections easily bend political guidelines. In Guangdong they say, "the mountains are high and the emperor is far away."

The sector of the population that Beijing cannot count on is Hong Kong's affluent middle class who are not as "immersed" in the mainland. The backbone of Hong Kong's prosperity, they are a jet-setting generation of local-born, Western-educated professionals in international trade and finance. Postwar baby boomers, they are now the movers and shakers who are more committed to Hong Kong than their parents.[47] Their social and emotional ties to China are relatively weak; their Chinese cultural identity is only partial, and their political idealism is influenced by Western criteria. They are skeptical of the claim of an inevitable place in history by Marxist-Leninist parties. Given the nature of Chinese politics, they are painfully aware of the uncertainty lying ahead. They know they have everything to lose. To add to their anxiety, their success story is in sharp contrast to the newest wave of refugees from rural China who now fill the lowest jobs in the local economy and who find the rhythm and texture of social life in Hong Kong perplexing and frustrating as the global city speeds toward the next century. The politics of difference is blatant. The tension is expressed in a host of cultural images. For the first time, unflattering remarks are heaped upon recent immigrants. There is a deliberate drawing of boundaries as "locals" and "aliens."

In the last five years, the middle class who are already nervous over their future are made more insecure by what they perceive as predatory acts of both officials and criminal elements from China. For months in 1988–1989, consumers in Hong Kong were plagued by vegetables from the border town of Shenzhen where farmers had dosed them with poisonous amounts of pesticides to increase their marketability. Violent robberies which involved shooting battles in broad daylight with submachine guns and Chinese-made grenades are blamed on illegal immigrants who worked as mercenaries. Hong Kong also loses a few thousand luxury cars every year, some of which find their way to official circles in Guangdong. The relationship between the Hong Kong marine police and Chinese border guards over seizing smugglers and their goods has become violent and confrontational. Outgunned, out speed, and outnumbered, the law enforcement forces in Hong Kong are utterly demoralized.[48]

Western-trained professionals, executives, and civil servants have the most to lose and the most painful choices to make. But many step up their plans for the future and "vote with their feet." A scenario based on government estimates foresees the total emigration in the decade of 1990–1997 to be between 550,000 and 700,000.[49] The exodus of this generation will have an impact, as severe shortages of qualified personnel are showing in the business communities, hospitals, and schools. In a study of emigration by occupation, it is shown that in 1987 and 1988, half of the emigrants were economically active, and 49.8 percent of the emigrants were professionals and administrative/managerial staff.[50] In desperation, the government planned to increase its support for higher education severalfold with the hope to retain at least a percentage of the graduates.[51]

The flow of capital outward is staggering. *Business Week* (September 23, 1991) had a special article on the situation for Canada. The amount each investor-immigrant takes to Canada is 1.5 million US dollars. Since 1984, 110,000 immigrants have landed in Canada, a group largely composed of professionals and investors. The number hit a record high of 29,000 in 1990 and an estimated another 200,000 will land by 1997. Capital flowing from Hong Kong to Canada averages two to four billion dollars per year. The Pacific has became Canada's largest trade partner, superseding the United States.[52] These émigrés are not refugees looking for menial work. The new immigrants constitute 3 percent of Canada's population but make up 10 percent of Canadian households owning assets over $200,000.[53]

Beijing accuses these emigrants of shirking responsibility, of draining the Hong Kong economy and creating instability, of showing a lack of confidence in their motherland. In sum, they have "betrayed" their cultural roots. But the politics of native roots does not have a convincing argument. For those who see a separation between cultural roots and citizenship, a Hong Kong identity does not naturally lead to support for regimes in Beijing. China's demand on their patriotism is as absurd as for the Queen of England to expect every Anglo-American to be loyal to the Crown. In the recent war of words between China and Britain over Governor Chris Patten's political proposals and the polarization of the Hong Kong population into pro-China and prodemocracy factions, cultural identity and patriotism have underlined the most heated issues. To the dismay of the Chinese leaders, 46.9 percent of the Hong Kong population in a recent survey continued to give Patten their support, despite vociferous and stinging attacks on Patten and the British business interests in the Chinese media which easily parallel the xenophobic tone and intensity of political rhetoric in the Cultural Revolution.[54]

Many who choose to stay in Hong Kong have been concerned enough with the affairs of China to become politically active.[55] The dramatic reactions in 1989 are an indicator of this activity. Hong Kong citizens raised 1.5 million dollars in a matter of days for the students during "Beijing Spring." When East Central China was literally under water in the summer of 1991, it was a similar group of prodemocracy professionals as well as popular performers who raised 75 million dollars overnight for the flood victims, a "patriotism" Beijing has swallowed not without ambivalence.

Moreover, the debate about democratizing the Hong Kong government before it becomes a part of China in 1997 has gathered momentum. In the 1991 elections for the legislative council, the liberal democrats won sixteen out of the eighteen seats allocated for direct election.[56] In the eyes of seasoned politicians, the campaign messages might seem naïve and the candidates inexperienced. But the election results are interpreted as a strong statement from the increasingly anxious and organized middle class: convergence with the Basic Law is important, but no more unquestioning deference to China for stability. The ironic point is that most of the elected legislators are not politicians but union leaders, doctors, teachers, and lawyers. Martin Lee, a British-trained lawyer, gained the highest number of votes. Soft-spoken in his Queen's English, he appears to have a stubborn conviction to play his traditional role as a concerned Chinese intellectual. His message is clear: he wants democracy and a degree of autonomy for Hong Kong as a safeguard against the inevitable encroachment of a regime which he considers self-righteous and unpredictable. His views are shared by younger professionals newly appointed or elected to the legislative council who now claim a share of the political limelight. In her speech to the Legislative Council backing Patten's political blueprint, the British-educated lawyer/company director Christine Loh demolished "the myth" behind convergence.[57] In response to China's recent threat to ignore the Sino-British agreements and to form its own legislative council and judicial organizations, Jacqueline Leong QC, chair of the influential Hong Kong Bar Association, publicly condemned Beijing's interference because she believes that Hong Kong's prosperity rests on judiciary independence and the rule of law.[58] To Beijing, this group of professionals are subversives precisely because they are committed to Hong Kong's future and are taking their Chineseness seriously.

Worse still for Beijing is the paradox of integration. China's intention to bring Hong Kong back into the Guangdong orbit has produced unexpected effects. Guangdong and in particular the Pearl River delta are assuming disproportional significance in the national economy. According to a report on the economic development of the region, Guangdong, with 5.6 percent of the nation's population, produced 9.2 percent of the Gross National Product (GNP) in 1990. In 1991, Guangdong exported 32 percent of national exports, of which the Pearl River delta was responsible for 74 percent. Foreign investment in the province and the delta respectively comprised 50 percent and 40 percent of the national total.[59] At the same time, Guangdong is detached from the rest of China by the powerful draw, via Hong Kong, of Western capitalist enterprises, of consumer culture and the freer intellectual linkages with the rest of the world. The mood in Guangdong during the spring and summer of 1989 was revealing. Cultural identity and political commitment to China, potentially problematic in history, made tenuous by the decade of reforms, were traumatically called into question by the events on the streets of Beijing.

It might have shocked policymakers in Beijing to realize that in the wake of June 4, 1989, they had to send special envoys to Guangdong to negotiate with the army. There was talk of civil war. The popular provincial head, Ye Xuanping, was eventually "promoted" to a position in Beijing but he continued to operate in Guangzhou. In reporting the June events, some China-owned newspapers in Hong Kong revolted, leading to the dismissal of a prominent editor of *Wenhui Pao*, followed by the eventual defection of the former head of the New China News Agency to the United States. When the Bank of China tried to cool the overheated economy by tightening the money supply for the unruly township enterprises in Guangdong, local managers stepped up their efforts to woo relatives overseas. For the first time, there was the hint of an integrated Guangdong-Hong Kong region declaring autonomous political status.

As in the past, the negotiation of cultural identity and the politics of difference in the 1990s are sustained by tensions in the public sphere as much as in private lives. South China continues to be unsettling for all concerned. From the way economic and political changes have progressed, it will be difficult for hard-liners in Beijing to choke off South China. The region has even captured the imagination of the political patriarch Deng Xiaoping during his recent trip. Although the Maoist revolution destroyed many cultural assumptions, the Beijing regime today recycles the old cultural identity in an effort to appropriate political allegiance from a region growing increasingly distant from it. Facing the encroachment, a rapidly liberalizing South China and Hong Kong are trying to redefine political expectations on a composite cultural terrain. Patriots and subversives are often the same group of people. When they flee, the political center cries traitor. When they turn around and act concerned, it cries subversive. Ironically, this exchange continues to lock the population of this region and Beijing over the affairs of China as a nation. How the tension is sustained or resolved depends on the regions' continual globalization as much as on the transformation of the Chinese polity. Whatever the outcome, it will not simply be an issue of an assertive regionalism breaking away from a political center, nor will it guarantee a standardizing cultural narrative. China as an experience will continue to have its many faces and meanings.

ACKNOWLEDGMENTS

This paper started as a presentation at a faculty dinner organized by the Yale Center for International and Area Studies. I thank James Scott, Deborah Davis, and William Kelly for comments on the paper and for theoretical inspiration. I also appreciate the comments from the participants at the authors' conference in September of 1992.

ENDNOTES

[1] See Helen Siu, "Recycling Tradition: Culture, History and Political Economy in the Chrysanthemum Festivals of South China," *Comparative Studies in Society and History* 32 (4) (October 1990): 765–94; Morris Rossabi, *China and Inner Asia from 1368 to the Present Day* (London: Thames and Hudson, 1981); Pamela Crossley, "Thinking About Ethnicity in Early Modern China," *Late Imperial China* 11 (1) (June 1990): 1–34; and Dru Gladney, *Muslim Chinese: Ethnic Nationalism in the People's Republic* (Cambridge, Mass.: Council on East Asian Studies, Harvard University, 1990).

[2] The idea of culture as a process, or as a moving target subject to constant reinvention, as Professor Robert Smith puts it, has become conventional wisdom in anthropology. See Sally F. Moore, *Law as Process: An Anthropological Approach* (London: Routledge and Kegan Paul, 1978); E. Hobsbawm and T. Ranger, eds., *The Invention of Tradition* (Cambridge: Cambridge University Press, 1983); and Sherry Ortner, "Theories in Anthropology Since the Sixties," *Comparative Studies in Society and History* 26 (1) (1984): 126–66.

[3] See Gladney, *Muslim Chinese*, chap. 2; Richard Fox, ed., *Nationalist Ideologies and the Production of National Cultures*, American Ethnological Society Monograph #2 (Washington, D.C.: American Anthropological Association, 1990); Barbara Ward, "Varieties of the Conscious Model: The Fishermen of South

China," in Michael Benton, ed., *The Relevance of Models for Social Anthropology* (London: Tavistock, 1965), 113–37; Fred C. Blake, *Ethnic Groups and Social Change in a Chinese Market Town* (Honolulu: The University Press of Hawaii, 1981); and Helen Siu and David Faure, "Down to Earth: The Territorial Bond in South China," (forthcoming).

[4]For similar observations and questions about a North-South dialogue in China, see Edward Friedman, "New Nationalist Identities in Post-Leninist Transformations: The Implication for China" (Hong Kong: The Hong Kong Institute of Asia-Pacific Studies, The Chinese University of Hong Kong, 1992). See also David Apter's paper in this issue of *Dædalus*.

[5]In this paper, South China refers to "Huanan," a region roughly within the provincial boundary of Guangdong.

[6]This is a point raised by Myron Cohen. See also Siu and Faure, "Down to Earth."

[7]See Carl L. Crossman, *The Decorative Arts of The China Trade* (Suffolk, England: Antique Collector's Club, 1991).

[8]Simon Murray, " 'Partnership of interest with China': a businessman's view," *Hong Kong Monitor,* December 1991. See also "The Fifth Tiger is on China's Coast," *Business Week,* 6 April 1992; and Willy Wo-lap Lam, "Coastal Areas to Seek Greater Autonomy," *South China Morning Post,* 29 October 1991, and "China's Renegade Province—Guangdong," *Newsweek,* 17 February 1992. In a November 1992 survey by the *South China Morning Post,* more people in Guangdong knew of Governor Chris Patten than their own governor.

[9]I have conducted fieldwork in the delta since 1974, spent a year in a market town in Zhongshan county in 1986, and have returned every year to other market towns. See "He Preaches Free Markets, Not Mao," *New York Times,* 11 May 1992.

[10]I was not surprised to hear the following statement by a former Party youth league leader turned private entrepreneur: "Chairman Mao once said that the scriptures are good, only that from time to time they had been recited by monks with crooked mouths. I wonder about the scriptures, it seems that they have distorted the mouths instead." Helen Siu, *Agents and Victims in South China: Accomplices in Rural Revolution* (New Haven: Yale University Press, 1989), chap. 13.

[11]These observations are echoed by Jonathan Unger who did fieldwork in towns in the eastern part of the Pearl River delta. Some of the criminal activities have spilled over the border to Hong Kong. Shoot-outs between Chinese mercenaries and Hong Kong police in the crowded streets of Hong Kong have become commonplace. See *South China Morning Post,* December 1992 and January 1993. The provincial government of Guangdong has periodically conducted mass public trials and executions of criminals. The most recent execution of forty-five criminals and the sentencing of over 1,100 were reported by *Yangcheng Evening News* and related in the *South China Morning Post* in Hong Kong, 11 January 1993.

[12]Myron Cohen, "Being Chinese: The Peripheralization of Traditional Identity," *Dædalus* 120 (2) (Spring 1991): 133.

13The Cold War atmosphere at the time probably gave the authorities plenty to worry about. The region was too close to the potentially "subversive" areas of Hong Kong, Taiwan, and Vietnam which were under heavy Anglo-American and French influence. Administrative autonomy was unthinkable. According to Pan Xiong, a former lecturer in Zhongshan University who participated in the surveys, much of the raw data remained classified. It is hard to verify his claims, but other scholars in China have confirmed the existence of raw data on a large number of minority groups. Volumes based on some of these data have been published in the recent decade. See Guangdong Sheng Renmin Zhengfu Minzu Shiwu Weiyuanhui, *Yangjiang yanhai ji Zhongshan gangkou shatian danmin yanjiu cailiao* (*Materials on the Dan fishermen along the Coast of Yangjiang and in the Sands of Zhongshan*) (Guangzhou: 1953).

14See the Introduction of Siu and Faure, "Down to Earth," for an analysis of that transformation. There is a vast anthropological literature on the symbolics of power associated with the position of being center. See Clifford Geertz, "Center, Kings, and Charisma: Reflections on the Symbolics of Power," *Local Knowledge* (New York: Basic Books, 1983), 124–46.

15See Liu Zhiwei, "Lineage on the Sands: The Case of Shawan," in Siu and Faure, "Down to Earth."

16See Nishikawa Kikuko, "Qingdai Zhujiang sanjiaozhou shatian kao" ("A Study of the Sands of the Pearl River delta"), trans. Cao Lei in *Lingnan wenshi* 2 (1985): 11–22. Originally published in *Tōyō gakuho* 63 (12) (1981): 93–136. In the reign of Qianlong, officials attempted to slow down the reclamation because it was causing flooding at the higher reaches of the Pearl River system.

17David Faure, *The Rural Economy of Pre-Liberation China: Trade Expansion and Peasant Livelihood in Jiangsu and Guangdong, 1870–1937* (Hong Kong: Oxford University Press, 1989).

18See Myron Cohen, "Lineage Organization in North China," *Journal of Asian Studies* (August 1990): 509–34.

19See David Faure, "The Lineage as a Cultural Invention: The Case of the Pearl River Delta," *Modern China* (January 1989): 4–36.

20See Susan Mann, *Local Merchants and the Chinese Bureaucracy, 1750–1950* (Stanford, Calif.: Stanford University Press, 1987).

21See David Faure, "What Made Foshan a Town? The Evolution of Rural-Urban Identities in Ming-Qing China," *Late Imperial China* 11 (2) (December 1990): 1–31.

22Ibid. For comparisons, see William Rowe, *Hankow: Conflict and Community in a Chinese City, 1796–1889* (Stanford, Calif.: Stanford University Press, 1989). For the twentieth century, see David Strand, *Rickshaw Beijing* (Berkeley: University of California Press, 1989), and Edward Rhodes, "Merchant Association in Canton, 1895–1911," in Mark Elvin and G. William Skinner, eds., *The Chinese City Between Two Worlds* (Stanford, Calif.: Stanford University Press, 1974).

23See Ye Xian'en and Tan Dihua, "Ming Qing Zhujiang sanjiaozhou nonyye shangyehua yu xushi de fazhan" ("Commercialization and the Development of Markets in the Pearl River delta during Ming and Qing"), *Guangdong shehui kexue* 2 (1984): 73–90.

[24]See Long Qingzhong et al., *Nanhai shenmiao* (*The Temple of the Nanhai Deity*) (Guangzhou: Guangzhou Shi Wenhua Ju, 1985).

[25]Despite their "modernizing" outlook, the overseas merchants had contributed much to what has been considered "traditional" cultural institutions such as ancestral estates and halls, village temples, communal granaries, and charity houses.

[26]Sun Lung-kee, "Zhongguo quyu fazhan de chayi," *Twenty-First Century* 10 (April 1992): 15–28.

[27]Ibid., 17.

[28]Benedict Anderson, *Imagined Communities: Reflection on the Origin and Spread of Nationalism*, rev. ed. (London: Verso, 1991).

[29]James Scott and Myron Cohen put this point to me as an observation and a question.

[30]For differing voices even under the most totalizing ideologies, see the theoretical works of James Scott, *Domination and the Arts of Resistance: Hidden Transcripts* (New Haven, Conn.: Yale University Press, 1990).

[31]Katherine Verdery, *National Ideology Under Socialism: Identity and Cultural Politics in Ceausescu's Romania* (Berkeley: University of California Press, 1991).

[32]Some of these British companies were pushing commodities into China. Some were large opium traders. See James Pope-Hennessy, *Half-Crown Colony: A Political Profile of Hong Kong* (Boston: Little Brown, 1969).

[33]For movements across the border and the effects on a rural community, see Patrick Hase, "Eastern Peace: Politics and Market in Shatoukok, 1825–1941," in Siu and Faure, "Down to Earth." Shatoukok, the border town between China and Hong Kong, was literally cut into two halves by the new political boundary in 1898.

[34]See Maurice Freedman, *Lineage Organization in Southeastern China* (London: Athlone, 1958); and *Chinese Lineage and Society: Fukien and Kwangtung* (London: Athlone, 1966); James Watson, *Emigration and the Chinese Lineage* (Berkeley: University of California Press, 1975); Rubie Watson, *Inequality Among Brothers: Class and Kinship in South China* (Cambridge: Cambridge University Press, 1985); David Faure, *The Structure of Chinese Rural Society: Lineage and Village in the Eastern New Territories* (Hong Kong: Oxf rd University Press, 1986); and James Hayes, *The Hong Kong Region, 1850–1ᵧₓ* (Hamden, Conn.: Archon Books, 1977).

[35]See a study of these merchants by Elizabeth Sinn, *Power and Charity* (Hong Kong: Oxford University Press, 1989). At a back room of the temple on Tai Ping Shan Street, thousands of tablets belonging to sojourners who had died were stacked. To the dismay of David Faure and myself, during a visit in 1991, we found that the temple caretaker had thrown away all the old tablets and replaced them with pieces of paper bearing only the names.

[36]In the late nineteenth century, many of the leading Cantonese agents for foreign companies in China were educated in British missionary schools in Hong Kong. The University of Hong Kong was established in 1911.

37Rey Chow, *Women and Chinese Modernity* (Minneapolis: University of Minnesota Press, 1990).

38See Liang Tao, *Origins of Hong Kong Street Names* (Hong Kong: Urban Council, 1992, in Chinese).

39See contrasting versions of what Hong Kong has accomplished. The annual *Hong Kong* reports through the years promotes the government views. *The Other Hong Kong Report* published by The Chinese University Press, Hong Kong, reveals hidden agendas and unintended results.

40See Siu-lun Wong, *Emigrant Entrepreneurs: Shang Industrialists in Hong Kong* (Hong Kong: Oxford University Press, 1988).

41See Siu-kai Lau, *Society and Politics in Hong Kong* (Hong Kong: The Chinese University Press, 1982), on population movements. See the section of the annual *Hong Kong* report on population and immigration for yearly figures.

42See Chow Wing-sun, "Xianggang mianlin renkou baozha" ("Hong Kong Faces Population Explosion"), *Qishi niandai* (November 1980): 23–36; and Li Mingkun, "Neidi laike de shehui gongneng" ("The Social Functions of Aliens from the Mainland"), *Qishi niandai* (December 1980): 59–60. For famine figures for the Great Leap Forward, see Mu Fu, "Zhonggong zhiguo de sanci dacuobai" ("The Three Political Failures of the Chinese Communists"), *Jiushi niandai* 177 (1984): 41–48.

43See Helen Siu, "Immigrants and Social Ethos: Hong Kong in the Nineteen-Eighties," *Journal of the Hong Kong Branch of the Royal Asiatic Society* 26 (1986) (1988): 1–16, on the experiences of some of these new immigrants. See also Chow Wing-sun, *Xianggang ren Xianggang shi* (Hong Kong: Ming Pao, 1987), for general transformations of Hong Kong society. See debates on this new rising "middle class" between Cheung Ping-leung, "Xin zhongchan jieji de muqi yu zhengzhi yingxiang," *Ming Pao Monthly* (January 1987): 10–15, and Lui Tai-lok, "Xianggang xin zhongchan jieji de teshe yu qianlu," *Ming Pao Monthly* (April 1987): 13–19.

44In 1990, the per capita GNP was approximately $12,000, approaching that of Australia and New Zealand. See *Hong Kong 1991* (Hong Kong: Government Information Service); see also an article on what the governor, Lord Wilson, has achieved in his five years in Hong Kong, *South China Morning Post*, 31 December 1991.

45People in Hong Kong are exposed to a concentrated dose of media through television, radio, newspapers, and magazines. On popular culture in Hong Kong, see Chow Wa-shan, *Zhou Runfa xianxiang (The Phenomenon of Zhou Runfa)* (Hong Kong: Qingwen, 1990); Lo Kwai-cheung, *Dazhong wenhua yu Xianggang* (Hong Kong: Qingwen, 1990); and Cheung Kin-ting, *Xiao zichan jieji zhouji (The Diary of a Petty Bourgeoise)* (Hong Kong: Chuangjian, 1992).

46See Akhil Gupta and James Fergeuson, "Introduction," *Cultural Anthropology* 7 (1) (February 1992): 6–23; and Ajun Appadurai, "Disjuncture and Difference in the Global Cultural Economy," *Theory, Culture and Society* 7 (1990): 295–310.

47Christine McGee, Ann Quon, and Louis Ng, "Power to the baby boomers," *South China Morning Post*, 2 January 1993.

48These episodes have been played up in both English and Chinese language newspapers in the last two years (1991–1992). See *South China Morning Post, The Hong Kong Standard, Ming Pao Daily,* and *Sing Tao Daily.* The frequent armed robberies appeared in newspaper headlines starting as early as 1984. See also Lo Tit-wing, "Law and Order," in Joseph Cheng and Paul Kwong, eds., *The Other Hong Kong Report* (Hong Kong: The Chinese University Press, 1992), 127–48; in the same volume, see Claudia Mo, "Disciplinary Forces: Police in the Limelight," 405–24.

49See Paul Kwong, "Emigration and Manpower Shortage," in Richard Wong and Joseph Cheng, eds., *The Other Hong Kong Report* (Hong Kong: The Chinese University Press, 1990), 297–337; and Lee Ming-kun, "Yimin chao yu guoke chingjie—guodu qi Xianggang ren de shehui yishi," *Xin bao caiqing yuekan* (January 1988): 26–30.

50See Kwong, "Emigration and Manpower Shortage," 303, quoting a study done by Pak-wai Liu and Stephen Tang.

51Emigration figures are between 40,000 to 60,000 per year. There was a jump after 4 June 1989. See Karen MacGregor, "Wealth with a heart," *The Times (U.K.) Higher Education Supplement* (29 November 1991). See also the *Hong Kong* annual report 1991 on the goals of the University and Polytechnic Grants Committee to increase tertiary education.

52For the close ties between Hong Kong and Canada, see Diana Lary, "Canada in Hong Kong," in *The Other Hong Kong Report,* 95–109.

53"Hong Kong Hustle is Heating Up Canada," *Business Week,* 23 September 1991.

54See Jonathan Braude, "Tide of public opinion swings behind Patten," *South China Morning Post,* 14 December 1992; and Doreen Cheung, "Jardines attacked in new salvo by Beijing," *South China Morning Post,* 18 December 1992.

55See the changing political dynamic as described by Siu-kai Lau, *Xianggang de zhengji gaige yu zhengzhi fazhan* (Hong Kong: Wide Angle Press, 1988).

56See Steve Tsang, "A Triumph for Democracy?" *Hong Kong Monitor* (December 1991) and local newspaper reports around September-October 1991. See also the report by the *New York Times,* 17 September 1991.

57Marita Eager, "Newcomer Loh speaks her mind and wins her spurs," *South China Morning Post,* 12 November 1992.

58Lindy Course, "QC condemns China threat, Legal profession urged to defend people's rights," *South China Morning Post,* 12 January 1993.

59See Pak-wai Liu et al., *Zhongguo gaige kaifang yu Zhujiang Sanjiaozhou de jingji fazhan* (Hong Kong: Nanyang Commercial Bank, 1992).

The Pearl River Delta

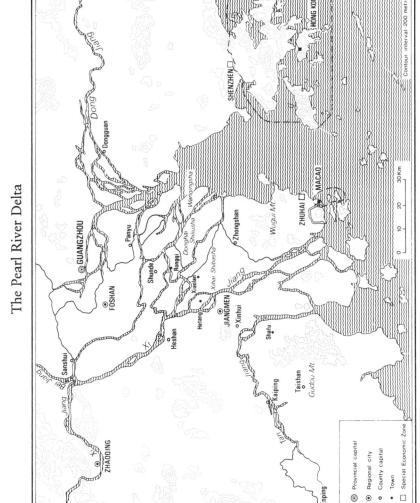

Helen F. Siu, *Agents and Victims in South China: Accomplices in Rural Revolution*, copyright © 1989. Reprinted by permission of Yale University Press.

Again and again we have said that we should never interfere in the internal affairs of the Chinese. But we know that this is only diplomatically, technically, or legally true. It cannot be historically true. For a half century at least, the United States has been a major and busy maker of Chinese history. Americans have fought three major wars in which, for one reason or another, China was a distinct contributing cause. Now the inconsistency can be reconciled, as a sense of common destiny of mankind has emerged from the rounds of conflict, and our understanding of the past is widened by current events. We cannot hold back this knowledge. What is more, when the entire record is reviewed in a worldwide perspective, the conclusions drawn should facilitate our understanding of other nations and civilizations still in various stages of the same struggle, in which the United States may again be involved. Maybe the agony can be avoided or at least lessened, with the Chinese experience as a hindsight.

Ray Huang

From *China: A Macrohistory*

Reprinted by permission of the author. Published by M. E. Sharpe, Inc., Armonk, New York, copyright © 1990.

William P. Alford

# Double-edged Swords Cut Both Ways: Law and Legitimacy in the People's Republic of China

WHEN WE THINK OF TRIALS IN the People's Republic of China (PRC), our minds turn first to the prosecutions that followed the suppression in June 1989 of the "Beijing Spring" prodemocracy movement.[1] From the first expedited proceedings leading to summary executions that same month[2] through the 1991 trials which the PRC government asserted "basically completed" cases arising from the events of 1989,[3] the weight of the Chinese criminal justice system was brought to bear upon hundreds of citizens who participated in or otherwise supported the students and workers who occupied their capital's main square and the world's imagination in the late spring of 1989.[4]

Our obligation to remain mindful of persons subjected to criminal punishment for their association with the Beijing Spring movement ought not to obscure a seemingly very different use of the law in contemporary China. Over the past year, an array of Chinese citizens, many of them prominent, have brought suit against organs and officials of their government and of the Communist Party, to which most of the plaintiffs belonged. They have alleged a variety of constitutional and legal transgressions, including defamation, physical mistreatment, improper seizure of private correspondence subject to constitutional protection, and other abuses of administrative power, and have sought remedies including injunctions against continued misuses of authority, compensation for economic and

*William P. Alford is Henry L. Stimson Professor of Law and Director of East Asian Legal Studies at Harvard Law School.*

reputational harm suffered, formal apologies, and independent investigations.

Although none of these cases has attained its stated legal objective—as the plaintiffs anticipated prior to filing their cases—that hardly diminishes their importance. They provide a valuable prism through which to examine Chinese legal and political reforms commencing after the Cultural Revolution[5] (which ran from 1966 to 1976). These reforms have neither been as full as the government's propaganda would have us believe[6] nor as fallow as its domestic and foreign opponents would like us to think.[7] This should not be surprising, given the mix of motives that lay behind them and the quandary that efforts to deploy legality in a highly instrumental fashion[8] pose for what Václav Havel has termed the post-totalitarian state—by which he means authoritarian regimes that have moved beyond "revolutionary excitement, heroism, dedication, and boisterous violence. . . . "[9] In so doing, they evoke notions of justice that run deeply through the course of Chinese history.

This article focuses on five of the most important cases: those brought by the novelist and former Minister of Culture, Wang Meng; the well placed journalist, Dai Qing; the outspoken philosophy professor, Guo Luoji; and two of the most celebrated dissidents imprisoned in the aftermath of the Beijing Spring, Wang Juntao and Chen Ziming. It commences by seeking to reconstruct these extraordinary and little publicized cases, and is followed by an effort to explore the range of motives that spurred these very different individuals to sue their government and Party. The article then seeks to explore through these cases the interplay of legality and power in the contemporary People's Republic of China as well as authoritarian societies more generally. It concludes with a brief consideration of the implications of these deployments of legality for a post-totalitarian China.

THE CASES

*Wang Meng*

Wang Meng's life in many respects exemplifies the vicissitudes of intellectuals throughout the history of the People's Republic of China. Although he joined the Party at age thirteen, two years prior to the People's Republic of China's foundation in 1949, and published his first novel while still a teenager,[10] Wang Meng was subjected to what was to be the first of a number of denunciations during the Anti-Rightist Movement of 1957.[11] Effectively barred from writing during the early years of the Cultural Revolution, Wang turned what was in essence an internal exile in Xinjiang into an opportunity to learn, immersing himself in the language and mores of the Uigher minority who occupy that border region. These political and social experiences, in turn, provided a reservoir from which poured forth a torrent of sophisticated modernist works commencing in 1980. Notwithstanding (or, some would suggest, because of) the strongly antisocialist realist character of his writing, Wang was named Minister of Culture during a relatively open period of the mid-1980s. Soon after the uprising of 1989, however, he was removed from office and criticized for his bourgeois thinking, as he had been in each of the three preceding decades.

The events leading to Wang's invocation of the state's formal legal processes in 1991 had their genesis in a short story he published in February 1989 while still Minister of Culture entitled "Jianyingde xizhou" ("Hard, Thin Gruel").[12] Wang's story, for which the Tianjin magazine *Xiaoshou yuebao* (*The Novel Monthly*) awarded him its *baihua jiang* (One Hundred Flowers Award) in 1990, centers around the efforts of four generations of a Chinese family to determine how to conduct their affairs and, in particular, what to eat. Concerned that the traditional Chinese breakfast of *congee* (rice gruel), steamed bread, and pickled vegetables is nutritionally inadequate and so, responsible for China's lack of progress and real stability, the family's sixteen-year-old scion abruptly switches the family's diet to Western food. A mere three days of such items as buttered toast and coffee with milk exhausts the family's monthly food allocation and, worse yet, leaves several members ill, including its loyal, if slightly corrupt, housekeeper of forty years. The disorder that ensues is only resolved with the introduction of a household election through which the family's eighty-eight-year-old patriarch is chosen to lead the family. He manages to restore stability, but not before the housekeeper, who has been highly skeptical of the while process, dies. In the end, although family members eat different items, rice gruel, steamed bread, and pickles remain their favorite fare.

Not all readers shared the *Xiaoshuo yuebao*'s enthusiasm for "Thin, Hard Gruel." On September 14, 1991, *Wenyi bao* (*The Literature and Art Gazette*), which is published under the auspices of the Ministry of Culture and is considered the Communist Party's most prominent vehicle for expressing its views on issues concerning the arts, ran a letter denouncing Wang and his story.[13] Written under the pseudonym Shen Ping, the letter cited an analysis of the story that appeared in the anti-Communist Taipei magazine *Zhongguo dalu* (*The Chinese Mainland*) to the effect that "Thin, Hard Gruel" was but a thinly veiled criticism of Deng Xiaoping, the People's Republic of China's octogenarian patriarch, and the program of reform that he and other of his generation had instituted. In order to continue the reform process, the letter continued, such attacks on China's leaders and political system should not be tolerated. Given the letter's contents, suggestions abound that it actually was written by or at the behest of *Wenyi bao*'s editor, Zheng Bonong,[14] who, presumably, would not have dared to attack Wang without at least the implicit approval of the then Acting Minister of Culture, He Jingzhi, who assumed office upon Wang's dismissal.[15]

Wang Meng responded by instituting a civil action against both Shen Ping and *Wenyi bao*,even though he remained a leading figure in the state directed Chinese Writer's Association, the entity that oversees professional authors and exercises a measure of control over the *Wenyi bao*.[16] In his complaint, Wang alleged violation of ARTICLE 120 of the 1986 General Principles of the Civil Law which recognized a citizen's right to protect his "name, likeness, reputation, or honor."[17] The suit further derided the suggestion that his story had been intended as a criticism of Deng Xiaoping or the reform efforts and chided Shen Ping for relying on a Taiwan magazine to interpret "Thin, Hard Gruel." His reputation could only be vindicated and the harm occasioned him arrested, the complaint contended, if the court ordered the defendants publicly to apologize for their libelous words and to pay him 2,000 *yuan* in compensation.[18]

Despite the assistance of the lawyer Zhang Sizhi who vigorously defended Wang Juntao a year earlier,[19] the local Beijing court where Wang initially sought to file his suit (the Chaoyang District People's Court) refused to accept his papers, asserting that it lacked jurisdiction over so highly placed a Party personage as a former Minister of Culture who was then still a Central Committee member. Wang thereupon filed his complaint with the Beijing Intermediate People's Court. It agreed to receive his filing, but within ten days and without a hearing, that court rejected his suit in a brief decision declaring, without intending irony, that Shen Ping's criticism fell within the bounds of "normal literary criticism" and therefore was not actionable legally.[20] Subsequent efforts by Wang to appeal the case and separately to call into question ex parte contacts between the Beijing Intermediate People's Court and the defendants prior to rendering its decision have proven unavailing. The controversy has remained in the public eye, however. Not only have publications such as *Dushu zhoukan* (*Reading's Weekly*) reported on the case in defiance of what is said to be a ban issued by the Party's Central Committee Propaganda Department,[21] but Wang has published two further pieces concerning the consumption of rice gruel. The first, "Wo ai he xizhou" ("I Love Thin Gruel"), published in the *Nongmin ribao* (*The Peasant's Daily*) in November 1991, attests to his particular affection for thin, hard gruel built up over years of travail but concludes by declaring that in the future "I believe we will all be eating better, more nutritious, more civilized and more pleasant food."[22] In the second piece, "Huashuo zhewan xizhou" ("Speaking about This Bowl of Gruel") which appeared in the December issue of *Dushu* (*Readings*), he portrays the original tale as one of "humor and satire [intended] to make fun of our people's shortcomings and weaknesses."[23]

## Dai Qing

However intricate the controversy swirling about Wang Meng and "Thin, Hard Gruel" may be, it pales before that concerning Dai Qing, whose history highlights many of the contradictions of Chinese factional politics from the late Qing dynasty (1644–1911) onward. Said to be a distant descendant of Pu Yi, the last Qing emperor, and the daughter of a revolutionary martyr, Dai Qing (who was born Fu Xiaqing and later known as Fu Ning) was adopted at age four by Ye Jianying, one of the People's Liberation Army's (PLA) ten marshals and a paramount leader of the People's Republic of China until his death in 1985.[24] Despite her training as a design engineer for the guidance system of intercontinental ballistic missiles, soon after the onset of the Cultural Revolution, she became a Red Guard and spent years in the countryside. At the end of the Cultural Revolution, through family contacts she joined the PLA, and became an intelligence agent, responsible for monitoring Eastern European writers, Western journalists, and other foreigners.[25]

Tiring, as she has put it, of having to "cheat people into believing you,"[26] in 1982 Dai arranged to join the staff of the *Guangming ribao* (*The Enlightenment Daily*), the principal state newspaper addressed to intellectuals (defined in the People's Republic of China as persons having at least a high school education). There, aided by links that included not only her adoptive father, but her adoptive brother, former Governor Ye Xuanping of Guangdong province (who is Marshal Ye's son), and her "godmother," Deng Yingchao (who was Zhou Enlai's widow, Premier Li Peng's stepmother, and a figure of political consequence in her own right), Dai embarked on a career as an investigative journalist. Although one might take issue with Geremie Barmé and Linda Jaivin's recent florid description of Dai's work during this period as "one of the most intriguing intellectual projects undertaken by anyone in China in the late 1980s,"[27] there is no denying that she produced a torrent of material—many pieces were published in the *Guangming ribao* and in other PRC media but some was barred from broad dissemination by the Party—that called into question the mainstream Communist Party treatment of a variety of issues and personalities, both past and present. These ranged from articles seeking to rehabilitate as yet unreconstructed victims of the Anti-Rightist and Cultural Revolution days, to exposés of abuses of power by many of China's more conservative contemporary leaders, to pieces that sought with un-usual vigor and directness to address the censorship of journalists and China's all too pervasive environmental degradation and gender discrimination.

Conservative Communist Party leaders were not the only ones to feel the wrath of Dai's pen. She has attacked persons standing at the edge of or outside of the Party who called for more substantial reform than the Party's more liberal leaders, such as Hu Yaobang, were willing to tolerate. She derided figures such as Liu Binyan, longtime investigative journalist, mocking his efforts to maintain a "second kind of loyalty."[28] Dai advocated what became known as *xin quanweizhuyi* (neo-authoritarianism), arguing in essence that China needed a benevolent authoritarian ruler akin to President Chiang Ching-kuo of the Republic of China in order to eventually end autocracy.[29]

In keeping with the type of concerns expressed in her support for a continued, more benevolent form of authoritarian rule in China, Dai took a more measured approach than most intellectuals toward the fledgling student and worker groups who were to occupy Tiananmen Square in the late spring of 1989.[30] Considering the movement politically naïve and likely to court a sharp response, she sought, without success, to persuade the demonstrators to evacuate the Square. In early June, she resigned from the Party. Despite her efforts to encourage the demonstrators to relinquish the Square, Dai was accused soon after June 4 in an article published in her own newspaper entitled "Dongluan jizhe Dai Qing" ("Reporter of the Turmoil Dai Qing") of being a "pawn of reactionary forces in and out of China" and was detained in Qincheng Prison for ten months.[31]

Freed from prison in 1990 and subsequently allowed to take up a fellowship at Harvard, Dai filed suit in late 1991 against both the author of the article and the *Guangming ribao*. Drawing on the legal logic of Wang Meng's case and her own legal research while imprisoned, Dai's complaint argues that by labeling her a supporter of the demonstrators and worse yet, a pawn of others, the article has damaged her reputation and she therefore seeks a public apology, relying on ARTICLE 120 of the General Principles of the Civil Code. "I don't dare to hope that my case will win," she informed Western journalists, "but even if I lose, it still shows that the Chinese people's understanding of law has increased. . . . "[32]

## Guo Luoji

Although Guo Luoji has been as unknown beyond the People's Republic of China as Dai Qing has been lionized, many thoughtful Chinese are of the opinion that it is Guo and individuals like him who warrant praise for having put into public play particularly bold and difficult questions regarding the character of Chinese political life. A distinguished professor of philosophy at Beijing University, Guo first ventured into the national political arena in 1979, during the prosecution of political dissident Wei Jingsheng, with an extraordinary essay entitled "Political Issues Can Be Discussed."[33] In the essay, published in *Renmin ribao* (*The People's Daily*), the official organ of the Chinese Communist Party (CCP) and China's most prominent newspaper, Guo raised serious questions as to whether the systemic problems in China's political culture that had given rise to the so-called Gang of Four continued even after their demise.

Guo Luoji's questioning incurred the wrath of Deng Xiaoping and other senior leaders; as a consequence, he was barred from publishing in Party organs. Undeterred and buoyed by the support of important personages such as then Party Chief Hu Yaobang, Guo instead continued to publish in *Renmin ribao* and elsewhere through the barely concealed ruse of a pen name. Though the name changed, the content continued to annoy conservative Party elders. In 1982, Guo was transferred from his post at Beijing University to the less prestigious Nanjing University and simultaneously removed from the membership rolls of the Communist Party.

In Guo's case, absence hardly made the heart grow fonder. He not only continued to express the type of views he had earlier espoused but he took the Party leadership to task for having ordered the PLA militarily to suppress the Beijing Spring movement and for the wave of repression that he saw subsequently sweeping China. As a result, in early 1991, the General Secretary of Nanjing University's Communist Party branch informed him that he was no longer politically qualified, which, in turn, meant that he was no longer competent to hold his professorial position. Later in the same year, the University announced, through the chair of the Philosophy Department, that Guo had become superfluous professionally and therefore could no longer lecture or supervise graduate students.[34]

Guo responded to the effort to terminate his professional existence by filing two related but distinct actions in the Nanjing City Intermediate People's Court—one directed against the Nanjing University Communist Party Committee and the other against Director Li Tieying of the State Education Commission, Nanjing University President Qu Qianyu, and Philosophy Department Chair Lin Dehong. In the former action, Guo argued that the Party's actions were in clear violation of ARTICLE 5 of the Constitution of the People's Republic of China which provides, inter alia, that ". . . all political parties. . . must abide by the Constitution and the law. . . " as said actions unfairly deprived him of fundamental political, economic, and social rights to which he was entitled by the Constitution as well as improperly limiting his legal right to travel internationally. The reasons invoked by the Party to justify its treatment of him, the complaint contended, consisted of little more than its displeasure with the objections that he had raised to the suppression of the Beijing Spring and to other abuses of power that he believed to be occurring in the Party. To penalize him for raising such objections, Guo continued, not only flew in the face of the *Communist Manifesto* and the People's Republic of China's 1991 *White Paper on Human Rights*, but was simply illogical, as it implied that one must support the leadership no matter what it did. This, he suggested, was the type of behavior that one would have anticipated from the Beiyang warlord government soon after the toppling of the Qing in 1911 or from the Guomindang in its early years, rather than from the Communist Party, given its professed ideals.[35] The situation, he concluded, could only be set straight by restoring his full rights, compensating him financially for the damage done both to his reputation and his wallet, and by taking to task those local Party officials who had undertaken the actions in question.

Guo's second action was equally bold. It accused the powerful head of the State Education Commission, Li Tieying, and Guo's superiors at Nanjing University of having violated both ARTICLE 42 of the Constitution, which guaranteed "the right as well as the duty to work," and ARTICLE 75 of the General Principles of the Civil Law, which indicated that a citizen's "lawful property" included "lawful income" and forbade "any group or individual" from illegally ". . . interfering with. . . or impounding, sequestering, freezing or confiscating [it]." China's newly implemented Administrative Procedure Law, continued the complaint, provided the authority needed to bring an action against these state employees in order to restore Guo's rights and to adequately compensate him for the reputational and economic harm occasioned.

On February 29, 1992, the Nanjing City Intermediate People's Court issued a brief written decision rejecting Guo Luoji's petitions on jurisdictional grounds, thereby avoiding the need to reach the merits, although it did grant Guo the right to appeal.[36] The Nanjing University Communist Party Committee, said the court, was an entity under the CCP and, as such, was not a state administrative agency. Accordingly, it was not amenable to suit under the Administrative Procedure Law. Nor, continued the court, was it in a position to review the decisions taken by the State Education Commission and Nanjing University regarding Guo's teaching status, as these were "internal decisions." Under ARTICLE 5 of the Administrative Procedure Law, it concluded, courts were only empowered to consider the legality, rather than the wisdom or propriety, of matters within an agency's area of administrative competence.

Guo availed himself of his right to appeal and in less than a fortnight filed a carefully crafted brief with the Jiangsu Province High People's Court.[37] The lower court, Guo argued, had confused important legal distinctions that he had taken pains to recognize in dividing his causes of action into two separate cases. After all, he reminded the appellate court, his initial case against the Party was premised on the Constitution and had implicitly left to the Nanjing City Intermediate People's Court the task of ascertaining which law provided the best vehicle for vindicating his constitutional rights,[38] given that China lacked a law on political parties.[39] The lower court's contention that his case should be dismissed because the Administrative Procedure Law was inapplicable to Party actions was illogical because it was the judges and not he, who had relied on this particular statute. Surely, he continued, it would be inappropriate now to deny him justice because the lower court had erred by incorporating arguments he had raised in one case into the other. In making these points, Guo reiterated, he was not opposing the CCP, but rather seeking—until such time as China had a comprehensive law on political parties and effective means for enforcing this and other legal limits—to help root out the abusive use of power, extremism, and corruption that were undercutting the Party's efforts to attain its avowed objectives.

The Nanjing City Intermediate People's Court ought also, continued Guo, to have answered the question he had raised as to who had made the decision barring him from leaving China to participate in an international conference. Had this decision been made by the proper state entities or by the Party, which, in theory, lacked the legal authority to decide such matters? If the latter had been the motive force, would not the decision be an even more inappropriate assertion of power, given that the Party had expelled him from membership and therefore theoretically had no ongoing nexus of control over him. In short, Guo suggested, was this not an illustration of the Party seeking to act as the "unwritten law beyond the law."

If the lower court's approach toward the Party's behavior was flawed, continued Guo's appeal, so, too, was its refusal to probe more deeply into his treatment at the hands of the educational bureaucracy. What was the difference between an internal and an external decision? Moreover, how could a decision be deemed internal to a governmental organization if it was based upon judgments formed by nongovernmental entities that were themselves said by the court to be immune from the Administrative Procedure Law and other measures designed to protect individuals from arbitrariness? More specifically, the State Education Commission and the University administration had found no fault with Guo's work as a teacher of philosophy, but had instead sought to remove him from his position because he had challenged the Communist Party. Would not these educational officials be less likely to have engaged in some of the repressive behavior of the post-June 4 period had they made their decisions on the basis of professional, rather than political considerations? Guo felt that the Jiangsu Province High People's Court should remand his cases to the Nanjing City Intermediate People's Court for reconsideration and should order local Party officials to refrain from pressuring him and instruct them instead to await a final decision from the courts.

Not surprisingly, the Jiangsu Province High People's Court rejected Guo's appeal without reaching its merits. Guo has since appealed further to the Supreme People's Court in Beijing but has yet to receive its judgment.[40] In the interim, he has been allowed to go abroad in order to take up a position as Visiting Scholar at Columbia University for the 1993 calendar year.

## Wang Juntao and Chen Ziming

The attempts of Wang Juntao, Chen Ziming, and their families to invoke the law to limit the abusive practices visited upon them have received even shorter shrift from the courts than those of Wang Meng, Dai Qing, and Guo Luoji. Although each of these alleged leaders of the demonstrations of 1989 was well under the age of forty at the time of the Beijing Spring, Wang and Chen had already had extensive experience with the law, having first been imprisoned for their roles in the 1976 Tiananmen Square protests commemorating the death of the former Premier Zhou Enlai and for subsequently running afoul of the police during the heyday of the so-called Democracy Wall in the late 1970s and early 1980s.[41] In the relatively more open climate of the mid-1980s, Wang and Chen founded the Beijing Institute of Social and Economic Science, which served as a base for their efforts to conduct independent survey research, translate and introduce major Western thinkers, report on economic phenomena in the Institute's own journal, and otherwise foster the process of greater openness both internally and with the world beyond China.

Despite these endeavors, as the Beijing Spring unfolded in April 1989, Wang and Chen initially avoided too prominent a role. With President Yang Shangkun's declaration of martial law on May 20, 1989, however, Wang and Chen moved to the foreground and joined with a number of intellectuals having links to reformists in the Party leadership to form the so-called Joint Liaison Group. Although they counseled nonviolence and sought a constructive resolution to the occupation of Tiananmen Square, these efforts were for naught and both fled soon after June 4.

Wang and Chen remained in hiding until they were captured in southern China in the autumn of 1989. Both were detained without formal arrest, in contravention of Chinese law, until early 1991, at which point they were labeled the "black hands behind the black hands" and sent to trial, accused of "conspiring to overthrow" the state and engaging in "counterrevolutionary propaganda and agitation."[42] Despite an extraordinarily courageous defense by their counsel, they were convicted of multiple charges of conspiracy and sentenced to thirteen years in prison.

Wang Juntao's suit grows out of his confinement, where, according to his family, he contracted hepatitis B and a number of other health problems.[43] Both during his lengthy pretrial detention and for months following his conviction in February 1991, Wang's wife, Hou Xiaotian, sought through public statements, addressed both to the People's Republic of China's leadership and the outside world, to highlight her husband's situation. When that failed, she endeavored to petition China's legislature, the National People's Congress.[44] In March 1992, as it became apparent that this and other avenues were unavailing, Hou brought suit against her husband's jailers for negligence in allowing him to contract hepatitis B, against the Supreme People's Procuracy for having confiscated his diary and recorder, against the Public Security Ministry for defamation in suggesting that Wang had a role in the attacks upon PLA troops, and against *Xinhua* (New China News Agency) for "mistakes in press coverage" in its portrayal of her husband's role in the Beijing Spring.[45] Despite the variegated nature of her complaint, Hou has had no more success than the other plaintiffs chronicled above.

Chen Ziming has had similar results. In December 1991, Chen's family filed suit on his behalf against *Xinhua* for having distributed a news story saying that he "had participated in and directly commanded" blockades against martial law troops in 1989, against *Renmin ribao* for reporting that he was apprehended in 1989 while trying to sneak out of China, and against both the State Education Commission and an affiliated publishing house for their treatment of his role in the events leading up to June 4, 1989.[46] Less than a month after these actions were filed in the District People's Court, they were rejected for being "too complex."[47]

MOTIVES

The difficulty of discerning motivation, the complexity of which we all too often underestimate, is compounded in these cases not only by geographic and cultural distance, but also by the very restrictions on direct expression that, broadly speaking, gave rise to these suits. To be sure, the plaintiffs have each indicated that they brought their suits to attain the specific legal relief asked for in them and to demonstrate their growing awareness of their legal rights.[48] Yet, clearly, there is far more involved when people who have been high enough within the system to understand its limitations and dissidents who have been particularly victimized by its brutality commence formal legal proceedings that they know have scant chance of being adjudicated on the merits, let alone resolved in their favor.

In striving to understand why Wang Meng, Dai Qing, Guo Luoji, Wang Juntao, and Chen Ziming chose to bring actions that they knew could not attain their stated legal ends, one can identify a number of possible rationale intended for a range of audiences. As individuals who had earlier sought to focus attention on abuses of power by government and Party through private remonstrations, critical writings, and interaction with foreign journalists, each of the five must have looked at the possibility of invoking the state's law in its courts as offering an extraordinary vehicle through which to give voice to vital concerns. After all, from 1978 onward, the People's Republic of China had gone to considerable lengths to highlight its work in legal development both at home and abroad.[49] The law reform effort provided China's post-Cultural Revolution leadership with a means for distinguishing itself from its immediate predecessors and otherwise enhancing its legitimacy even as it also expressed the desire of some in leadership circles to prevent the recurrence of the very type of arbitrary abuse of power through which they had suffered. These undertakings also had the added benefit of providing the legal infrastructure that many in top positions felt necessary both to spur the growth of the domestic commodity economy and to convince foreign business more comfortably to part with the capital and technology China so sorely needed. And, after June 1989, further revision of state law was for some an expedient way of addressing the many human rights charges leveled at the People's Republic of China and so, of shoring up Beijing's damaged international credibility.[50]

The very effort that the People's Republic of China's leadership focused on building up and publicizing the formal legal system goes far to explain its appeal to individuals otherwise having difficulty in making their voices heard. The mere act of filing a complaint enables litigants to juxtapose publicly the gap between the state's professed ideals and lived reality with a rare drama, clarity, and moral force—whether their goal be to attack particular individuals and institutions without appearing vengeful or to raise more systemic questions about legitimacy. Litigation further poses a profound dilemma for the authorities by requiring, in effect, that the state either provide the litigant a day in court to make his case or appear to be acting in hypocritical disregard of processes that it has labored hard to publicize. The very real possibility that the state might choose the latter course, as it did in each of these cases, only enhances litigation's attractiveness. Through litigation, plaintiffs are able not only to reveal what they believe to be prior wrongdoing, but can also look forward to the government further undercutting its own legitimacy through its handling of their cases. Indeed, it may not be too irreverent to suggest that some of these litigants, including Wang Meng, might well have been disappointed had the court accorded them full procedural justice, as that would have denied them the chance to make their larger points about the legal and political climate.

If the particular instrument of a lawsuit against the ruler and its agents is a relatively new one in Chinese society, it bears more than a faint echo of a very deeply rooted tradition—namely, that of the virtuous official confronting corrupted authority in the name of higher ideals.[51] In its classic embodiment, the courtier often stands falsely accused by the very persons whose wickedness is responsible for misdirecting the ruler, but he is ultimately less concerned with personal vindication than with alerting the ruler to the moral calamity that awaits, absent a return to the higher virtues pursuant to which society is to be directed. This image is perhaps most powerfully evident in the example of Chu Yuan (338–278 B.C.), the loyal minister of the preimperial state of Chu (403–221 B.C.), who was driven to suicide by his heroic, but futile, attempts to alert his ruler to the dangers posed by those close to the throne misusing the authority vested in them.[52] Indeed, at least from the time of the Grand Historian Sima Qian (145–90 B.C.) onward,[53] the story of Chu Yuan, a lyric poet who devoted much attention during his time as an official to reforming his state's laws, has taken on a mythic quality and has been deployed by a range of actors from Confucian scholar-officials to the CCP. More prosaically, at least from China's first imperial legal code of the Qin (221–206 B.C.),[54] false accusations have been treated with particular severity throughout Chinese history[55]—as well they might when one considers the paucity of ways available for individuals to vindicate themselves in a society that has relatively limited avenues of public expression.

That figures such as Chu Yuan took on something of a mythic quality in Chinese history does not, of course, necessarily mean that one can attribute contemporary actions to their enduring force. The actions of Hou Xiaotian and other family members determined to spare their loved ones additional suffering or those of Dai Qing and others enjoying access to groups close to power would seem to owe little to such imagery. On the other hand, it is hard to read some of these cases, and particularly the elegant prose of Guo Luoji, without sensing at least a measure of self-identification with the ideal of the loyal but incorruptible official who feels compelled to speak out.[56]

In speaking out, Chu Yuan was chiefly addressing his ruler and fellow officials. The litigation that Wang Meng, Dai Qing, Guo Luoji, Wang Juntao, and Chen Ziming have undertaken has enabled them simultaneously to voice their concerns to a range of audiences. Clearly, such suits are capable of speaking to a variety of actors within the regime itself, going beyond the specific individuals and institutions named as defendants to encompass both the leadership and those lower level functionaries responsible for the disposition of their cases. Such litigation seeks to embarrass those in high leadership positions by exposing either the limitations of their power or the artificiality of their promises or both.[57] At the same time, it also forces more ordinary administrative personnel to confront what Havel describes as the anxiety that lurks behind despotism by peeling away the protective layering of legality.[58] Given the novelty of the post-Cultural Revolution legal system and the relatively modest sophistication of most officials working in it, there is considerably less likelihood that judges and other personnel would resort to a carefully embroidered shroud of strict adherence to legal doctrine to mask the law's larger moral choices as John Dugard[59] and Robert Cover,[60] respectively, suggest was the case with some South African and antebellum American jurists. Nonetheless, the judicial responses to the five cases, ranging from the excessively formalist response of the Nanjing Intermediate People's Court to Guo Luoji's petition to the rumored ex parte contacts between the Beijing Intermediate People's Court and the defendants in Wang Meng's case, leave the impression that some Chinese judges have not been unaware of the dissonance these cases have posed between the law as written and as applied.

In bringing their cases, the five appear also to have sought audiences beyond those currently controlling the corridors of power or carrying out its missions. For some, litigation seems to have provided a rallying point for political allies enmeshed in factional struggles high within elite circles. This may have been the case with Wang Meng, who has been a point person for what are described as more open, liberal forces vying with more doctrinaire Marxists for control of the Ministry of Culture, the state writer's association, and other entities concerned with culture, broadly defined.[61] It may also be pertinent with respect to Dai Qing, given how directly she has been tied to so-called reformist circles within the top leadership.[62]

In addition, a number of the litigants and their supporters have been able to use their cases as masterful educational tools—boldly highlighting and legitimating experiences and reactions that many have shared but have yet to articulate or translate into action. Wang Meng's case in particular seems to have struck a resonant cord among PRC scholars abroad, many of whom, pondering no doubt how inconceivable such an action would have been even five years ago, have taken it as a sign, perhaps too optimistically, of a new faith in legality. But the value of these cases as pedagogy has by no means been restricted to the intelligentsia and others in the elite; the *Nongmin ribao* has reported on Wang's case to millions across the land, as indicated above, in defiance of Party orders.

Foreigners have been another audience. The families of Wang Juntao and Chen Ziming have sought through their litigation to galvanize foreign support, especially in jurisdictions such as the United States for which appeals to rights and formal legality are believed to hold particular force. This potential impact of litigation has not been lost on the leadership. As the *Wenyi bao* noted with obvious irritation soon after Wang Meng's unsuccessful suit against it, persons bringing such actions do

> not care about winning the case but aim to create sensational news headlines in society... passed on to overseas media... [This has the potential] to start trouble which could eventually create political news with an international color or a political incident... That would be going too far.[63]

Finally, one should not discount audiences as yet unborn. Guo Luoji has sought to associate himself with officials courageously but loyally challenging authority to expose wrongdoing and point the state toward greater rectitude. Even if such efforts are futile, as was the case with Chu Yuan, history at least holds the promise of some solace for those falsely accused and wrongly punished.

THE INTERPLAY OF POWER AND LEGALITY

The five cases that form the focus of this article suggest the limits of both power and legality in contemporary authoritarian societies. As a regime seeks to move beyond the type of arbitrary and often violent assertions of power that characterized large periods of Stalin's Soviet Union or Mao's China to Havel's post-totalitarian state, it encounters a need for at least the trappings of formal legality. Whether undertaken to limit the recurrence of terror, to shore up legitimacy in domestic or foreign eyes with the demise of the Cold War in Europe, to spur economic development at home, or to ease integration into the international marketplace, a certain core of public, positive laws, professional legal personnel, and state institutions holding forth the promise of regularity and predictability are needed.

Ironically, the aforementioned imperative has the effect of fostering far greater liberalization than any such regime could ever have intended. In essence, the regime has not only through its law provided a legal, moral, and political vocabulary with which those who wish to take it to task might articulate their concerns, but also, by developing its court system, has proffered these individuals a singular platform from which their concerns might be broadcast. In seeking to deploy formal legality for highly instrumental purposes, the regime has unwittingly handed its opponents a keenly honed instrument through which to seek to accomplish their own, very different ends. So it is, for example, that Guo Luoji has been able in a skillfully ironic fashion to use the legal system—through his demand that the Nanjing Intermediate People's Court identify the statute needed to vindicate constitutional rights infringed by the Party and the call in his appellate brief for a Political Party Law—to drive home the point that even when fully enforced, that system is simply inadequate for the task of cabining abuses of the Party.

In noting that legality may be a dual-edged sword, we ought not to overstate its force. Mundane problems of competence have the potential to rob it of much force; judges may lack not only the political will but also sufficient suppleness with the law to devise workable technical solutions to complex problems. More importantly, there can be no denying that when threatened, such regimes still possess the willingness and capability rapidly and effectively to turn this weapon against its opponents or even to abandon the law altogether. But it also should be observed that any such stripping away of the formal legal system's espoused neutrality, predictability, and fairness ultimately carries with it considerable cost in terms of the very objectives that the regime was seeking to reach when it undertook to build its laws, legal personnel, and legal institutions.[64] And the greater the regime's instrumental use of legality to consolidate its hold on power, secure international stature, and rapidly move ahead economically, the more vulnerable it ultimately is to the use of this weapon against it.

Our pleasure in seeing a double-edged sword turned against those we deem oppressive ought not to prevent our recognizing that such a weapon has the potential to inflict much harm even in the hands of those whose opposition to oppressive behavior we applaud. We who enjoy the luxury of relative freedom and security cannot avoid seeming to be gratuitous when we criticize dissidents and victims who have very limited legal and other tools when they use those tools in a highly instrumental fashion. Nonetheless, we ought not to allow the seeming goodness of a cause to blind us to the ways in which proponents of that cause may fall victim to elements of the very behavior that they object to in their efforts to address oppression. As the current drive in many Eastern European jurisdictions rapidly to generate and implement lustration laws illustrates, the habits of instrumentalism developed while in dissent may be hard to shake when one takes the levers of power.[65]

To return to the example of the People's Republic of China, it is too early to know what Chinese justice might look like if and when individuals such as those written about in this article have the chance to mold it in a more affirmative way than at present. After all, there is clearly more than a commitment to legality at play when someone such as Wang Meng, who has been a lifelong advocate of intellectual openness, employs the legal system to attack political opponents for criticizing his writing, even if they had the broader political agenda of discrediting him. To note this is not to disparage Wang and others who have brought these cases, but to urge that as we take full note of their courage and ingenuity, we remain honest observers of what they are doing, mindful of the instrumental fashion in which China's elites have throughout history so frequently deployed the law. For only when China's elite and masses alike recognize the possibility of law aspiring to serve higher ideals of justice, as well as immediate political purposes, will China be able to move away from being, as Guo Luoji has put it, a country possessed of ". . . an unwritten law beyond the written law. . . . "

ACKNOWLEDGMENTS

I would like to thank my colleagues at the Harvard Law School (HLS) to whom an earlier version of this paper was presented in July 1992. I also wish to acknowledge other friends who made many a constructive suggestion. In particular, I want to thank Makau Wa Mutua, Deputy Director for the Human Rights Program at HLS, who artfully fuses passion and reflectiveness about issues of human rights; Yu Xingzhong, HLS doctoral candidate, for his generosity and insight in tracking down key materials and carefully critiquing this paper; Margot Landman and Stanley B. Lubman for their usual incisive and insightful comments; David Huntington, HLS 1993, for his helpful research assistance; Melissa Smith, for her patient and talented stylistic, grammatical, and secretarial assistance; and Nancy Hearst, Director of the Fairbank Center for East Asian Research Library, for her bibliographic guidance. None of them, however, are in any way responsible for the views expressed or errors contained herein.

ENDNOTES

1There is a vast literature concerning the Beijing Spring and its immediate aftermath. See Han Minzhu, *Cries for Democracy: Writings & Speeches from the 1989 Chinese Democracy Movement* (Princeton: Princeton University Press, 1990) and Geremie Barmé and Linda Jaivin, *New Ghosts, Old Dreams: Chinese Rebel Voices* (New York: Times Books, 1992).

2The truncated trials leading to these executions are discussed in Amnesty International, AI Index ASA 17/60/89, *People's Republic of China: Preliminary Findings on Killings of Unarmed Civilians, Arbitrary Arrests and Summary Executions Since June 3, 1989* (London: Amnesty International, August 1989).

3Department of State, "China," *Country Reports on Human Rights Practices for 1991*, report submitted to the Committee on Foreign Affairs, the House of Representatives and the Committee on Foreign Relations, the Senate (Washington, D.C.: Government Printing Office, 1992), 809.

4Asia Watch, *Two Years After Tiananmen* (New York: Asia Watch, 1991). Beyond those formal prosecutions in the courts of the People's Republic of China, "there are still no reliable figures indicating how many" individuals were placed in *laogaidui* (labor reform camps) pursuant to less formal administrative processes. Hongda Harry Wu, *Laogai—The Chinese Gulag* (Boulder, Colo.: Westview Press, 1992), 20.

5The Great Proletarian Cultural Revolution is generally agreed by Chinese and Western scholars alike to have been disruptive of normal political, economic, and social life and is widely referred to as China's "ten lost years." The death count from it is unknown, but many estimate that over one million people died from violence or malnutrition. See Roderick MacFarquhar, *Origins of the Cultural Revolution* (London: Oxford University Press, 1974).

6For a particularly exaggerated example, see the PRC government's *White Paper on Human Rights, Guowu yuan xinwen zhu, Zhongguo de renquan zhuangkuang* (State Council Information Office, "Human Rights in China") (Beijing: 1991).

7See, for example, Human Rights Watch, *World Report 1992* (New York: Human Rights Watch, 1991). In their sincere determination to do what they believe best, Asia Watch, Amnesty, and certain other international human rights groups treat the Chinese criminal justice system as unreservedly violative of human rights. They fail to recognize that for all its many abusive characteristics and practices, the Chinese system is appreciably more complex than can be captured in so simple a dismissal (as arguably the civil cases that form the basis of this article suggest). Nor do they heed the nuanced fashion in which many Chinese who are as sincere and dedicated to human rights as they view their own legal system and the question of what are universal human rights in a Chinese context. See William

Alford, "Making a Goddess of Democracy from Loose Sand: Thoughts on Human Rights in the People's Republic of China," in Abdullahi An-Na'im, ed., *Human Rights in Cross-Cultural Perspectives: A Quest for Consensus* (Philadelphia: University of Pennsylvania Press, 1992), 65.

[8] At some level, all uses of legality are instrumental. When speaking of instrumentalism, I mean the willingness of states or individuals to use legality as an instrument to achieve their policy objectives but to depart from it when compliance with the law no longer serves the attainment of such ends. The tendency of some American legal academics to belittle the effort to distinguish between law and politics is regrettable and suggests an inability to grasp the reality of life in societies where the distinction is, indeed, all too routinely ignored.

[9] Václav Havel, *The Power of the Powerless* (New York: M. E. Sharpe, 1985).

[10] For more background on Wang and his writing, see Wendy Larsen, ed., *Wang Meng, Bolshevik Salute* (Seattle: University of Washington Press, 1989).

[11] The Anti-Rightist Movement was launched in June 1957 to deal with intellectuals and others whose devotion to the Communist Party was seen as suspect in the aftermath of the Hundred Flowers Movement of 1956–1957. Estimates are that between 500,000 and one million people were labeled as rightists and, in many instances, removed from their jobs and sent to the countryside. As General Secretary of the Communist Party, Deng Xiaoping played an active part in directing the Anti-Rightist Movement. See MacFarquhar, *Origins of the Cultural Revolution*.

[12] Wang Meng, "Jianyingde xizhou" ("Hard, Thin Gruel"), *Zhongguo zuojia* (*The Chinese Writer*) (February 1989). The story is reprinted in *Minzhu zhongguo* (*Democratic China*) (November 1991): 28.

[13] This letter is reproduced in *Minzhu zhongguo* (November 1991): 30.

[14] Nicholas Kristof, "Beijing Journal: Writer Scolded: Plays His Ace with a Lawsuit," *The New York Times,* 20 November 1991.

[15] He Jingzhi's principal claim to fame is that he wrote the libretto for one of the eight revolutionary operas that could be performed during the highly restrictive years of the Cultural Revolution. Under He's stewardship as Acting Minister, the Ministry of Culture was seen as a redoubt of ideological hard-liners suspicious of the cultural liberation of the mid- and late-1980s. See "Chinese Arts Polluted by the West: Minister," *Agence France Presse,* 10 October 1991.

[16] The complaint that Wang filed with the court is reprinted in *Ming bao yuekan* (*The Bright Paper Monthly Magazine*) (December 1991): 46.

[17] Zhonghua renmin gongheguo minfa tongze (The General Principles of the Civil Law of the People's Republic of China) promulgated on 12 April 1986 and effective from 1 January 1987. The General Principles provide a framework for a civil law order, many pieces have been promulgated in recent years but have not yet been integrated into a coordinated whole.

[18] Two thousand *yuan* are worth approximately US $350 which is equivalent to more than one half a year's salary for many Chinese intellectuals.

19Zhang's heroic efforts are described in Liao Ran, "Wang Juntao de bianhu lushi Zhang Sizhi" ("Wang Juntao's Defense Lawyer Zhang Sizhi"), *Zhongguo zhi chun (China Spring)* (June 1991): 26. For more on Wang Juntao, see Hou Xiaotian, "On the Prosecution of Wang Juntao," *Human Rights Tribune* 2 (April 1991): 16.

20The decision of the Beijing Intermediate People's Court is reprinted in *Ming bao yuekan* (December 1991): 48.

21Kristof, "Beijing Journal: Writer Scolded."

22Wang Meng, "Wo ai he xizhou" ("I love thin gruel") *Nongmin ribao (The Peasant's Daily)*, 14 November 1991.

23Wang Meng, "Huashuo zhewan xizhou" ("Speaking about this Bowl of Gruel"), *Dushu (Readings)* (December 1991), reprinted in *Ming bao yuekan* (December 1991): 49. See also Anne Sytske Keyser, "Wang Meng's Story 'Hard Thin Gruel': A Socio-Political Satire," *China Information* 7 (2) (Autumn 1992): 1.

24Su Wei, "Zu ling lishi dai lei kan: yue shou Dai Qing" ("Enough of an Impression for History to Cry: Examining Dai Qing"), *Ming bao yuekan* (January 1992): 50 and (February 1992): 89; Sheryl WuDunn, "Beijing Journal: Trading Cloak and Dagger for Pen and New Ideals," *The New York Times,* 27 December 1991; Perry Link, *Evening Chats in Beijing: Probing China's Predicament* (New York: W. W. Norton & Co., 1992), 144–49 and 283–85; and Geremie Barmé, "The Trouble with Dai Qing" *Index on Censorship* 21 (8) (September 1992): 15.

25WuDunn, "Beijing Journal: Trading Cloak and Dagger for Pen and New Ideals."

26Ibid.

27Barmé and Jaivin, *New Ghosts, Old Dreams,* xviii.

28Ibid., 171.

29See Su Wei, "Enough of an Impression for History to Cry."

30Based on discussions with Dai, February 1992, Cambridge, Mass.

31Hu Nan, "Dai Qing: Yige pei shou zhengyi de ren" ("Dai Qing: A Person who is Ready to Engage in Debate"), *Zhongguo zhi chun* (August 1991): 25. Dai Qing's account of her imprisonment entitled "Wode ruyu" is excerpted in *Index on Censorship* 21 (8) (September 1992): 20.

32Janet Snyder, "Chinese Woman Dissident Plans to Sue Newspaper," *Reuters,* 10 December 1991. It is rumored that early in 1993, the *Guangming ribao* dismissed Ms. Dai.

33Guo's troubles are said to have begun when "he gave Chairman Mao's daughter a borderline-pass grade for Marxist philosophy." Andrew Zhang, "Speaking Out Despite the Cost," *Human Rights Tribune* 3 (2) (Summer 1992): 6. For a personal history of Guo, see Hu Ping, "Yu wu sheng chu ting jing lei" ("Without song everywhere you can hear the frightening thunder"), *Zhongguo zhi chun* (March 1992): 14. Guo also recounts a portion of his difficulties with the Party in Beijing and in his early years in Nanjing in "Guo Luoji de shangsukuang" ("Guo Luoji's Appeal"), reprinted in *Zhongguo zhi chun* (May 1992): 44. See also Pitman Potter, "Administrative Litigation and Political Rights in China," *Human Rights Tribune* 3 (2) (Summer 1992): 6.

34These facts are recounted in Guo's complaints filed with the Nanjing City Intermediate People's Court. They are reprinted in "Guo Luoji konggao Li Tieying" ("Guo Luoji Sues Li Tieying"), *Zhongguo zhi chun* (March 1992): 9.

35Ibid.

36Jiangsu sheng Nanjing shi zhongjie renmin fayuan, Xingzheng caidingshu (Jiangsu Province, Nanjing City Intermediate People's Court, Administrative Judgment), reprinted in *Zhongguo zhi chun* (May 1992): 48.

37Ibid.

38Although the People's Republic of China's Constitution indicates that it grants extensive rights to citizens, the document does not provide individuals with a mechanism for redressing transgressions of said rights. Legal actions by nationals of the People's Republic of China to vindicate such rights cannot be premised on the Constitution itself but must invoke a statute that also has been violated. This difficulty in availing oneself of protections to which one is entitled from the state is reminiscent of problems in "enforcing" the fiducial bond that Confucian thought posited between ruler and subject. Rulers had an obligation to provide for the physical and moral sustenance of the populace, but there was little that could be done, short of lèse-majesté, to call a ruler indifferent to his obligations to task. For more on this fiducial bond, see William Alford, "The Inscrutable Occidental: Roberto Unger's Uses and Abuses of the Chinese Past," *Texas Law Review* 64 (1986): 915.

39Guo's suggestions to suitable contents for such legislation are contained in Guo Luoji's Appeal. See Snyder, "Chinese Woman Dissident Plans to Sue Newspaper."

40Guo's petition to the Supreme Court is reprinted in "Guo Luoji de shensushu" ("Guo Luoji's Appeal"), *Zhongguo zhi chun* (February 1993): 67.

41For background on Wang and Chen, see Sarah Lubman, "China Dissidents," *United Press International,* 12 February 1991; and Bruce Shu, "Silent Victims of Tiananmen Square," *Agence France Presse,* 13 November 1991.

42Ibid.

43"Chinese Dissident Sues Prison for Mistreatment," *Agence France Presse,* 10 March 1992.

44William Brent, "Dissident Appeals for Help for Chinese Political Prisoners," *Agence France Presse,* 11 February 1992.

45"Chinese Dissident Sues Prison for Mistreatment."

46David Schlesinger, "Chinese Dissident Not Allowed to Sue the Government," *Reuters,* 17 January 1992.

47Ibid.

48WuDunn, "Beijing Journal: Trading Cloak and Dagger for Pen and New Ideals." For more on Dai's familiarity with the law, see Dai, "Wode ruya."

49The law reforms of the post-Cultural Revolution era are sketched out in Anthony Dicks, "The Chinese Law Reforms in the Balance," *China Quarterly* 119 (1989): 540. For a further discussion of the goals of the People's Republic of China's leadership in undertaking law reform during this period, see William Alford, "'Seek Truth from Facts,'—Especially When They are Unpleasant: America's Understanding of China's Efforts at Law Reform," *UCLA Pacific Basin Law Journal* 8 (1990): 177; William Alford, *To Steal a Book is an Elegant Offense: Intellectual Property Law in Chinese Civilization* (Stanford: Stanford University Press, forthcoming); and Donald Clarke, "Regulation and its Discontents: Understanding Economic Law in China," *Stanford Journal of International Law* 28 (1992): 283.

50See, for example, *White Paper on Human Rights.*

51For a discussion of that tradition, see Laurence Schneider, *A Madman of Ch'u: The Chinese Myth of Loyalty and Dissent* (Berkeley and Los Angeles: University of California Press, 1980).

52Ch'ü Yuan's life and the mythology that subsequently grew surrounding it are reconstructed and explored in Schneider, *A Madman of Ch'u*. Of particular interest are the ways in which he was elevated to national exemplar status during the 1950s, being described as the forerunner of a "revolutionary romanticism" of which Mao Zedong was said to be the foremost contemporary practitioner. Ibid., 159.

53See the biography of Ch'ü Yuan in *Records of the Grand Historian of China: Translated from the Shih-chi of Ssu-ma Ch'ien*, vol. 1, trans. Burton Watson (New York: Columbia University Press, 1961), 499–516.

54Qin legal texts devote considerable attention to false accusation. See the *Qin lü da wen* (*Answers to Questions Regarding Qin Statutes*), trans. and annotated in A. F. P. Hulsewé, *Remnants of Ch'in Law; An Annotated Translation of the Ch'in Legal and Administrative Rules of the 3rd Century B.C. Discovered in Yün-meng Prefecture, Hu-pei Province, in 1975* (Leiden: E. J. Brill, 1985), 131–33, 149–51.

55For a discussion of the penalties for false accusation during the early Qing dynasty (1644–1911), see Huang Liu-hung, *A Complete Book Concerning Happiness and Benevolence: A Manual for Local Magistrates in Seventeenth Century China*, ed. Djang Chu (Tucson: University of Arizona Press, 1984), 353.

56Without investing the point with undue significance, one might note that the *Wenyi bao*—the paper sued by Wang Meng—published a special issue in 1953 devoted to what it described as "Four Giants of World Culture"—Copernicus, Rabelais, José Marti, and Ch'ü Yuan. Schneider, *A Madman of Ch'u*, 160–61.

57Harold Berman suggests the possibility that these plaintiffs may have been motivated in part by awareness either of the efforts of European Communists early in the twentieth century to stage "counter-trials" designed to uncover what they believed to be the hypocrisy of the capitalist states they sought to transform or by debates among Soviet dissidents as early as the late 1960s as to whether use of the legal system further legitimated the Communist Party's hold on power. Letter by Harold Berman to the author, 28 August 1992.

58Havel, *The Power of the Powerless*, 69–78. For practical examples of what Havel is discussing, see Hugo Frühling, "Repressive Politics and Legal Dissent in

Authoritarian Regimes: Chile 1973–1981," *International Journal of the Sociology of Law* 12 (1984): 351.

59John Dugard, *Human Rights and the South African Legal Order* (Princeton: Princeton University Press, 1978). For an intriguing study from a jurisprudential viewpoint of the moral dilemma such cases pose, see David Dyzenhaus, *Hard Cases in Wicked Legal Systems: South African Law in the Perspective of Legal Philosophy* (London: Clarendon Press, 1991).

60Robert Cover, *Justice Accused: Antislavery and the Judicial Process* (New Haven: Yale University Press, 1975). Cover skillfully portrays the philosophical and psychological conundrum confronting judges charged with enforcing the slave laws. A recent study of German judges during the war years suggests that many went further than even formalism dictated in aiding the Nazi regime. Ingo Müller, *Hitler's Justice: The Courts of the Third Reich* (Cambridge, Mass.: Harvard University Press, 1991). Political trials more generally are the subject of a number of scholarly works, including Otto Kirchheimer, *Political Justice: The Use of Legal Procedure for Political Ends* (Princeton: Princeton University Press, 1961); Judith Shklar, *Legalism: Law, Morals and Political Trials* (Cambridge, Mass.: Harvard University Press, 1986); and Ron Christenson, *Political Trials: Gordian Knots in the Law* (New Brunswick: Transaction Books, 1986).

61It is worth noting that the Fourteenth Plenum of the Chinese Communist Party meeting in October 1992 removed both Wang and his archly conservative successor He Jingzhi from the Party's Central Committee. Geremie Barmé describes Wang Meng's political circle in "A Storm in a Rice Bowl: Wang Meng and Fictional Chinese Politics," *China Information* 7 (2) (Autumn 1992): 12.

62As her bold 1989 examination of the case of Chu Anping demonstrates, Dai Qing was well aware of the political uses to which formal legality might be put.

63"Beijing Court Rejects Daring Suit by Ousted Culture Minister," *Reuters,* 22 October 1991.

64As Jürgen Habermas observes, "Legality can create legitimation when, and only when, grounds can be provided to show that certain formal procedures fulfill material claims to justice under certain institutional boundary conditions." Jürgen Habermas, *Legitimation Crisis*, trans. Thomas McCarthy (Boston: Beacon Press, 1975).

65Stephen Engelberg, "The Velvet Revolution Gets Tough," *The New York Times Magazine*, 31 May 1992.

There are no concerns more central to Confucianism than the concern with the ethical gap between norms and actualities or the concern with the capacity of human moral agents to bridge the gap. The individual human being must, to this extent, possess at least *in potentia* an autonomous individual life of his own separate from the "whole" of the sociopolitical order which seems to have no inbuilt "holistic" power to preserve its own norms. Here only the individual components can preserve the whole. Even in the Taoism of Lao-tzu and Chuang-tzu, the individual human being possesses the fatal negative power to detach himself from the whole of the *tao*. Chinese holistic thought as a shared cultural assumption—like shared cultural assumptions elsewhere—creates not finished solutions but a vast problematique.

Benjamin I. Schwartz

From *The World of Thought in Ancient China*

*Wang Gungwu*

# To Reform a Revolution: Under the Righteous Mandate

W HEN THE REPUBLIC OF CHINA WAS proclaimed on January 1, 1912, Sun Yat-sen called its government that "of a revolutionary era." Two months earlier, when he was in the United States and heard that the uprising in Wuchang was succeeding, he thought that only the governments of the United States and France, which had had their own republican revolutions, would support the Chinese revolution, while the German, Russian, and Japanese governments would not. British support was crucial. Britain was the Great Power in the East. If it sided with Russia, Japan, and Germany against the new Republic, then French and US support would not have been enough. Sun Yat-sen hoped to use public sympathy in Britain to persuade the government to back his rebellion. Although the government was undecided, the people were sympathetic. When he reached London a month later, he spoke of the unstoppable tide of enlightenment and progress which would soon enable revolutionary China "to join the civilized and freedom-loving nations of the world."[1] Thus, China acquired parts of a modern face. Sun Yat-sen saw the Republic as having broken from the past and from all the futile efforts to reform and save the imperial Confucian system. It had become part of modern world history—there was to be no looking back.

A new generation of educated Chinese, including Mao Zedong, picked up the call during the May Fourth Movement after 1919 and many wanted China to go much further. This second generation produced the leaders who established the People's Republic of China

---

*Wang Gungwu is Vice-Chancellor of The University of Hong Kong.*

in 1949 as an advanced country in "the vanguard of world revolution." Mao Zedong himself was impatient to realize this ideal and finally launched a violent "cultural" revolution to achieve that goal. Consciously or not, he did so by putting on parts of a Chinese face, invoking features of authority and power which had the effect of reversing recent trends and restoring older political values and structures.[2]

After his death, the word "reform" regained efficacy and replaced the word "revolution" in China's policies and goals. Since the disintegration of Soviet power after 1989, the word revolution has lost its universal appeal even more rapidly. The Chinese word for reform, *gaige*, is now used for everything. *Geming* (revolution), however, is widely greeted with indifference and a tinge of fear. Some of the third generation of educated Chinese have shown, especially during the decade leading to the tragedy at Tiananmen on June 4, 1989, that they are prepared to contemplate radical changes amounting to yet another revolution in political and cultural values. What do these words, reform and revolution, *gaige* and *geming*, tell us about modern Chinese, the country's struggle to free itself from the past, and the brave new world it has so much wanted for its people?

The question reminds us that it has always been difficult to approach any subject about one civilization using terms derived from another. Should we use indigenous terms in original contexts to try and portray reality as the local people see it themselves? Should we translate the terms as best we can, but interpret them in language familiar to the foreign audience we write for? Or, should we assume a oneness of history and accept the language of discourse dominant at any one time and define everything accordingly? These are old questions for which answers become even more difficult when we deal with what appears to be global events in modern history. The more complex the phenomena and the more entangled the current developments are in a civilization's traditions, the harder it is to understand and explain what is happening, and least of all to predict future changes.

Not surprisingly, this is especially difficult with events in China. The tight-knit cultures within its borders hide a great deal, even from its own people. Its long history of dynastic empires thrusting out beyond existing borders or pulling into itself, and its image as a country which had experienced cycles of cultural and institutional sameness have been especially misleading. Certainly the size of territory and population had led its rulers, whether Imperial, nationalist or Communist, to give priority to, and use all available resources to ensure unity and conformity, and to encourage bureaucratic simplification of the institutions of social and political control. If necessary, reality could always be made to fit the current ideology.

Students of modern Chinese history cannot but be struck by the distance between hopes, intentions, and goals of every generation and the compromises, betrayals, and what may be described as the burdens of China's history. Another kind of distance is that between the modern ideal of seeking to meet the needs and demands of the ordinary people (however defined) and the reality of their helplessness in the face of the traditions of centralized power. There are also other kinds of cultural distance derived from the dissonances between imported ideas and technologies, on the one hand, and native pride and inspiration on the other.[3] Whichever kind of distance it is, our efforts at explaining contemporary China remain a continuous struggle, because each manifestation of distance is not created by mere ignorance or naïveté, nor even by dishonesty. It is implicit in the idea of China, whether as a country, a civilization, an empire, a nation-state, a cultural subcontinent, or an integral part of an interdependent world.

It is in this context that the words reform and revolution, as taken from Western and world history and applied to China, are explored here. In their Chinese manifestations, revolution is compared with *geming*, the tradition of a violent but righteous (Heavenly) mandate to rule which is deeply rooted in Chinese history, and reform with *gaige* which is often taken for granted and rarely explicit as each dynasty renews and strengthens itself.[4] These comparisons immediately bring out the fact that there are many paradoxes prevailing in China today.

Among them are those which suggest that the old men of today who had launched the Communist revolution now want nothing but reform and the younger ones who have tired of revolution are willing to contemplate a new kind of revolution to replace the one that had failed. This may not really be so, nor is it unique to the Chinese. Much depends on what meanings are attached to words like reform and revolution and what qualities are emphasized. For example, if the speed and dimensions of change are stressed in the definition of each word, reform suggests the gradual improvement of a workable system and revolution connotes a total comprehensive change that has been swiftly, and often violently, achieved. On the other hand, if it is the protagonists who deserve attention, then it may matter whether they have organized for changes from above to meet elite interests or from below to establish new and more responsive power structures.

In the language of modern scholarship, reform and revolution, reformists and revolutionaries, are opposed in order to assist analysis. In reality, the contrasts apply best only during a specific period when the differences seem clear cut. Once past the time when sharp distinctions can be made, however, successful reforms could lead to radical change and even amount to a revolution, and revolutions that faltered or failed might need to be saved by reforms.

In that context, China today may be no different. It could be demonstrated that the revolutions of 1911 and 1949 have successively lost their way. When the first failed to deliver on its promises, a new set of leaders tried to save China by the second, a more thorough and genuine revolution. But when the second also faltered, ironically despite desperate attempts to galvanize the people to greater efforts at revolution, the old leaders fell back on reform in order to save what they had. Suddenly the rhetoric was significantly changed and all the good words connected with reform were brought in to replace the strident expressions associated for decades with revolution. This change of direction may not be peculiar to China. Much of it may be compared with developments elsewhere and conform to modern political and economic imperatives. Nevertheless, there are unique features in the Chinese condition that reflect subtle continuities and recall a powerful and not yet forgotten past.

These features mark the ambivalent face of China. China has a distinctive intertwining of past and present—a past that had once seemed so unchangeable, a present which now defies predictability. The search for modernization in China has given this relationship a new manifestation. In addition, we have been led to an image of apparent elusiveness by the prism of our modern analytical concepts like reform and revolution. These words as applied so richly to Western history should be adequately lucid. But, in Chinese, they both have ancient roots that are evocative and layered with meanings which have persisted to this day.

The term *gaige* may be set beside other modern terms for reform like *weixin, ziqiang,* or *bianfa,* but the strong echoes of historic efforts to save the country or a dynasty are unmistakable whichever term is used.[5] Revolution as in modern England, France, and the United States is more complicated, but the word *geming* is not a bad translation, even though it was first used in China more than 2,500 years ago to describe the victories of Tang and Wu, founders of the Shang and Zhou dynasties, respectively. Given the dynastic connotations of the term, they remind us of the concept of mandate, whether in its traditional sense of *tianming* (Mandate of Heaven), or the modern idea of "given power" as mandate. The latter would be translated as *shouquan*; that could mean, for example, the mandate of the people, which is an openly demonstrable form that could be compared with Mencius' idealized *tianming*.[6] In this essay, I shall combine the two senses of heavenly and secular by using the phrase "righteous mandate." It helps to remind us that there are always echoes of the past in the Chinese present. This paper will attempt to use such resonances to explore what lies behind the ambivalent face of China.

## REVOLUTION

Every Chinese person alive today has lived with the idea of *geming* as revolution since his or her youth. How many meanings has that word had? When Sun Yat-sen, the first internationally acknowledged leader of revolution in China, was asked a question in London, and in English, in 1896 about his *"revolutionary* business," he avoided answering the question but, later the same day, he claimed, again in English, to have been arrested "for sending a memorial for *reform.*"[7] He had read enough of Western history to know the difference between the two words and was being evasive. In fact, he had been plotting the overthrow of a failed dynasty ruled by the Manchu, hated foreigners in the eyes of the many southern Han Chinese who supported him. The Qing rulers (1644–1911) and their literati functionaries saw him primarily as a rebel as did many of his admiring followers who wanted nothing more than to rebel successfully with him.

It is doubtful that Sun Yat-sen thought that what he was saying to his followers when he founded his *Xingzhong Hui* (Revive China

Association) in 1895 was in the language of modern revolution. He was at that stage influenced by the traditions of the secret societies of South China and *Xingzhong* was more likely to have echoed the idea of *Zhongxing* (dynastic restoration) used during the reign of the Tongzhi emperor thirty years earlier, after the Taiping rebellion was finally crushed in 1864.[8] The inversion of *Xingzhong* and *Zhongxing* brings out a difference between the 1860s and the 1890s, between restoration of imperial power and national (Han Chinese) revival, but implicit in both is an evolving patriotism about the dignity and power of an ancient state, sustained by a great civilization. This civilization-state had experienced a considerable battering by the Western powers, and the humiliating defeat by the Japanese in 1894–1895 was, especially for the Han Chinese elites, the last straw.

Soon after the failure of his first attempt at open rebellion in Guangzhou in 1895, Sun Yat-sen saw the word *gemingzhe* (revolutionary) applied to him in the Japanese press and he quickly recognized what he stood for. The ambiguity in the term *geming*, however, remained between the traditional sense of overthrowing a dynasty that had lost its Heavenly Mandate and the modern meaning of replacing a political system that was no longer viable, by force of arms if necessary. For Sun Yat-sen and his young lieutenants, this ambiguity was probably useful. They were aware that the vast majority even of their own followers were not ready to accept that their modern ideals were derived principally from studying Western political institutions. What most Chinese really understood was the idea that the Qing dynasty's mandate was near its end and therefore the time had come to replace it. Already, for practical reasons, there had begun the fudging of foreign ideas that needed to be explicated in Chinese terms.

In 1894, Sun Yat-sen sent a memorial advocating reform to the Qing senior minister, Li Hongzhang. At that time, the *yangwu* (Western affairs) experts who offered modernizing reforms for the *ziqiang* (self-strengthening) of the dynastic system had suffered a loss of power because of the disastrous defeats by the Japanese. They were soon challenged by a new group of younger literati who wanted radical changes to the system, comparable to Japan's Meiji Restoration or *weixin* (another way of expressing renewal through transformation).[9] They failed and were accused of trying to stage a *zhengbian* (coup). In traditional language, this was treason punishable by death and indeed six of the leaders were executed. Historians have now settled for the equally traditional term *bianfa* (changing the laws) to describe what this younger group led by Kang Youwei was prepared to do. The term traces back to the reforms of Shang Yang (fourth century, B.C.) which transformed the Qin state before it unified the whole of China; after that, the most famous example of *bianfa* was the lifelong effort by Wang Anshi to reform the Northern Song dynasty (960–1279). Nevertheless, conservatives in China have always frowned on the idea of *bianfa* and the self-strengtheners, the conservative *yangwu* experts, were no less hostile to what Kang Youwei and his supporters advocated.[10]

In this way, the reform camp was split between the conservatives and the radicals, those still in high office within the system and those now outside the court, including those who were outlaws outside the country. Facing these reformers, who made half-hearted attempts to unite with Sun Yat-sen's more or less revolutionary groups, were those who sought to change the mandate altogether, *geming* instead of *bianfa*. As Mary Wright and her colleagues have demonstrated, neither camp was talking about reform and revolution as understood through the history of the English, the French or the Americans.[11] It would be another two decades or more into the twentieth century, after the reformists had failed and the revolutionaries of 1911 had won, before a new generation of intellectuals began to see the need to redefine *geming* and equate it with modern Western examples of revolution.

By that time, revolution had acquired another dimension and many turned to it in the shadow of the October Bolshevik Revolution in Russia. These young activists sought to divert the Chinese people from their traditional historical operas, novels, and the connotations of dynastic change so deeply rooted in their consciousness. They sought a cultural or *mentalité* revolution: it was antisuperstition, anti-Confucian, antireligion as well as anti-Imperialist and ultimately anti-Western and even xenophobic. It was a real baptism in several fierce currents of hostility in search of what the new kind of *geming* should stand for.[12]

After eliminating several alternative ideologies inspired by more or less Western political parties, there remained only nationalism and socialism, both protean words that could be applied to many situations. For example, nationalism could encompass *liberté, égalité, fraternité* as well as capitalism, socialism, and representative democracy while socialism could be accommodated by liberal democrats, Communists as well as Fascist dictators. Not very helpful for clear thinking idealists, one must say, but being very modern and equated with world trends and universalistic movements, both conformed to the laws of modern history. There was certainly enough differentiation for two major political parties to emerge in China to fight a bitter civil war.

Although the two parties did combine briefly for a national salvation anti-Japanese war, there was no hope of any reconciliation and eventually the socialist definition of revolution won a decisive victory over the nationalist one. After 1949, what was considered the more genuinely revolutionary force thrust the lesser one out of the mainland of China. Historians after that were extolled to adopt a holistic interpretation of what appeared to be the apotheosis of a modern revolution on par with that of the French and the Soviets and on a larger scale than all the great revolutions that had gone before. Clearly, there could be discerned a common thread of an elitist departure from the past, spurning the Great Tradition in favor of a new modern/Western (including Marxist and Soviet) and populist/peasant Chinese culture, an ideology and polity that would, together and thoroughly, redefine *geming* as revolution for every Chinese, regardless of their class origin.[13]

The grand view of revolution appeared *both* sinicized and global, the object of new pride because it laid the foundations of a new Chinese civilization that could f~ ~e down the world. It is now doubtful how much substance ~ay behind the rhetoric, the violent action, and frenetic political campaigns that followed for the next three decades. Even if there was substance, there was hardly enough time for the new worker-peasant military-industrial complex to replace the literati-peasant military-agrarian one that had dominated China for two thousand years. What was certain, however, was that Sun Yat-sen and his nationalist and Communist heirs had broken the dynastic mold by violent revolution. There would be no more Sons of Heaven. Theirs was the Republic or People's Republic, and the modern Chinese nation had been given a fresh start.

But it is also true, among ordinary Chinese steeped in myths and local lore, that the new leaders could yet be thought to have founded a new kind of dynastic structure, ruling till death without office or title of any kind, becoming ancestors entombed in mausoleums, possibly even new deities in revived temples or protagonists doomed to become tragic wandering spirits. In addition, had they not, like many of their predecessors in history, turned on one another in succession as revolutionary leaders, first in civil wars and then during the Great Leap Forward and the Cultural Revolution? It has not helped that both their brands of nationalism and socialism led to comparative poverty on the mainland and that similar socialisms that celebrated their revolutions and had been so dominant elsewhere in a once hopeful world collapsed altogether. The recent experiences after a decade of extensive economic reforms in China and after the end of the Soviet Union have begun to undermine the *geming* which a whole generation of Chinese had redefined. At the very least, they threaten to cancel out the many efforts by the present Chinese leaders to distinguish their market socialism from the capitalist democracies, on the one hand, and from the residual continuities of the Great Tradition on the other.

There has, in short, been a return to historical ambiguity here. This is a feature of modern Chinese culture that has persisted through the century more strongly than the idealists and revolutionaries expected. The ambiguity has acquired fresh intensity now that erstwhile revolutionaries speak so passionately of reform. The idea of reforming a revolution grates against the more familiar one of *consolidating* a revolution and has to be seen as a contradiction in terms. But, in the Chinese context, it not only brings back echoes of reform at the beginning of modern Chinese history in the late nineteenth and early twentieth century, it also calls for a reappraisal of the deep-rooted idea of *geming* itself.

The reform that is now so strongly espoused cannot avoid being compared with what is normally associated with the *yangwu* experts and the *bianfa* radicals of the nineteenth century. The reformers in China today have chosen yet another term, *gaige,* to distinguish their reforms from the earlier ones. This term, too, has an honorable ancestry. Although it is not identified with any dynasty or period in history, it also has, by common usage, connotations of removing old ways and replacing them with new ones, but usually by peaceful means. The questions that have brought about continual debates and divisions, however, have always been: which of the old had to change, how quickly, and how new the new had to be.

REFORM

On the surface, there is so much today that reminds us of the bitter struggle at the center between the *yangwu* self-strengtheners and the radical supporters of the Hundred Days Reform in 1898. On the periphery, a few bold activists, with some outside support, try to harass both groups. Indeed, it is tempting to produce a collage which mounts a number of modern names, faces, and slogans beside or on top of the comparable ones from the period of Li Hongzhang, Kang Youwei, and Sun Yat-sen. Of course, nothing would quite fit, nor should we expect it to. If they did fit, and China appears to have returned to square one after one hundred years and countless millions of lives sacrificed, that would certainly be reason for despair. But there are times, as through a distorting mirror, that the audience feels that it is looking at the same old picture. What they actually see, of course, is the ambivalent face of China. A few examples to show what this means for various reform measures will suffice to suggest what is happening. They range from the insistence on minimal change to attempts at grudging reform, from clearly radical ideas to policies revealing both indecision and confusion.

The example of minimal change in an area widely perceived as needing urgent reform is in the power structure. Although the network of cadres within Zhongnanhai today are obviously different from the Qing court mixture of Manchu-Mongol-Han aristocrats and officials, the determination to change the political and ideological framework as little as possible is remarkably familiar. All the reformist vocabulary skirts what the Qing court and the Chinese Communist Party (CCP) both regard as the moral core of their respective belief systems.[14] This includes the image of Deng Xiaoping as the "head of the household," the retired elder, without office or title, with something like an untestable mandate; the myth of nonexistent factionalism; and, most of all, the sacred rituals of political succession. The last is particularly striking, down to the long-lived untitled ruler governing from behind the curtains awaiting some yet unforeseeable opportunity to pick the right heir.

The reality is much more complicated. The power structure today, borrowed at the same time as the revolutionary ideology, may be alien in origin, but through the efforts of Mao Zedong was adapted to Chinese usage.[15] It successfully crushed the old world of landlords and literati, and their family-dependent commerce, but built its power base on a neotraditional alliance of peasant armies and state-controlled workers.[16] Though the rhetoric is new, the structure is built on historically familiar groups of majority interests.

Thanks to decades of abuse and mismanagement under several overenthusiastic revolutionary leaders, the power structure has rapidly lost credibility as one that was intended to fully replace the Confucian state. The revolution has done enough to insure that there is no return to the decrepit imperial system, but it has not yet been accepted as its permanent replacement.[17] The disasters that have befallen all the Communist states around the world during the past few years make it unlikely that the Chinese people will ever accept that Communist system in its original form.

Perhaps that is recognized by those still in power. Is this why they have concentrated on reforms in other spheres, in part because they need to keep control of the structure in order to stay in power longer? Is it possible that successful nonpolitical reforms may save them from ever having to change the structure and the ideology that supports the regime? Or, is it because any call for political reform must raise the specter of *geming*, or a total change in the regime? This would be gambling for very high stakes indeed, not only for the future of the Party's elites and their revolution, but also for that of the country and the people. But, most immediately for the Chinese people, the series of selective reforms is intended to prevent the need for another revolution, or at least to avoid reminding the people about *geming*.

## Economic Reform

Among the areas selected for reform, that of economic reform has been agreed to by most in China. People seem to have been enthusiastic about, and grateful for, the small freedoms that enable them to trade, to profit from productive labor, to learn new technologies from abroad, and even to enjoy themselves. This is nothing new; it is simply a return to some of the little pleasures and privileges that the Chinese people had earlier in the century under the previous regime and during the centuries before, under the last two dynasties.

All the same, the package of reforms aimed at stimulating the economy is more systematic than anything earlier regimes attempted; there is a decisiveness about ends and means in the efforts to achieve dramatic results that is in fact quite new. Clearly these include modern responses to the new international trading system, to the mature capitalism that produced the system, and to the growing pace of technological progress. Because the Asian Pacific neighborhood has undergone a sea change, China has a chance to become an economic power, if not to restore its traditional position of superiority, then to at least take its rightful place as one of the region's modern and leading nation-states.

Still, what one sees on the whole is grudging economic reform, constrained by the need to avoid any change that might weaken the existing power arrangements and ideological shibboleths. It seems to be pushed in directions which favor those cadres and networks trusted by the power center and close to officialdom. This power center is clearly determined to prevent the emergence of an indigenous merchant class. The minimal reform approach reflects traditional concerns about protecting the political structure and existing groups of elites and their families in every possible way. The fear of an indigenous merchant class is harder to understand given the anxiety to encourage foreign capitalists, including those of Chinese descent, businessmen from capitalistic Hong Kong and Taiwan as well as more recent overseas Chinese emigrants. They are invited to be active and invest in increasingly large sectors of the Chinese economy.

If the reforms are intended to be modern, why is there no place for those of merchant background still living in China to resume their professions, to maximize the commercial and industrial benefits they could bring to the country? The reforms have encouraged independent business activity principally at the lower levels; they are applied only minimally to the enterprises managed by the state. One cannot resist comparisons with the *yangwu* self-strengtheners who believed that one of the economic reforms China badly needed was to have high-minded officials supervise entrepreneurial merchants.[18] In fact, the reforms today have gone further than that: China today has policies in place to train a commercially sensitive bureaucratic cohort to buy and sell for China, to market China's manufactures at home and abroad, and to supervise foreign and overseas Chinese capitalists operating in China. But these measures are carried out with ambivalence, using recognizably Marxist-Leninist language softened by traditional merchant values and capitalistic managerial standards.[19]

*Population Reform*

Reform does not preclude radical ideas. On the contrary, some reforms require drastic action before anything can change. This is particularly true of an enormous country with such a large population. The *yangwu* experts were never radical and the *bianfa* reformers were not allowed to be radical. In contrast, the present regime in China, going against the exhortations of their revolutionary hero Mao Zedong, adopted one of the most radical reform policies the Chinese people have ever experienced.[20] I refer to the one-child policy as a measure for population control, which is really an essential part of radical economic reform. If it succeeds in the face of persistent resistance, even partially, it will not only help to raise the standard of living of the people but also do more to transform the whole fabric of traditional society than any other single reform in Chinese history. This, of course, is merely a policy of reform. It would not have been anything that would have interested professional revolutionaries like Sun Yat-sen and Mao Zedong, yet it could be potentially more revolutionary in effect than most measures those two leaders advocated.

Radical reforms of this nature may be compared with the industrial revolution which took several decades to take effect in every country, and with the urban, both bourgeois and proletariat, revolution that changed everyone's life-style and produced the most effective population control results in history. Is the one-child policy reform then an example of a modernizing *revolutionary* breakthrough, fundamentally departing from tradition? This is only a superficial ambiguity of language. A deeper ambiguity stems from the fact that the policy cannot succeed voluntarily. It would have to be accompanied by crude indoctrination methods at all levels of education and training. It would have to be supported by strong authoritarian measures, together with draconian ways of intervening in the private lives of every individual in the country.

With these decisions coming from above, it recalls the traditional policies of *yimin shibian* (moving people to support border areas as military colonies) and *yimin tongcai* (moving people to ease economic conditions, usually for the survival of whole districts because of famine or other natural disasters) when the traditional state transported millions of people over long distances, often against their will.[21] These were population redistribution measures for reasons of security and livelihood and not, of course, for purposes of population control. Certainly they were carried out when China had fewer people and more undeveloped land. But the application of interventionist state power in social engineering is well within the tradition. The difference is that of degree: modern systems and technology can penetrate deeper and the effects can be much more drastic and even irreversible and, if sustained for long periods, nothing less than revolutionary.

## Intellectual Reform

The reform of any structure can produce much indecision and confusion, but nowhere is the uncertainty more manifest than in the present regime's policy on intellectuals.[22] The idea of *zhishi fenzi* (intellectuals) is ambiguous. It distinguishes them from the scholar gentry who traditionally shared power at the top and wielded great power in the countryside. At the same time, these intellectuals could also be recognized as new types of experts and professionals who could be treated as "knowledge workers" in the socialist workers' state. Had it been possible to remain clear and consistent about such definitions, this would have given intellectuals both respectability among other workers and allowed them to partake of the power the working class was supposed to have. It would also have freed them from the stigma of association with the traditional *shi* (mandarin-literati) and placed them among the benign category of *gong* (artisan). In this way, they could have been accepted as a sort of literate artisan subclass instead of being seen as ambitious and discontented remnants of the overthrown scholar gentry.

But this was not to be for several reasons. The *shi* tradition was so strong in Chinese history that the modern intellectuals could not easily escape the sense of moral and spiritual responsibility for the future of the state and for Chinese civilization. They would not be content to become better educated artisans. At the very least, in modern terms, they would claim the status of professionals, with all the connotations of independence, autonomy, and self-regulation. In addition, access to higher learning and intellectual output outside

China has confirmed the belief that there is an important role for freethinking intellectuals in any modernization process. It is not enough for them to be loyal and well-trained technocrats. The privilege of having knowledge required that they actively participate in the checks on, if not the exercise of, power on behalf of the people and the nation. This self-chosen role of independent critic has caused great difficulty for the policy on intellectuals, whether under Mao Zedong or Deng Xiaoping.[23]

The reason for this confusion and ambiguity is the fact that most people in China look upon the Party cadres as having seized the reins of power from the traditional mandarins. Their monopoly of power both at the center and in the provinces has impressed everyone. As long as they also manifested a similar aura of moral integrity and respect for learning, they would indeed be seen as having successfully replaced the old discredited literati. The new revolutionary elites were expected to be superior, more modern, efficient, and caring than the corrupt representatives of a bankrupt tradition.

But the four decades after 1949 clearly showed that this was not so, partly because these cadres were no more immune to abuses of power than mandarins, and partly because they would not tolerate the independently critical role that the modern intellectuals want. What added to the indecision in the Party's policy on intellectuals was that forty years of indoctrination could not eliminate the intangible heritage of the literati nor prevent the assimilation of the professional and intellectual ideal from the world outside. There is no greater ambiguity in China today than in the efforts to reform and redefine the relationship between what the Party wants from the new generations of intellectuals who had grown up since 1949 and what these intellectuals want for themselves.

There remains the ambiguity underlying the meaning of revolution, expressed as *geming*, eighty years after the fall of the last dynasty. This new kind of *geming* as revolution is quite different from changing dynasties in an unchanging China; it represents a major break with the past, comparable to the massive change that followed the unification of China under the Qin-Han empire. Indeed, innumerable comparisons have been made both within and outside of China with what the First Emperor Qin Shihuang in the third century B.C. achieved and the present. The primary one is that this regime did not last any longer than the Qin dynasty of only a few decades which was followed suddenly by *geming* and a new dynasty.[24]

It must be clear that the 1949 Revolution did produce a social upheaval. What is doubtful is the picture of unchanging China since the fall of the Qin dynasty. As long as this remains the perception outside China, and as long as such images permeate discourse within intellectual circles in China, the term *geming* would be, despite its origins in Chinese history, considered inappropriate for application to the dynastic changes during the intervening two thousand years. Instead, the modern *geming* should only be equated with revolution as understood in Western Europe, the United States, and the Soviet Union. If this should become the only legitimate meaning of the word, I suggest that it will diminish our understanding of the role of the past in China's current development. If this and other similar terms taken from classical texts should assume only the meanings of the Western words they have been used to translate, it would reduce our ability to provide the many-layered explanations needed for the many more interesting faces of modern China.

The common view about imperial China says that there have been dozens of dynasties since the fall of Qin in 206 B.C. Most of them were overthrown by violence, but continuity was greater than change under each new ruling house. Therefore, *geming* (changing the mandate) consisted largely of a change of dramatis personae and a similar cyclical plot accompanied by some moving of furniture on the stage of history. The Confucian rhetoric of the Mandate of Heaven remained more or less the same and served no more than as a device to say that one group was no longer worthy to hang on to power and had to be replaced by another. Thus, the picture of stagnation and little progress for China.

We need to distinguish the minor changes of dynastic houses from the major political upheavals that launched powerful new dynasties. The former would come under the phrase *gaichao huandai* (change of ruling houses); they had no effect on the political system they inherited and they fit the stereotype of being mainly a change of personnel. Most of these occurred during long periods of disunion between the fall of the Han dynasty and the rise of the Tang dynasty, and a few occurred when the Tang fell in the tenth century. Of the fifty-five or so dynasties recognized in official histories, more than forty belong to this category and they occupy about five of the twenty-one centuries of imperial history. The remaining sixteen centuries saw six major dynastic houses. The founding of each of these, especially the founding of the Tang, the Song, the Yuan, the Ming, and the Qing, would clearly count as having experienced a real change of *geming* (mandate).

For the past thousand years, each change of the four major dynasties, the Song, the Ming, the Yuan, and the Qing, had been accompanied by great violence, disorder, and transformation of the political structures, more gradual in the Song though no less far-reaching, but brutal and oppressive in the other three. The empire's economy remained primarily agrarian throughout and its wealth came mainly from the toil of its peasants. Imperial rhetoric governing all four dynasties was carefully made consistent with the orthodox ideology and endorsed by court historians. These facts, however, should not be allowed to diminish the extent of *geming* (political change) under each of the dynastic mandates which the Chinese people experienced before the 1911 Revolution. Given the record of such experiences over the centuries, most people at the end of the Qing dynasty were prepared to take the political restructuring offered by the Republican Nationalists in their stride. Similarly, when that was followed by further transformations introduced by the CCP, there was also willing acceptance of them all as the results of the new mandate still recognizable in the modern use of the term *geming*.

Only those who lost out in the competition for power were aggrieved and only those Confucian loyalists who saw the damage done to the fabric of their most ancient and glorious civilization were outraged. For the rest, whether inside or outside the country, they looked to the social and economic betterment to come with expectation and hope. If the new righteous mandate brought about a successful uplifting in the standards of living and a more secure livelihood for everyone, and therefore wealth for the country as a whole, so much the better. But their experiences and the tradition of *geming* as the righteous mandate promised them that the social and economic benefits would come over time, with effective reform coming after the revolution of violent political change was over.

It is with this background in mind that one understands why, for the present regime, *geming* is now a word of the past and *gaige*, especially economic reform, the key to salvation and progress. *Geming* is historically associated with violence and upheavals and the people have had enough of those during the two decades from 1956 to 1976, if not the years from 1911 to 1949. *Gaige,* on the other hand, assumes that the *political* structure is here to stay. The structure may need improvement in order to survive, but this can come about when the necessary economic reforms are achieved: the raising of the standard of living from subsistence levels, the enrichment of the country in order to enable it to play its proper role in world affairs, and, if safe and necessary, a greater opening of the country to foreign and modern ideas about technology, culture, and life-style. Political reform at this stage is seen as a dangerous ambiguity, easily confused with *geming,* or a new mandate to overthrow the regime and replace it by another.

CONCLUSION

What of the future? I referred earlier to China's present which now "defies predictability." What follows, therefore, is highly speculative but not groundless. Reports of what the Chinese elites are preparing for, taken together with the country's immediate and deep-rooted history, suggest that some speculations are more probable than others. From this China-focused point of view, there remain fears among the Party elites that even the *gaige* that they have sponsored may endanger their power structure. In the longer run, their economic reforms could lead to some form of "peaceful evolution" that ultimately amounts to a revolutionary, or as they see it, a retrograde or reactionary, change from socialism to capitalism.[25] Such fears could be a reflection of their insecurity verging on paranoia, but these fears are not unjustified if retaining their present power structure is the final objective of the current economic reforms.

These reforms, however carefully and grudgingly implemented, will engender changes which in turn will produce further need for change. Indeed, many moderate critics of the present regime look forward to precisely the chain reactions that would ultimately bring about a fundamental shift in the political system. But this does not mean *geming,* another change of mandate or a violent revolution. On the contrary, if skillfully managed by the successors of the present generation of leaders, they could themselves be the beneficiaries of such a shift when it comes. This may not be the same as the liberal democratic revolution which others may hope for. But when it becomes clear that *geming* is undesirable and any revolutionary action unnecessary, a new generation of political leaders allied to loyal and experienced technocrats may be ready to produce an improved, more representative, responsible, and accountable system of government that might win over liberal and democratic lobbies.[26]

Outside China and drawing upon historical examples in other parts of the world, the "peaceful evolution" argument seems less likely. But those who reject this scenario do not necessarily agree as to why they disbelieve in it. The two main kinds of speculation are also influenced by different sets of modern events. Those knowledgeable about the nature of market economies and the kinds of infrastructures they need, including an open and fair political and legal environment, would be skeptical of China's present authoritarian and inefficient framework of government. They see China as just another modernizing nation-state, but one which had adopted a Communist system of government. Therefore, what happened to Communist governments elsewhere will soon happen in China.[27] They believe that modernizing economic reforms without concurrent political reforms will not succeed, and that the consequent economic failures will soon bring the whole structure down. They expect dramatic changes to happen quickly; when they do, they would produce something like a modern revolution that follows when reformists fail. This view may be underestimating the capacity of the Chinese people to produce enough economic successes to offset the political inadequacies of the system and the corruption and incompetence of its officials. But there is clear evidence that all Communist systems find it very difficult to adapt to market conditions.[28] The Chinese face an uphill struggle.

There are other commentators who are more fearful of the nature of authoritarian governments supported by a politicized military and are also aware of recent Chinese history. They expect that the political and military factions at the center who represent nobody but their narrow selfish interests will fight openly for power when key members of the Old Guard die. If that happens, the administration will break down, massive discontent will surface, and forces demanding political rights and freedom will be unleashed. Those more optimistic in their speculations believe that, after perhaps years of disorder and division, political progress will be made and something like a liberal democratic revolution would be given a chance to win the final victory. Those less sanguine would despair at the damage that prolonged civil war could bring to China as a unified state and to the fabric of Chinese society and culture. They would have little hope for a strong and prosperous China after such a period of division and no reason to expect that liberal and democratic ideals could succeed in the impoverished country that resulted.

Such speculations depend on whether the Chinese people would react as other peoples under similar circumstances or whether their patterns of behavior would be more deeply influenced by the cultural determinants they have inherited. If most Chinese have become modern by following the ways of the peoples of Western Europe and North America and do, in fact, think and act wholly in terms of the modern concepts of reform and revolution, then analogies can easily be drawn with their modern counterparts elsewhere. What this essay suggests is that, despite the experience of revolution in 1911 and then in 1949, it may be too early to assume that this is so.[29] Throughout Chinese history, it has always taken great force to move the people to make major changes to their way of life, even more to provoke them to political action. For most of them, the difference between modern revolution and the more familiar *geming* could hardly be significant. Everyone appears to know that *geming* as revolution has already taken place: the Republic had become part of modern world history and the People's Republic tasted the bitter fruits of "world revolution." As long as this transforming struggle to join the civilized and freedom-loving nations of the world is still garlanded with a righteous mandate, no further *geming* as revolution would seem to be called for. If the mandate has not been exhausted, another drastic *geming* would not be necessary. Until then, most Chinese would be content with *gaige,* especially if the reforms generated are to strengthen or save not only the existing system or regime, but also the country and possibly the civilization as well.

ENDNOTES

[1]Interview with a journalist of *The Strand Magazine* in London, "My Reminiscences," *The Strand Magazine* 43 (255) (March 1912): 301–307, trans. and collected in *Sun Zhongshan quanji,* vol. 1 (Beijing: Zhonghua Press, 1890–1911), 547–58. The Proclamation in Nanjing by Sun Yat-sen on 1 January 1912 is collected in *Sun Zhongshan quanji,* vol. 2, 1–3. In 1942, *geming* or the so-called Right of

Revolution was noted as "a sort of ideological preparation for democratic institutions which, there is good reason to hope, will enable [China] in the future to assume her rightful place among the world's great democracies," in Derk Bodde, *Essays on Chinese Civilization,* ed. Charles Le Blanc and Dorothy Borei (Princeton: Princeton University Press, 1981), 138. (reprint of an essay, "Dominant Ideas in the Formation of Chinese Culture," first published in the *Journal of the American Oriental Society* 62 (December 1942): 293–99).

2Wang Gungwu, "Juxtaposing Past and Present in China Today," *The China Quarterly* (London) 61 (March 1975): 1–24; also in a collected volume of my essays, *The Chineseness of China: selected essays* (Hong Kong: Oxford University Press, 1991), 209–29.

3Such distances can be measured in terms of industrial entrepreneurship, political action, philosophy, scientific education, literature, and the arts. See Jonathan D. Spence, *The Gate of Heavenly Peace: the Chinese and their revolution, 1895–1980* (New York: Viking Press, 1981); and W. J. F. Jenner, *The Tyranny of History: The Roots of China's Crisis* (London: Allen Lane/ The Penguin Press, 1992). For an earlier period, Leo Ou-fan Lee, *The Romantic Generation of Modern Chinese Writers* (Cambridge: Harvard University Press, 1973), provides a valuable framework for understanding the present. For developments during the past decade, see Geremie Barmé and John Minford, eds., "Seeds of Fire: Chinese Voices of Conscience," *Far Eastern Economic Review* (Hong Kong) (1986), and Geremie Barmé and Linda Jaivin, eds, *New Ghosts, Old Dreams: Chinese Rebel Voices* (New York: Times Books, 1992).

4Benjamin I. Schwartz, *The World of Thought in Ancient China* (Cambridge: The Belknap Press of Harvard University Press, 1985), 102–17. The concept of reform was often expressed through Heavenly warnings that suggested that something was seriously wrong. See Michael Loewe, "The Religious and Intellectual Background," *The Cambridge History of China: The Ch'in and Han Empires, 221 B.C.-A.D. 220,* vol. 1 (Cambridge: Cambridge University Press, 1986), 708–13.

5Both *gai* and *ge* in the term *gaige* appear under the same hexagram *Ge* in *I Ching* (*The Book of Changes*) and both explain and extend the idea of change in the context of "great progress and success" and "coming trom what is correct," implying improvement and reform. Raymond Van Over, ed., *I Ching,* trans. James Legge (New York: The New American Library, 1971), 249–52.

6The term *geming* also appears under the hexagram *Ge* in *I Ching.* In its direct association with *tianming* (Mandate of Heaven), it is most fully developed in *Mencius,* Book IV, Part A of D. C. Lau's translation (New York: Penguin Books, 1970), 117–27.

7*Daily Chronicle,* 24 October 1896 and *Evening Standard,* 24 October 1896; both quoted in J. Y. Wong, *The Origins of an Heroic Image: Sun Yat-sen in London, 1896–1897* (Hong Kong: East Asian Historical Monographs, Oxford University Press, 1986), 169, 172.

8The language of the constitutions of the Xingzhong Hui of Honolulu (1894) and Hong Kong (1895) may be compared with that in the proposal for reform which Sun Yat-sen sent in 1894 to Li Hongzhang. *Sun Zhongshan quanji,* vol. 1, 8–24. For his early association with secret societies and other traditional groups, see

Harold Z. Schiffrin, *Sun Yat-sen and the Origins of the Chinese Revolution* (Berkeley: University of California Press, 1968), 56–97, and Lilia Borokh, "Notes on the early role of secret societies in Sun Yat-sen's republican movement," in Jean Chesneaux, ed., *Popular Movements and Secret Societies in China, 1840–1950* (Stanford: Stanford University Press, 1972), 135–44.

⁹Ting-yee Kuo and Kwang-Ching Liu, "Self-strengthening: the pursuit of Western Technology," in John K. Fairbank, ed., *The Cambridge History of China, vol. 10: Late Ch'ing, 1800–1911, Part I* (Cambridge: Cambridge University Press, 1978), 491–542, and Hao Chang, "Intellectual change and the reform movement, 1890–1898," in John K. Fairbank and Kwang-Ching Liu, eds., *The Cambridge History of China, vol. 11: Late Ch'ing, 1800–1911, Part 2* (Cambridge: Cambridge University Press, 1980), 274–338.

¹⁰Hsiao Kung-chuan, *A Modern China and a New World: K'ang Yu-wei, Reformer and Utopian, 1858–1927* (Seattle: University of Washington Press, 1975), and Hao Chang, *Chinese Intellectuals in Crisis: Search for Order and Meaning (1890–1911)* (Berkeley: University of California Press, 1987). See also James T. C. Liu, *Reform in Sung China: Wang An-shih (1021–1086) and his New Policies,* Harvard East Asian Studies, no. 3 (Cambridge: Harvard University Press, 1959).

¹¹Mary C. Wright, ed., *China in Revolution: the First Phase, 1900–1913* (New Haven: Yale University Press, 1968); a more recent account is Michael Gasster, "The republican revolutionary movement," in Fairbank and Liu, eds., *Late Ch'ing, Part 2,* 463–534.

¹²Chow Tse-tsung, *The May Fourth Movement: Intellectual Revolution in Modern China, 1915–1924* (Cambridge: Harvard University Press, 1960), and Lin Yu-sheng, *The Crisis of Chinese Consciousness: Radical Anti-traditionalism in the May Fourth Era* (Madison: University of Wisconsin Press, 1978). See also Vera Schwarcz, *The Chinese Enlightenment: Intellectuals and the Legacy of the May Fourth Movement of 1919* (Berkeley: University of California Press, 1986), and Benjamin I. Schwartz, "Themes in intellectual history: May Fourth and after," in John K. Fairbank, ed., *The Cambridge History of China, vol. 12: Republican China, 1912–1949, Part 1* (Cambridge: Cambridge University Press, 1983), 406–50.

¹³Wang Gungwu, *China and the World since 1949: The Impact of Independence, Modernity and Revolution* (London: Macmillan Press, 1977), and "Outside the Chinese Revolution," *The Australian Journal of Chinese Affairs* (Canberra) (23) (January 1990): 33–48.

¹⁴The essays in S. R. Schram, ed., *Foundations and Limits of State Power in China* (London: University of London, School of Oriental and African Studies and The Chinese University of Hong Kong Press, 1987), provide an excellent background to this question, notably, Marianne Bastid, "Official Conceptions of Imperial Authority at the End of the Qing dynasty," 147–85, and David S. G. Goodman, "Democracy, Interest and Virtue: the search for legitimacy in the People's Republic of China," 291–312.

¹⁵Two studies by Frederick C. Teiwes explore this topic most successfully: *Leadership, Legitimacy and Conflict in China* (London: Macmillan, 1984) and *Politics at Mao's Court: Gao Gang and Party Factionalism in the Early 1950s* (New York: M. E. Sharpe, 1990). See also Lucian W. Pye, *The Mandarin and the*

*Cadre: China's Political Cultures* (Ann Arbor: Center for Chinese Studies, University of Michigan, 1988), 135–73.

16Wang Gungwu, "China: 1989 in Perspective," *Southeast Asian Affairs 1990* (Singapore: Institute of Southeast Asian Studies, 1990), 71–85.

17Tang Tsou, *The Cultural Revolution and Post-Mao Reforms: a Historical Perspective* (Chicago: University of Chicago Press, 1986). Three of the essays are particularly insightful: "Back from the Brink of Revolutionary-'Feudal' Totalitarianism," 144–88; "Political Change and Reform: the Middle Course," 219–58; and "Reflections on the Formation and Foundations of the Communist Party-State in China," 259–334.

18Albert Feuerwerker, *China's Early Industrialization: Sheng Hsuan-huai (1844–1916) and mandarin enterprise* (Cambridge: Harvard University Press, 1958), and Wellington K. K. Chan, *Merchants, mandarins and modern enterprise in Late Ch'ing China* (Cambridge: Harvard University Press, 1977).

19Dorothy J. Solinger, *Chinese Business Under Socialism: The Politics of Domestic Commerce, 1949–1980* (Berkeley: University of California Press, 1984); also "Capitalist Measures with Capitalist characteristics," *Problems of Communism* 38 (January-February 1989): 19–33, and "Urban Entrepreneurs and the State: the merger of state and society," in Arthur Lewis Rosenbaum, ed., *State and Society in China: The Consequences of Reform* (Boulder: Westview Press, 1992), 121–41. Three studies in Brantly Womack, ed., *Contemporary Chinese Politics in Historical Perspective* (Cambridge: Cambridge University Press, 1991), are updates of the central issues raised by Solinger: Edmond Lee, "A bourgeois alternative? The Shanghai arguments for a Chinese capitalism: the 1920s and the 1980s," 90–126; Peter Nan-shong Lee, "The Chinese industrial state in historical perspective: from totalitarianism to corporatism," 153–79; and Hong Yung Lee, "From revolutionary cadres to bureaucratic technocrats," 180–206.

20Song Jian, "Population development—Goals and Plans," in Liu Zheng et al., *China's Population: Problems and Prospects* (Beijing: New World Press, 1981), 25–31; Judith Banister, *China's Changing Population* (Stanford: Stanford University Press, 1987); and John S. Aird, "Coercion in Family Planning: Causes, Methods and Consequences," in *China's Economy looks Towards the Year 2000: vol. 1, The Four Modernizations* (Washington, D.C.: U.S. Congress, 1986), 184–221.

21This ancient tradition was perfected during the period of the Warring States, fourth-third centuries, B.C.; Hsu Cho-yun, *Ancient China in Transition: an Analysis of Social Mobility, 722–222 B.C.* (Stanford: Stanford University Press, 1965).

22Merle Goldman, *China's Intellectuals: Advise and Dissent* (Cambridge: Harvard University Press, 1981), provides the most lucid account of the shifts in policy since 1949. This has been updated in Merle Goldman, "The Intellectuals in the Deng Xiaoping Era," in Rosenbaum, ed., *State and Society in China*, 193–218.

23The Communist Party's recent policies towards intellectuals are examined in Part Four of *China's Intellectuals and the State: In Search of a New Relationship*, ed. Merle Goldman, Timothy Creek, and Carol Lee Hamrin, Harvard Contemporary China Series (Cambridge: The Council on East Asian Studies, Harvard University,

1987), 253–74, 275–304. The contradictions in the idea of "knowledge workers" contributed to the breakdown of order during the Cultural Revolution; see Lynn T. White III, *Policies of Chaos: The Organizational Causes of Violence in China's Cultural Revolution* (Princeton: Princeton University Press, 1989). The political distance between the regime and young intellectuals seems to have grown during the 1980s; see Han Minzhu, ed., *Cries for Democracy: Writings and Speeches from the 1989 Chinese Democracy Movement* (Princeton: Princeton University Press, 1990).

[24]Many historians and polemicists in Taiwan and on the mainland have drawn attention to these analogies. The practice reached a climax during the Cultural Revolution, especially in the early 1970s. See Wang Gungwu, "Burning Books and Burying Scholars Alive: Some Recent Interpretations Concerning Ch'in Shih-huang," *Papers of Far Eastern History* (Canberra) (9) (1974): 137–86.

[25]There have been several terms in use in the Chinese media on the mainland: "bourgeois liberalization," "peaceful transformation," and "peaceful evolution." All have played a part in internal and external political debates and struggles; see Hsi-sheng Ch'i, *Politics of Disillusionment: The Chinese Communist Party Under Deng Xiaoping, 1978–1989* (New York: M. E. Sharpe, 1991), 257–76.

[26]This issue has been passionately argued by many commentators. One of the clearest statements to date is Edward Friedman, "Permanent Technological Revolution and China's Tortuous Path to Democratizing Leninism," in Richard Baum, ed., *Reform and Reaction in Post-Mao China: The Road to Tiananmen* (New York: Routledge, 1991), 162–82.

[27]Victor Nee and David Stark, eds., *Remaking the Economic Institutions of Socialism: China and Eastern Europe* (Stanford: Stanford University Press, 1989), examine this view critically. See Cyril Zhiren Lin, "Open-ended Economic Reform in China," 95–136; Martin King Whyte, "Who Hates Bureaucracy? A Chinese Puzzle," 233–54; and the opening essay by the editors, "Toward an Institutional Analysis of State Socialism," 1–31.

[28]Two thoughtful essays in Baum, ed., *Reform and Reaction,* are Connie Squires Meaney, "Market Reform and Disintegrative Corruption in Urban China," 124–42, and Jean C. Oi, "Partial Market Reform and Corruption in Rural China," 143–61.

[29]Tsou Tang, "The Tiananmen tragedy: the state-society relationship, choices, and mechanisms in historical perspective," in Womack, ed., *Contemporary Chinese Politics,* 265–327.

*Andrew J. Nathan and Tianjian Shi*

# Cultural Requisites for Democracy in China: Findings from a Survey

HINESE POLITICAL CULTURE IS OFTEN cited as an obstacle to the realization of democratic aspirations.[1] Its undemocratic attributes are generally thought to include authoritarianism, passivity, ignorance of politics, fear of politics, and intolerance. The first national sample survey of Chinese political culture allows a more nuanced look at some related attributes and their distribution among the population. Some of the specific findings are surprising, and the overall pattern suggests that political culture may affect democratization in more complex ways than usually acknowledged.

Until now, evidence concerning the nature of Chinese political culture has been drawn from interpretive studies.[2] We use this term to describe studies that are characteristically based on documentary sources, interviews, and field observation. Interpretive studies seek to identify complex sets of attitudes, or syndromes, of values, beliefs, and practices, which are thought to be distinctive of, or even unique to, a given culture, or to a broad section of its population, often over a long span of time.[3]

When implemented well, the interpretive approach to the study of political culture has marked strengths. These include the ability to characterize the culture of a whole people or of large social segments; the ability to attend both to broad themes in a culture and to nuance, contradiction, levels of meanings, and dialectical relationships; and the capability to use documents and other historical evidence to retrieve information about the belief and value systems of the past.

*Andrew J. Nathan is Professor of Political Science at Columbia University.*

*Tianjian Shi is Assistant Professor of Political Science at the University of Iowa.*

The approach also has weaknesses. These include a tendency to imprecision when specifying referents (what the belief or attitude in question consists of); frequent ambiguity of propositions (who is said to have believed what at what time, and with what effect); an inability to provide rigorous, intersubjectively reliable evidence that the propositions are more true than alternative propositions (are the Chinese really more authoritarian than some other people?); a tendency to tautological arguments about the effects of culture on behavior, since behavior itself is often used as an indicator for the existence of a belief or attitude; the inability to describe with precision the distribution of attitudes among the population; and the inability to carry out analytical procedures to distinguish the effects of sociodemographic attributes on cultural attitudes or the effects of attitudes on behavior. In short, even the best interpretive work consists of broadly stated, loosely specified insights using ill-defined terms, meaning different things to different readers, and making statements that may or may not be true.

These weaknesses multiply when a cross-cultural comparison is attempted. For example, Chinese are said to be more collectively oriented, Americans more individualistic. But interpretive studies cannot give precise or reliable answers as to what this means, how large the difference is, whether the contrast really exists, and how different sectors of the two populations vary among themselves.

An alternative to the interpretive approach, the survey approach, has been widely applied to the study of democratic political systems, but has not been used very much in the study of Chinese culture.[4] Its research tool is the sample survey, whose use requires precise sampling methods, sophisticated interviewing techniques to assure reliability, scoring and scaling techniques to sort and organize responses in categories related to theoretical variables, and statistical analysis and inference.[5] In this approach, political culture is conceptualized as the distribution of values, attitudes, and beliefs towards politics among a population.[6] The unit of observation is the individual. Culture is an aggregative concept referring to the pattern of attitudes among the population or a specified subset.

When implemented well, the survey approach has certain advantages. These include clear specification of referents, disambiguation of propositions, empirical reliability of findings, the ability to measure variation in cultural attributes among a population, the potential ability to measure change over time if serial surveys are done, avoidance of tautology in the specification of relations between culture and behavior, and the ability to perform a wide range of statistical analyses, including analyses of the effects of sociodemographic variables on culture, and of cultural variables on political behavior.

The method also has disadvantages. Aside from its technical difficulty, these include the inability to go back in time except under special circumstances, the technique's flattening or simplifying effect on the cultural attributes which can be measured, and the intrinsic inability to identify attributes which are or might be culturally unique, except in a trivial sense. We discuss these advantages and problems later in the paper.

Prior to the study reported here, no one had done a survey of Chinese political culture that was based on a random sample and hence permitted statistical induction.[7] A few studies by foreign scholars employed multiple émigré interviews, but the numbers of respondents were too small and the samples too unrepresentative to make induction possible.[8] In the 1980s, scholars in China began to conduct surveys, some of which touched on political-cultural topics. According to Dong Li, during the period from 1979 to 1991, Chinese scholars conducted at least 181 surveys concerning political attitudes.[9] Only one was national in scope, Min Qi's *Chinese Political Culture*, carried out in 1987 under the auspices of the Beijing Social and Economic Research Institute.[10] All the Chinese surveys on which we have information, including Min Qi's, were methodologically flawed in terms of sampling, question formulation, and interview techniques. Min Qi's study, for example, severely undersampled women, older citizens, rural residents, and other key sectors of the population.

This paper reports some results from a survey conducted in China in 1990 which is, so far as we know, not only the first scientifically valid national sample survey done in China on political behavior and attitudes, but the only valid national-level sample survey on the political behavior and attitudes of the general populace ever done in a Communist country.[11] (See Appendix for details.)

The survey assessed approximately fifty political-cultural variables, too many to examine in a single paper. As a first step, we have selected for discussion certain items which involve the cultural requisites for democracy, and which were designed to permit cross-national comparison. Most of them were adapted from two classic studies—Gabriel Almond and Sidney Verba's *The Civic Culture* and the International Social Survey Program (ISSP).[12] We are comparing China in 1990 to other countries in 1959–1960 and 1985 respectively, and to countries that were democratic at the time of their surveys.[13] These time gaps and system differences present no obstacle to comparison as long as we take account of them in the analysis.

The study of political culture emerged from curiosity about the prerequisites for stable democracy, especially the relationships between citizens' subjective orientations and democratic stability. Theorists have stressed the importance to the democratic process of such values as the belief in popular sovereignty, commitment to the equality of citizens, and the principle of majoritarian decision making with adequate protection of minority rights.[14] In a recent study of Russian political culture, James Gibson and Raymond Duch identified five values conducive to democracy: *1)* the belief in the legitimacy of democratic institutions; *2)* beliefs about authority relationships between government and the governed; *3)* confidence in the capacity of the government; *4)* political and interpersonal trust; and *5)* the belief in the possibility of cooperation and the legitimacy of conflict.[15]

We focus here on three dimensions of political culture which we believe are fundamental to democracy: first, do citizens perceive the government as salient to their lives, as having an impact on themselves and their families? Second, do people believe that they have the capability to understand and engage in politics? Third, to what extent are citizens prepared to be tolerant of those who hold different political beliefs?

We show that while some of the attitudes associated with democracy are less prevalent in China than in some other countries, Chinese political culture today is neither especially traditional nor especially totalitarian. Our findings lead to two kinds of concluding reflections: on the prospects for democracy in China and on cultural distinctiveness—not only China's cultural distinctiveness, but the notion of cultural distinctiveness as it appears from the perspective of the survey approach to culture.

THE PERCEIVED IMPACT OF GOVERNMENT

One of the cultural requisites commonly cited for democracy is that citizens perceive the actions of government to be salient to their lives. An awareness of the impact of government is thought to generate interest in politics and a desire to participate in the political process. The classic question to assess this attitude was asked by Gabriel Almond and Sidney Verba, authors of *The Civic Culture,* who separately measured citizens' perceptions of national and local government impact. We asked the same two questions in China.[16] Our results are displayed with Almond and Verba's in *Tables 1* and 2.

TABLE 1. Estimated Degree of Impact of the Local Government on Daily Life, by Nation

| Percentage who say local government has: | China | United States | United Kingdom | Germany | Italy | Mexico |
|---|---|---|---|---|---|---|
| Great effect | 5.4% | 35% | 23% | 33% | 19% | 6% |
| Some effect | 18.4 | 53 | 51 | 41 | 39 | 23 |
| No effect | 71.6 | 10 | 23 | 18 | 22 | 67 |
| Other | — | — | — | — | 2 | — |
| Do not know | 4.6 | 2 | 3 | 8 | 18 | 3 |
| Total percentage | 100.0 | 100 | 100 | 100 | 99 | 100 |
| Total number | 2896 | 970 | 963 | 955 | 995 | 1007 |

Actual text of the question used in *The Civic Culture*: "Now take the local government. About how much effect do you think its activities have on your day-to-day life? Do they have a great effect, some effect, or none?"

Actual text of the question used in China: "Now let's discuss the local government. How much effect do you think its activities have on your day-to-day life? Do they have a great effect, some effect or none?"

It is striking that so few Chinese citizens perceive their government as having an impact on their daily lives. Whether China's system is now or ever was totalitarian is a subject of debate,[17] but few would question that the Chinese government is more intrusive in citizens' lives and deals with a broader scope of policy than most other governments. Yet, approximately 72 percent of Chinese citizens stated that both national and local governments had no effect on their daily lives, figures comparable in the Almond and Verba data only to Mexico. As in most of the other nations, slightly more Chinese attributed the influence to local rather than to the national government, but the difference was not great.

TABLE 2. Estimated Degree of Impact of the National Government on Daily Life, by Nation

| Percentage who say national government has: | China | United States | United Kingdom | Germany | Italy | Mexico |
|---|---|---|---|---|---|---|
| Great effect | 9.7% | 41% | 33% | 38% | 23% | 7% |
| Some effect | 11.7 | 44 | 40 | 32 | 31 | 23 |
| No effect | 71.8 | 11 | 23 | 17 | 19 | 66 |
| Other | — | 0 | — | — | 3 | — |
| Do not know | 6.7 | 4 | 4 | 12 | 24 | 3 |
| Total percentage | 100.0 | 100 | 100 | 99 | 100 | 99 |
| Total number | 2896 | 970 | 963 | 955 | 995 | 1007 |

Actual text of the question used in *The Civic Culture*: "Thinking now about the national government [in Washington, London, Bonn, Rome, Mexico City], about how much effect do you think its activities, the laws passed and so on, have on your day-to-day life? Do they have a great effect, some effect, or none?"

Actual text of the question used in China: "Now let's discuss the national government in Beijing. About how much effect do you think its activities have on your day-to-day life? Do they have a great effect, some effect or none?"

Do differences in the structure of public administration in China help explain the low salience of national and local governments? Unlike the five nations referred to in *The Civic Culture,* the structure of government in China extends below the local (provincial and county) levels to the urban neighborhood and rural village committees, the so-called "grass-roots level of government," and below these to the work units which are officially nongovernmental.[18] Even if Chinese citizens are unaware of the impact of the national and local government, they may perceive the impact of the village/neighborhood level of administration, which performs many distributive and redistributive functions important to local residents. *Figure 1* reveals that, indeed, a higher percentage of respondents perceive an effect on their lives from the village/neighborhood level of administration than from the national or local levels. But the numbers are still remarkably low.

It is also possible that the low Chinese totals result from different groups of citizens paying attention to the impact of different levels of government, each focusing on the level that most concerns him or her. If a different group of citizens were aware of the impact of each level of the government, then the groups added together would make for a widespread awareness of government at one level or another. However, *Figure 2* shows that this is not the case. Nearly 60 percent

Figure 1. Perceived Impact of National and Local Government and Neighborhood or Village Committee on Daily Life by Type of Household Registration

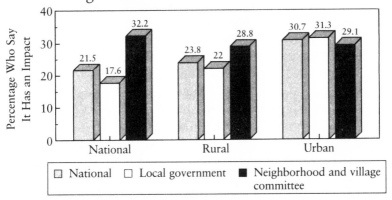

Figure 2. Perceived Impact of Government

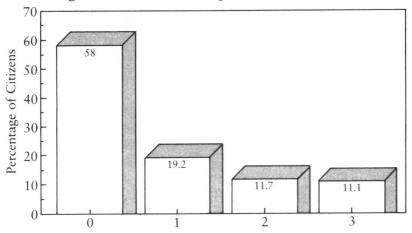

Number of Levels with Perceived Impact

of the population attributes no impact to any of the three levels of government.

In any society, awareness of the government is likely to vary with such individual attributes as urban residence and education. If the population is heavily weighted towards persons who are less likely to be aware of the impact of government, the overall level of awareness might be low in the population as a whole because of the population's composition rather than because of the nature of the culture. Modernization theory suggests that urban Chinese might be more aware of the impact of government on their lives than rural residents. According to this theory, economic development expands the proportion of higher status roles in a society, involves tensions and strains among social groups, produces an expansion of the functions of the government, and raises the saliency of an individual's identity as a member of the national state. These trends usually lead to higher levels of political mobilization.[19] Since urban China is more developed than rural China, urban residents might be more aware of the impact of government than their rural cousins.

When we subdivided our sample into urban and rural sectors as shown in *Figure 1,* we found that, as expected, more urban than rural residents attributed some influence to the national and local governments.[20] But the urbanites did so at levels below all the *Civic Culture* nations except Mexico. Unlike rural residents, urban residents perceived no substantial difference in the influence of the three levels of the administration.

In the *Civic Culture* nations, awareness of the government's impact varied with educational level. Italians and Mexicans without formal education had a very low level of awareness of the impact of the national and local governments.[21] In China, 25.7 percent of our sample was illiterate and another 30 percent had educations at or below the primary level.[22] This suggests that the differing aggregate levels of awareness among the six countries might be due to differences in the educational makeup of national populations. *Table 3* shows that in China, as elsewhere, the perceived impact of the national government varies substantially with the level of education, with less-educated respondents less likely to perceive an impact by the government on their daily lives. In both China and Mexico, the high proportion of less-educated citizens in the total population partly explains why the aggregate estimate of the impact of the government is low.

But the data also reveal that at each educational level, Chinese respondents are less aware of the impact of the government than similarly educated respondents in the other five nations. About half as many Chinese with no formal education perceive the national government to have an impact as do uneducated Italians and

TABLE 3. Educational Differences in the Perceived Impact of the National Government, by Nation

| Percentage who say national government has: | None | Primary or less | Some Secondary | Some University |
|---|---|---|---|---|
| **China** | | | | |
| Some effect | 12.0% | 17.2% | 27.4% | 61.2% |
| No effect | 75.3 | 77.1 | 68.1 | 36.1 |
| Other | 0.0 | 0.0 | 0.0 | 0.0 |
| Do not know | 12.7 | 5.7 | 4.5 | 2.3 |
| Total percentage | 100.0 | 100.0 | 100.0 | 100.0 |
| Total number | 687 | 869 | 1276 | 64 |
| **United States** | | | | |
| Some effect | | 73 | 89 | 96 |
| No effect | | 17 | 10 | 4 |
| Other | | 0 | 0 | 0 |
| Do not know | | 10 | 1 | 0 |
| Total percentage | | 100 | 100 | 100 |
| Total number | | 339 | 443 | 188 |
| **United Kingdom** | | | | |
| Some effect | | 70 | 76 | 92 |
| No effect | | 25 | 21 | 8 |
| Other | | 0 | 1 | 0 |
| Do not know | | 4 | 2 | 0 |
| Total percentage | | 99 | 100 | 100 |
| Total number | | 593 | 322 | 24 |
| **Germany** | | | | |
| Some effect | | 69 | 83 | 92 |
| No effect | | 18 | 14 | 8 |
| Other | | 0 | 0 | 0 |
| Do not know | | 14 | 2 | 0 |
| Total percentage | | 101 | 99 | 100 |
| Total number | | 792 | 123 | 26 |
| **Italy** | | | | |
| Some effect | 24 | 48 | 72 | 85 |
| No effect | 17 | 20 | 19 | 13 |
| Other | 6 | 3 | 2 | 2 |
| Do not know | 53 | 29 | 7 | — |
| Total percentage | 100 | 100 | 100 | 100 |
| Total number | 88 | 604 | 245 | 54 |
| **Mexico** | | | | |
| Some effect | 25 | 30 | 35 | 57 |
| No effect | 65 | 68 | 62 | 41 |
| Other | — | — | 2 | — |
| Do not know | 10 | 2 | 1 | 3 |
| Total percentage | 100 | 100 | 100 | 101 |
| Total number | 221 | 656 | 103 | 24 |

Mexicans. For those with primary educations, the gap was 55.8 percent between Chinese and Americans, 52.8 percent between Chinese and Britons, 51.8 percent between Chinese and Germans, 30.8 percent between Chinese and Italians, and 12.8 percent between Chinese and Mexicans. Even among persons with university educations, the Chinese are substantially less likely to perceive a national government impact, with gaps ranging from 20 to over 30 percent. The sole exception is Mexico: Chinese with university educations are slightly more likely than similarly educated Mexicans to perceive an impact of the national government on their daily lives.

The initial impression remains unshaken: compared to citizens in the five democratic nations studied in 1959–1960 in *The Civic Culture,* Chinese citizens in 1990 were relatively unaware of the impact of the government on their daily lives even when education is held constant. But the Chinese profile did not depart far from that of the Mexicans thirty years earlier, when Mexico was already considered a democracy, although not yet a highly developed one. In Almond and Verba's terms, Chinese citizens today are still relatively parochial;[23] the workings of even the grass-roots levels of administration remain obscure to the majority.

According to conventional wisdom, the state in communist systems exercises close control over society. Our data are not about the objective role of the state, but about the subjective perceptions of ordinary citizens. We seem to have found a gap between the two. Although the regime in China controls the daily lives of citizens more totally than was the case in the five nations studied by Almond and Verba, fewer citizens are able to identify such control. We do not know what mechanisms are at work to produce this paradox— whether the regime manages to make its subjects overlook its control over their daily lives or whether the citizens contrive to ignore the regime's control as a way of managing the psychological tension that it induces. In any case, the finding suggests that the Chinese regime enjoys a "safety cushion" of popular underestimation of its role, which may to some extent blunt demands for democracy.

POLITICAL EFFICACY

The sense of efficacy is a powerful determinant of people's involvement in politics. Whether or not citizens can influence politics, their beliefs about whether they can do so help guide their political behavior. Feelings of efficacy motivate people to engage in political activities, while the absence of these feelings evokes political apathy and withdrawal. Some researchers consider efficacy a key indicator of the health of a democratic system.[24]

Political efficacy was originally defined as "the feeling that individual political action does have, or can have, an impact upon the political process."[25] Two different operationalizations of the concept have been popular in the literature. Almond and Verba concentrated on whether citizens believe that they have the capacity to wield influence. They differentiated political efficacy into subject and citizen "competence." The former refers to a person's awareness of his or her rights to fair and equal treatment from the government, the latter to his or her awareness of the ability to influence the government.[26] The approach associated with the Survey Research Center (SRC) of the University of Michigan puts more emphasis on the perceived responsiveness of political institutions than on the respondent's sense of his or her own capabilities.[27]

Subsequent research demonstrated that both approaches are valid. Political efficacy is a multidimensional phenomenon containing two separate components. One is internal efficacy, which consists of beliefs about one's competence to understand and participate in politics. The other is external efficacy, which refers to beliefs about the responsiveness of the government.[28] Internal efficacy in turn contains two subdimensions: the belief in one's ability to understand complicated political issues and the belief in one's ability to act politically. The former component affects the likelihood that people engage in politics; the latter affects the level and patterns of participation.

Some measures of internal efficacy in China are displayed in *Table 4*. The table shows that slightly less than half (47.3 percent) of our respondents deemed themselves able to understand work unit issues as well as other people. In relation to the national government, the percentage of persons with a sense of efficacy dropped to 31.9 percent.[29] About 20 percent of the population believed that they could be as good a leader in their work unit or village as others, and 16.8 percent had confidence in their ability to serve as government leaders.

TABLE 4. Internal Efficacy

| Percentage who report they: | Understand work unit affairs as well as others | Understand national affairs less well than others | Can be as good a unit leader as any others | Can be as good a government leader as any others |
|---|---|---|---|---|
| Strongly agree | 17.6% | 16.5% | 8.4% | 6.1% |
| Agree | 29.7 | 32.6 | 14.1 | 10.7 |
| Not sure | 5.5 | 4.7 | 4.2 | 3.3 |
| Disagree | 24.6 | 23.3 | 29.9 | 27.3 |
| Strongly disagree | 8.0 | 8.6 | 24.8 | 32.3 |
| Do not know | 14.6 | 14.3 | 18.6 | 20.2 |
| Total percentage | 100.0 | 100.0 | 100.0 | 99.9 |
| Total number | 2896 | 2896 | 2896 | 2896 |

Actual text of the question: Do you strongly agree, agree, disagree or strongly disagree with the following statement: "I think that my understanding of the situation in our work unit is no worse than other people's"; "I think that my understanding of national affairs is not as good as ordinary people's"; "I think that I would not be a worse work unit leader than other people"; "I think that I would not be a worse government leader than other people."

*Table 5* shows the results from a similar but different question, which asks the respondent to rate his or her understanding of the issues facing the nation, the local government, and the unit. Self-rated understanding of unit affairs is again higher than self-rated understanding of local or national-level affairs. Nearly 50 percent of the respondents felt that they understood the "important issues facing [their] work unit" very well or relatively well, compared to 19.9 percent for local issues and 17.9 percent for national-level issues. Taken together, the figures from *Tables 4* and *5* demonstrate a substantial gap in internal efficacy when one moves from the grass-roots level of administration to formal government institutions.

*Tables 6* and *7* place these Chinese figures in the context of comparable figures from *The Civic Culture*. Chinese citizens generally scored lower on this measure than citizens of other nations, but they did not lag behind the Italians and the Mexicans in all respects. Although fewer Chinese than Italians or Mexicans claimed to understand either national-level or local issues "very well," the sum percentage of Chinese understanding national-level issues "relatively well," "depends," and "poorly" was higher than in Italy and Mexico, and the percentage claiming to understand national-level affairs "not at all" was lower than in Mexico.

TABLE 5. Understanding of National-Level, Local, and Unit Affairs

| Percentage who say they: | National affairs | Local affairs | Unit affairs |
|---|---|---|---|
| Understand very well | 0.9% | 1.9% | 15.4% |
| Understand relatively well | 17.0 | 18.0 | 31.9 |
| Understand poorly | 37.5 | 32.7 | 23.0 |
| Do not understand at all | 41.5 | 44.8 | 25.9 |
| Do not know | 3.1 | 2.7 | 3.9 |
| Total percentage | 100.0 | 100.0 | 100.0 |
| Total number | 2896 | 2896 | 2896 |

Actual text of the question: "Regarding the important international and domestic issues facing our country, how well do you think you understand them? How about the important issues facing the city (county, or district)? How about the important issues facing your work unit (village), do you understand them very well, relatively well, not very well, or not at all?"

TABLE 6. Understanding of National-Level Affairs

| Percentage who say they: | China | United States | United Kingdom | Germany | Italy | Mexico |
|---|---|---|---|---|---|---|
| Understand very well | 0.9% | 7.2% | 8.0% | 13.1% | 6.6% | 1.5% |
| Understand relatively well | 17.0 | 37.9 | 36.3 | 35.1 | 19.9 | 6.4 |
| Depends on the issue | — | 2.1 | 1.8 | 7.5 | 4.1 | — |
| Understand poorly | 37.5 | 37.0 | 35.5 | 24.3 | 23.7 | 44.8 |
| Do not understand at all | 41.5 | 14.6 | 15.5 | 14.7 | 33.7 | 44.4 |
| Do not know | 3.1 | 1.1 | 2.9 | 5.3 | 12 | 2.8 |
| Total percentage | 100.0 | 100.0 | 100.0 | 100.0 | 100.0 | 100.0 |
| Total number | 2896 | 970 | 963 | 955 | 995 | 1008 |

Actual text of the question used in *The Civic Culture*: "Thinking of the important national and international issues facing the country—how well do you think you can understand these issues?"

Actual text of the question used in China: "Regarding the important international and domestic issues facing our country, how well do you think you understand them?"

Turning to external efficacy, the best-established measures would have been too sensitive to ask in China.[30] As a surrogate, we used Almond and Verba's measure of "output affect," which, besides feasibility, offered the opportunity for further comparison with the *Civic Culture* countries. The question asks about the respondent's expectation of equal treatment at a government office. In view of China's reputation for government corruption and abuse, it comes as a surprise to find in *Table 8* that Chinese citizens in 1990 were not very different from Germans, Italians, and Mexicans at the time of

TABLE 7. Understanding of Local Affairs

| Percentage who say they: | China | United States | United Kingdom | Germany | Italy | Mexico |
|---|---|---|---|---|---|---|
| Understand very well | 1.9% | 21.0% | 17.5% | 24.8% | 15.0% | 5.4% |
| Understand relatively well | 18.0 | 43.5 | 36.8 | 36.8 | 23.3 | 13.4 |
| Depends on the issue | — | 1.0 | 1.0 | 7.6 | 3.3 | 0.1 |
| Understand poorly | 32.7 | 22.9 | 25.2 | 17.9 | 19.3 | 47.2 |
| Do not understand at all | 44.8 | 10.2 | 14.2 | 7.1 | 26.5 | 32.9 |
| Do not know | 2.7 | 1.3 | 5.2 | 5.8 | 12.6 | 1.0 |
| Total percentage | 100.0 | 100.0 | 100.0 | 100.0 | 100.0 | 100.0 |
| Total number | 2896 | 970 | 963 | 955 | 995 | 1008 |

Actual text of the question used in *The Civic Culture*: "How about local issues in this town or part of the country. How well do you understand them?"

Actual text of the question used in China: "How about important issues facing the city (county, or district), how well do you think you understand them?"

*The Civic Culture* surveys in their expectation of equal treatment. The percentage of Chinese who expected equal treatment was a little lower than the Germans and a little higher than the Italians. Overall, a majority of Chinese respondents thought they would be treated equally by a government office.

Most political culture variables are strongly affected by respondents' educational levels.[31] Output affect is no exception. In China, education's impact on the expectation of equal treatment displays an unusual pattern. *Figure 3* shows that in four of the five *Civic Culture* nations, the expectation of equal government treatment increases with the level of education. In the United States, Britain, and Germany, although education has a positive impact on people's expectation of fair government, the less educated do not expect to be treated categorically differently from the more educated.[32] In Italy and Mexico, the overall percentage of those expecting equal treatment is lower, and the differences between the more educated and the less educated are more marked. In Mexico, only 19 percent of the people with no education expect equal treatment compared to 68 percent of those with a university education: a spread of 49 points. In all six countries, except China and Italy, the expectation of equal treatment increases linearly with every step in the educational ladder.

In China and Italy, the relationship between education and output affect is curvilinear. The expectation of equal treatment increases with respondents' educational levels up to a certain point and then

TABLE 8. Expectation of Treatment by Governmental Bureaucracy, by Nation

| Percentage who say: | United States | United Kingdom | Germany | China | Italy | Mexico |
|---|---|---|---|---|---|---|
| They expect equal treatment | 83% | 83% | 65% | 57.0% | 53% | 42% |
| They do not expect equal treatment | 9 | 7 | 9 | 24.2 | 13 | 50 |
| Depends | 4 | 6 | 19 | — | 17 | 5 |
| Other | — | — | — | 9.1 | 6 | — |
| Do not know | 4 | 2 | 7 | 9.8 | 11 | 3 |
| Total percentage | 100 | 98 | 100 | 100.1 | 100 | 100 |
| Total number of cases | 970 | 963 | 955 | 2876 | 995 | 1007 |

Actual text of the question used in *The Civic Culture*: "Suppose there were some question that you had to take to a government office—for example, a tax question or housing regulation. Do you think you would be given equal treatment—I mean, would you be treated as well as anyone else?"

The text of the question used in China: "Suppose there were some issue that you had to take to a government office. Do you think you would be given equal treatment? I mean, would you be treated as well as anyone else?"

reverses itself. In Italy, in 1959, 30 percent of the most disadvantaged group expected equal treatment by the authorities. The expectation increased with each increase in education up to the level of secondary school. But the expectation of equal treatment among the most advantaged group, people with some college education, was 6 percent less than among those with secondary school education.

The shape of the curve in China is remarkable. Slightly more than half of the most disadvantaged group expect equal treatment by the government, a figure much higher than that of Italy and Mexico. The figure increases slightly with the level of education, but only up to the primary school level. Beyond this level, the advantage imparted by education not only disappears but becomes negative. Those with some secondary education are 5 percent less likely than those with some primary education to expect equal treatment, and those with some university education are nearly 17 percent less likely to hold this expectation.

In short, while the least-educated Chinese have the strongest output affect among the nations studied, the best-educated Chinese have the weakest. The decline associated with education is so sharp that Chinese with college educations are 6 percent less likely than

## Figure 3. Expectation of Equal Treatment by Government Authorities, by Education

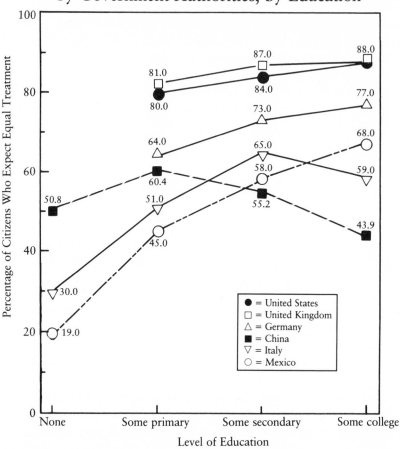

their most educationally disadvantaged countrymen to expect equal treatment. Compared to college graduates in other countries, Chinese college graduates are more than 44 percent less likely to expect equal treatment than Americans and Britons, 33.1 percent less likely than Germans, 24.1 percent less likely than Mexicans, and 15.1 percent less likely than Italians.

When a person feels he cannot achieve his goals through conventional participation, one logical choice is to turn to unconventional political activities—either to oppose the political system, take advantage of its loopholes, or simply to express frustration and dissatisfaction. Findings from a 1988 survey in Beijing showed that political activities of these types are indeed associated with college education in China.[33] Our findings on output affect help to explain why.

The findings also show how a cultural attitude considered conducive to democracy may also help buttress authoritarianism. The relatively high Chinese figures on output affect dovetail with findings from the 1988 Beijing survey that many Chinese citizens have developed a range of techniques for exerting influence on the bureaucracy despite the authoritarian nature of China's political system.[34] This sense among ordinary people of having access to the system may help explain why political dissatisfaction among intellectuals has not struck many sparks among the broader population, especially in rural areas where the less-educated are concentrated. Together with the widespread ignorance of the government's impact noted above, the reservoir of confidence in the government among less-educated Chinese may have helped the authoritarian regime to survive. But the implications of the high system affect are not necessarily adverse to democracy. It might also help to stabilize the society during a transition to a more open system and give a new democratic system a grace period to establish itself.

POLITICAL TOLERANCE

Political tolerance is associated with two principles underlying the democratic process: the commitment to the equality of citizens and the protection of minority rights. Both require tolerance for the viewpoints and political activities of its opponents. Some students of democracy consider tolerance the essential ingredient of democratic politics. As pointed out by Gibson and Duch, "without tolerance, widespread contestation is impossible, regime legitimacy is imperiled, and a numbing conformity prevails."[35]

Interpretive studies have portrayed Chinese political culture as intolerant. According to Lucian Pye, for example, "the dominant emotion of modern Chinese politics has been a preoccupation with hatred coupled with an enthusiasm for singling out enemies." Pye states that Chinese political culture knows no equals, only superiors and inferiors, and that the Chinese perceive a sharp divide between friend and foe.[36] Using the survey technique, we can compare Chinese levels of intolerance to those elsewhere, compare intolerance in different domains (speaking, teaching, and publishing), and determine which sectors of the Chinese population are more or less intolerant.

Since *The Civic Culture* contains no measure for tolerance, we selected a series of items from the ISSP for comparison. The position presented in the 1985 ISSP survey was, "There are some people whose views are considered extreme by the majority. Consider people who want to overthrow the government by revolution."[37] The respondent was then asked whether he or she thought that such people should be allowed to express their views in a public meeting, express their views as a teacher in a college, and express their views by publishing articles or books. We adapted the question to the Chinese setting by stating, "There are some people whose ideology is problematic, for example, they sympathize with the Gang of Four."[38] We then asked the same three questions.

*Figure 4* presents the figures for China and for the six highly developed democratic ISSP countries. It reveals that the Chinese are indeed the least tolerant among the seven nations. Fewer than 20 percent of the Chinese respondents were willing to allow sympathizers of a deviant viewpoint to express their views in a meeting, as compared to 40 to 75 percent of the populations in the other countries. When asked about teaching, Chinese tolerance levels were even lower, standing at 10.3 percent of the population, but the gap between China and the other countries was not as large. Tolerance for publishing unpopular ideas was again low in China (10.3 percent), with the range in the other countries extending from 51.8 percent to 70.3 percent.[39]

Political tolerance is normally associated with education: the less educated are less tolerant and more authoritarian.[40] Are the lower levels of tolerance in China attributable to generally lower levels of education, or does the tolerance gap remain when educational subgroups are compared across nations? *Figure 5* breaks down tolerance for speaking at a meeting, by level of education. As in other countries, in China education has a strong positive impact on tolerance. But at each level of educational attainment, Chinese respondents are less tolerant than people in other countries.

By far the most intolerant group in all the countries studied were the Chinese illiterates.[41] *Figure 6* provides a profile of this group. It shows that illiterates are heavily concentrated among persons above age forty (that is, who were born in 1950 or before), and that within

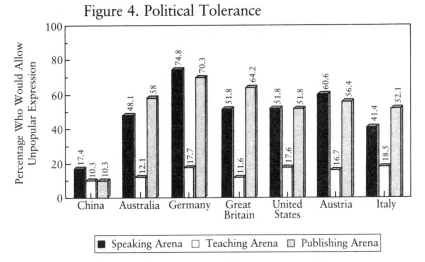

Figure 4. Political Tolerance

this group illiteracy is especially widespread among females resident in rural areas.

*Figure 6* demonstrates how survey research can allow us to look some distance into the past. The curves give insight into the distribution of educational opportunities in China from 1920 to 1972. They confirm that most urban male children and many rural male children were given some education in the early Republican period, show that virtually no education was given to rural females until about 1930, and suggest that a fraction of urban females were given some education starting about 1920.[42] A number of refinements of this analysis are possible, but these rough figures are sufficient to illustrate the retrospective use of survey data.[43]

The data suggest that average tolerance levels in China are likely to increase as older illiterates are replaced by later-born, better-educated citizens.[44] Even so, *Figure 5* shows that even the better-educated in China are less tolerant than their opposite numbers in the other countries studied. Tolerance levels in China may remain lower than those in democratic countries for some time, even with changes in the educational makeup of the population.

PROSPECTS FOR DEMOCRACY

We have presented data on only three sets of attitudes out of many that are theoretically related to democracy. Political scientists have

## Figure 5. Tolerance for Speaking at Meeting, by Education and Country

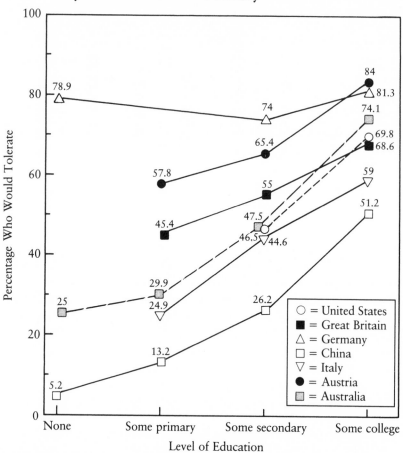

established no minimum thresholds for perceived saliency of government, internal and external efficacy, and tolerance in democratic societies. And political culture is but one of the several sets of conditions that affect the prospects for democracy. So our data justify no sweeping conclusions.

Some patterns in the data suggest potential difficulties if the Chinese political system begins to democratize. Relatively low levels of awareness of government's impact, system affect, and tolerance may pose impediments to democratization. People may be unmotivated to engage in politics and may favor the repression of ideas that

Figure 6. Illiteracy Rates, by Gender and
Age Group

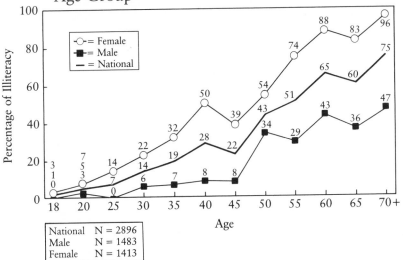

| National | N = 2896 |
| Male | N = 1483 |
| Female | N = 1413 |

they do not agree with. It is not clear whether the educated elite have sufficiently high levels of political tolerance to set an example for the rest of the population. Although educated Chinese are more likely to be aware of the impact of government, to feel able to understand and influence government, and to tolerate political speech by disliked groups, they are substantially less likely to hold democratic orientations than people of the same educational levels elsewhere.

The distribution of output affect in relation to other variables gives cause for both concern and hope. Although educated people are most likely to be aware of the influence of government and are more confident of their ability to understand and engage in politics, they are least likely to expect fair treatment from the government. They know that government policy can have a great effect on their lives, but they do not expect government officials to treat them equally. This contradiction may create psychological tension akin to what Ted Gurr calls "status reversal," an attitude Gurr considers conducive to outbreaks of rebellion.[45] If so, it helps to explain why this group has been the most likely to engage in regime challenging activities and why they may do so again.

The cultural profile of the rest of the population is virtually the reverse. They have a relatively low sense of the government's impact, relatively low internal efficacy, and relatively high system affect. In short, they are somewhat insulated from and satisfied with the government. The contrast between the two patterns suggests that if a political crisis between the regime and the intellectuals occurs again, the majority of the population may once again not offer much backing for the demands for democratic change. But if this is true, the implications for a democratic outcome are uncertain. The attitudinal gap between the educated and the uneducated that now helps to stabilize the regime may moderate the violence of a regime transition and provide a reserve of deference to help an infant democracy survive.

Nothing in our data supports the theory that Chinese political culture is an absolute bar to democracy. When compared to residents of some of the most stable, long-established democracies in the world, the Chinese population scored lower on the variables we looked at, but not so low as to justify the conclusion that democracy is out of reach. In general, as theory predicts, the more urban and educated sectors showed more democratic attitudes, supporting expectations derived from modernization theory that China's culture will move closer to the patterns characteristic of democratic countries as the economy grows. Once in place, a democratic regime could speed the pace of cultural change by actively inculcating the popular attitudes it needs to survive.

CONCLUSION: CULTURAL DISTINCTIVENESS AND UNIVERSAL ATTRIBUTES

Because this issue of *Dædalus* is concerned with questions of cultural distinctiveness and universalism, we have selected for analysis a few attributes for which comparative data are available. In each case, the distribution of attitudes in China both resembles and differs from the distributions in other countries. The data show China's culture to be distinctive, but only distributionally, not categorically. The attributes are universal, only the distributions are particular.

This finding, however, is in a sense an artifact of our approach. The survey method inevitably illuminates how Chinese citizens stand, compared to citizens of other countries, along universal or potentially universalizable dimensions of analysis, as well as how Chinese vary among themselves. In contrast to the interpretive method employed by most other research on Chinese political culture, survey results can never take the form of generalizations about all Chinese and how they differ from all non-Chinese. Surveys measure attributes which exist (whether they have been measured or not) in some degree everywhere, and they assess variation in the distribution of these attributes within and across one or more populations.

Of course, it is possible to ask a survey question which makes sense in only one culture, thus demonstrating the uniqueness of the culture. But this uniqueness would be an artifact of the way the question was asked and in that sense trivial. What is universal about a given norm or attitude is that which can be expressed in universal language (i.e., translated from language to language in a form that is understood within each language); what is distinctive about it is that which is expressed in a way that is understood in only one language. The norm or practice itself is intrinsically neither universal nor particular. An attitude can be shifted from the category of the unique to that of the universal, either linguistically or by going up or down the ladder of abstraction. *Kuan-hsi,* for example, is culturally unique, but particularism (of which *kuan-hsi* is an example) is universal.

By the same token, findings of cultural distinctiveness are equally an artifact of the interpretive approach. In this approach, cultural attributes are conceptualized with such specificity or complexity that what is portrayed is by definition unique. Ambrose King's informative discussion of *kuan-hsi* and network building in an earlier issue of *Dædalus* provides an example.[46] If we were to ask Americans whether they function through *kuan-hsi,* they would say no, because they would not know what we were talking about. If we were to ask them whether they sometimes get things done through networks or connections, or whether they consider it proper to help a relative or friend under certain circumstances, or whether it is important to cultivate personal relations with people from whom one wishes to get favors, many of them would say yes, perhaps as many in the United States as in China.

If King is describing something distinctively Chinese, it is not because the component cultural attributes are distinctive to China, but because the author has formulated a complex of attitudes and behaviors which is unique as a whole and by definition. Such a claim of uniqueness is not accessible to proof by survey research, because the survey technique of measurement requires the breakup of a cultural complex into measurable components. Since such components are cross-culturally measurable, they are bound to some degree to be cross-culturally existent. Cultures, then, are unique synthetically, universal analytically. Both the distinctiveness and nondistinctiveness of cultures are not facts about cultures, but artifacts of the ways in which cultures are studied.

APPENDIX: THE SAMPLE AND THE SURVEY

This analysis is based on a survey conducted in December of 1990, in cooperation with the Social Survey Research Center of People's University of China (SSRC). The sample was designed to be representative of the adult population over eighteen years old residing in family households at the time of the survey, excluding those living in the Tibet Autonomous Region.[47] A stratified multistage area sampling procedure with probabilities proportional to size measures (PPS) was employed to select the sample. Since the political structure in the rural areas is different from that of urban areas, political culture and behavior in the countryside may be different from that in cities and towns. In order to obtain separate estimates for rural and urban areas, we divided the whole population into two domains: the rural domain and the urban domain. Poststratification technique was used to create a valid national sample.

The Primary Sampling Units (PSUs) employed are *xian* (counties) for the rural domain and *shi* (cities) for the urban domain. Before selection, counties were stratified by region and geographical characteristics and cities by region and size. The Secondary Sampling Units (SSUs) were *xiang* (townships) in rural areas and *qu* (districts) or *jiedao* (streets) in urban areas. The third stage of selection was villages in the rural domain and *juweihui* (neighborhood committees) in the urban domain. For both domains, households were used at the fourth stage of sampling.

In the selection of PSUs, the 1986 National Population Data Book[48] was used as the data base to construct the sampling frame. The number of family households for each county or city was taken as the measure of size (MOS) in the PPS selection process.

For the subsequent stages of sampling, population data were obtained from local public security bureaus or governments. At the village and neighborhood committee levels, lists of *hukou* (household registrations) were obtained from police stations. In places without household registration, lists were obtained by field count.

The project interviewed 3,200 people, and 2,896 questionnaires were collected, which represents a response rate of 90.5 percent.

The survey instrument was constructed in the United States and pretested in Beijing in December of 1988. After thorough analysis of the pretest, we revised the questionnaire. College students of sociology and statistics were employed as field interviewers. Before the field work, project members went to China to train the interviewers in field interviewing techniques.

ACKNOWLEDGMENTS

The authors acknowledge the support of National Science Foundation grant INT–88–14199, a grant from the United Daily News Cultural Foundation, and the assistance of the Opinion Research Center of China, Social and Economic Research Institute of Beijing, under directors Chen Ziming and Wang Juntao.

ENDNOTES

[1]See, for example, Lucian W. Pye with Mary W. Pye, *Asian Power and Politics: The Cultural Dimensions of Authority* (Cambridge, Mass.: Harvard University Press, 1985); Lucian W. Pye, *The Mandarin and the Cadre: China's Political Cultures* (Ann Arbor, Mich.: Center for Chinese Studies, 1988); Andrew J. Nathan, *Chinese Democracy* (New York: Knopf, 1985); and various articles in "The Living Tree: The Changing Meaning of Being Chinese Today," *Dædalus* 120 (2) (Spring 1991).

[2]Pye, *Mandarin and Cadre*, 8, uses this term.

[3]Well-known examples of this kind of work dealing with China, besides those cited above, include Lucian W. Pye, *The Spirit of Chinese Politics* (Cambridge, Mass.: MIT Press, 1967); Benjamin I. Schwartz, *China's Cultural Values* (Tempe, Ariz.: Center of Asian Studies, 1985); and Richard H. Solomon, *Mao's Revolution and the Chinese Political Culture* (Berkeley, Calif.: University of California Press, 1971).

[4]Outstanding examples of the use of this approach include Gabriel A. Almond and Sidney Verba, *The Civic Culture* (Princeton, N.J.: Princeton University Press, 1963; abr. ed., Boston: Little, Brown, 1965; abr. ed. reprint, Newbury Park, Calif.: Sage Publications, 1989); Alex Inkeles and David H. Smith, *Becoming Modern: Individual Change in Six Developing Countries* (Cambridge, Mass.: Harvard University Press, 1974); Samuel H. Barnes et al., *Political Action: Mass Participation in Five Western Democracies* (Beverly Hills, Calif.: Sage Publications, 1979); Ronald Inglehart, *Culture Shift in Advanced Industrial Societies* (Princeton, N.J.: Princeton University Press, 1990); and Scott C. Flanagan et al., *The Japanese Voter* (New Haven, Conn.: Yale University Press, 1991).

[5]Gabriel A. Almond, "The Study of Political Culture," in *A Discipline Divided* (Newbury Park, Calif.: Sage Publications, 1990), 142.

[6]According to Ibid., 143–44, political culture consists of the set of subjective orientations to politics in a national population or subset of a national population; has cognitive, affective, and evaluative components; is the result of childhood socialization, education, media exposure, and adult political experiences; and reflects and affects political and governmental structure and performance.

[7]A possible exception is a survey conducted by the State Statistical Bureau for Ronald Inglehart on materialism and postmaterialism. At the time of writing this paper, we do not know the details of this study. Statistical induction is the process of generalizing from the characteristics of a sample to the characteristics of the population from which it was selected.

[8]See, for example, Paul J. Hiniker, *Revolutionary Ideology and Chinese Reality: Dissonance Under Mao* (Beverly Hills, Calif.: Sage Publications, 1977); Solomon, *Mao's Revolution*; Susan L. Shirk, *Competitive Comrades: Career Incentives and Student Strategies in China* (Berkeley, Calif.: University of California Press,

1982); Nathan, *Chinese Democracy*; William L. Parish and Martin King Whyte, *Village and Family in Contemporary China* (Chicago: University of Chicago Press, 1978); and Martin King Whyte and William L. Parish, *Urban Life in Contemporary China* (Chicago: University of Chicago Press, 1984).

[9]Dong Li, "Public Opinion Polls and Political Attitudes in China, 1979–1991," Ph.D. diss. in progress, Columbia University.

[10]Min Qi, *Zhongguo zhengzhi wenhua* (Kunming: Yunnan renmin chubanshe, 1989). By national, we mean covering the entire Chinese mainland with the possible exception of certain remote and lightly populated areas.

[11]Previous large-scale studies of mass behavior in communist societies were based on surveys of emigrants. The largest were reported in Alex Inkeles and Raymond A. Bauer, *The Soviet Citizen* (Cambridge, Mass.: Harvard University Press, 1959) and James R. Millar, ed., *Politics, Work, and Daily Life in the USSR: A Survey of Former Soviet Citizens* (New York: Cambridge University Press, 1987). Since the fall of communism, the survey enterprise has accelerated in the postcommunist societies, but national level surveys remain rare. We are aware of surveys in progress by Arthur H. Miller (Russia, Ukraine, and Lithuania); James Gibson (Russia); Samuel Barnes and Peter McDonough (Eastern Europe); and Sidney Verba, Cynthia S. Kaplan, and Henry E. Brady (Russia and Estonia).

[12]The ISSP is a continuing program of cross-national collaboration conducted in Australia, Germany, the United States, Great Britain, Austria, and Italy. It brings together preexisting national social science projects and coordinates research goals by adding a cross-national perspective to the individual national studies. See *International Social Survey Programme, Role of Government—1985 Codebook ZA-NO. 1490* (Ann Arbor, Mich.: ICPSR, University of Michigan).

[13]We define democracy as a system of authentically competitive elections for national and local offices. Authentic competition requires freedom of political organization, freedom of political speech, the right of citizens to run for office, and the secret ballot.

[14]Almond and Verba, *Civic Culture*; J. Roland Pennock, *Democratic Political Theory* (Princeton, N.J.: Princeton University Press, 1979), 236–59; and Robert A. Dahl, *A Preface to Democratic Theory* (Chicago: The University of Chicago Press, 1956). Some works stress cultural prerequisites for democratization; some stress cultural requisites for the stability of democratic systems. Although the two arguments are logically distinct, the attributes cited are generally the same.

[15]James L. Gibson and Raymond M. Duch, "Emerging Democratic Values in Soviet Political Culture," in Arthur H. Miller, William M. Reisinger, and Vicki L. Hesli, eds., *Public Opinion and Regime Change: The New Politics of Post-Soviet Societies* (Boulder, Colo.: Westview Press, 1993), 71.

[16]Almond and Verba, *Civic Culture*, 79–88; abr. ed., 46–52. Of course, the term "local government" refers to different objects in different countries; this partially explains different levels of awareness in different countries. In China, for example, people may think it is the "party" or "cadres" and not the "government" that affects their lives locally. But if one anticipates this and asks a different question in each country, the results cannot be considered comparable. Generally, the most equivalent stimulus is the one that uses the most similar language. After getting an

initial measure of differences across countries based on an equivalent stimulus, one can ask additional questions to explore hypotheses that one thinks may explain cross-national differences.

[17]Revisionist views have been presented by Vivienne Shue, *The Reach of the State* (Stanford, Calif.: Stanford University Press, 1988), and Victor Nee, David Stark, and Mark Selden, eds., *Remaking the Economic Institutions of Socialism: China and Eastern Europe* (Stanford: Stanford University Press, 1989), among others.

[18]Parish and Whyte, *Village and Family in Contemporary China*; Whyte and Parish, *Urban Life in Contemporary China*; and Jean C. Oi, *State and Peasant in Contemporary China: The Political Economy of Village Government* (Berkeley, Calif.: University of California Press, 1989).

[19]Samuel P. Huntington and Joan M. Nelson, *No Easy Choice* (Cambridge, Mass.: Harvard University Press, 1976), 43–45.

[20]We distinguish rural and urban sectors by the respondent's type of household registration. The actual place of residence at the time of the survey may be different, but the household registration establishes an individual's legal permanent residence, and usually corresponds to the actual place of residence.

[21]Almond and Verba, *Civic Culture*, 86; abr. ed., 52.

[22]These figures accord closely with those for the population as a whole derived from census data, testifying to the accuracy of our sample.

[23]Almond and Verba, *Civic Culture*, 17–19; abr. ed., 16–17.

[24]See among others, Norman H. Nie, G. Bingham Powell, Jr., and Kenneth Prewitt, "Social Structure and Political Participation: Developmental Relationships," Parts I and II, *American Political Science Review* 63 (2) (1961): 361–78; and 63 (3) (1961): 808–32; Lester Milbrath and M. L. Goel, *Political Participation: How and Why Do People Get Involved in Politics?*, 2d ed. (Chicago, Ill.: Rand McNally, 1977), 58–59; Russell J. Dalton, *Citizen Politics in Western Democracies* (Chatham, N.J.: Chatham House Publishers, 1988), 50; and M. Stephen Weatherford, "Measuring Political Legitimacy," *American Political Science Review* 86 (1) (March 1992): 149–66.

[25]Angus Campbell, Gerald Gurin, and Warren E. Miller, *The Voter Decides* (Evanston, Ill.: Row, Peterson, 1954), 187.

[26]Almond and Verba, *Civic Culture*, 214; abr. ed., 168–69.

[27]Campbell, Gurin, and Miller, *The Voter Decides*.

[28]Stephen C. Craig, Richard G. Niemi, and Glenn E. Silver, "Political Efficacy and Trust: A Report on the NES Pilot Study Items," *Political Behavior* 12 (3) (September 1990): 290.

[29]To avoid response set, some questions are asked in a positive form, some in a negative form; for national-level political understanding, a "disagree" answer indicates efficacy.

[30]For example, "People like me don't have any say about what the government does."

[31]Milbrath and Goel, *Political Participation*, chap. 3 and 4.

[32]Almond and Verba, *Civic Culture,* 110–11; abr. ed., 73–74.

[33]They are explored in Tianjian Shi, "Political Participation in Beijing: a Survey Study," Ph.D. diss., Columbia University, 1992.

[34]Ibid.

[35]See among others, Larry Diamond, Juan Linz, and Seymour Martin Lipset, eds., *Democracy in Developing Countries: Asia,* vol. 3 (Boulder, Colo.: Lynne Rienner, 1989), 16–17; James L. Gibson, "The Political Consequences of Intolerance: Cultural Conformity and Political Freedom," *American Political Science Review* 86 (2) (June 1992): 338–56; and Gibson and Duch, "Emerging Democratic Values," 72.

[36]Lucian W. Pye, *The Spirit of Chinese Politics,* new ed. (Cambridge, Mass.: Harvard University Press, 1992), 67–84.

[37]*International Social Survey Programme, Role of Government—1985 Codebook.*

[38]The Gang of Four is a very different stimulus from revolution, but we would have endangered our project if we had raised the question of overthrowing the government in China. The Gang of Four was the most equivalent feasible stimulus we could think of. Many of the population attribute their suffering during the Cultural Revolution to the Gang of Four. In the early 1980s, the regime carried out a purge of alleged sympathizers of the Gang, expelling many from the Party and giving prison terms to some.

[39]These figures are net of "don't know" answers, which constituted 18.0 percent on speaking, 20.9 percent on teaching, and 21.2 percent on publishing. The high "don't know" percentages indicate that for many respondents the question was too controversial to answer.

[40]Seymour Martin Lipset, *Political Man,* exp. and updated ed. (Baltimore, Md.: Johns Hopkins University Press, 1981), chap. 4; and Gibson, "Political Consequences," 346.

[41]This is with the exception of the two cases from the American sample who had no formal education and were intolerant. We deleted them from the display becau.e their tiny number makes the association between education and intolerance in their case statistically insignificant.

[42]These findings are consistent with those of Evelyn Sakakida Rawski, *Education and Popular Literacy in Ch'ing China* (Ann Arbor, Mich.: The University of Michigan Press, 1979).

[43]We could recalculate the figures in terms of urban and rural places of birth instead of urban and rural places of current household registration, and correct for disproportionate deaths above the national average in each population segment in order to recover the population makeup of earlier time periods.

[44]Our data show that tolerance levels in China decrease sharply with age.

[45]Ted Robert Gurr, *Why Men Rebel* (Princeton, N.J.: Princeton University Press, 1970).

[46]Ambrose Yeo-chi King, "Kuan-hsi and Network Building: A Sociological Interpretation," *Dædalus* 120 (2) (Spring 1991): 63–84.

[47] Transportation in Tibet is difficult since there is no railroad and the highway system is not well developed. Many Tibetans do not speak Chinese. It is difficult to find qualified interviewers who can work there effectively. For these reasons, we decided to exclude Tibet from this study.

[48] Ministry of Public Security, *Population Statistics by City and County of the People's Republic of China, 1986* (Beijing: Map Publishing House of China, 1987).

With the swift collapse of the Soviet Union late in 1991 and its transformation into a commonwealth dominated by Russia, India found itself without the superpower support she had enjoyed since 1971. Prime Minister Rao wisely sought to mend India's troubled relations with her largest Asian neighbor, China, welcoming Premier Li Peng to New Delhi in December 1991. Though no agreement was reached on the long-contested Sino–Indian border, both nations promised to try to increase trade and to foster more "cordial" relations based on "mutual understanding" and educational and cultural exchanges. With more than 100,000 Tibetan refugees from China living in northern India, New Delhi kept close watch and strict martial control over irate Tibetan protesters thoughout Premier Li's visit. A return to the Nehru era of Sino–Indian friendship and cooperation seemed to have dawned by the end of that historic five-day visit, for despite China's long-standing friendship with Pakistan, Premier Li said nothing about Kashmir while he was in India.

In many ways then India appears to revert to past traditions, beliefs, aspirations, attitudes, and friendships as she moves forward toward the twenty-first century. Hindu faith in cyclical patterns of time, rolling from kalpas of golden light to eras of dismal darkness and back again over eons and yugas to the brightest dawn of Brahma's new day helps sustain most Indians through troubled ages of suffering and pain, for *Dharma's* wheel turns upward as well as downward. Thus, the more India changes, the more *Indian* she remains, her present reflecting myriad-facets of her past, antiquity anticipating her future, even as the Universal All is symbolized by the spherical fullness of *Om*!

Stanley Wolpert

From *A New History of India,* fourth edition

*Ying-shih Yü*

# The Radicalization of China in the Twentieth Century

S INCE THE TURN OF THE CENTURY, a radical mode of thinking has dominated the Chinese mind. The history of Chinese thought in the twentieth century may be interpreted as a process of rapid radicalization. As a matter of fact, never in China's long intellectual tradition of over 2.5 millennia had she been as thoroughly radicalized as in modern times.

Radicalism in the Chinese intellectual tradition, however, has its limits. The critique developed within the tradition is essentially an internal one. Traditional critics in general and Confucians in particular have tended to take the *Way* (*Tao* or *Dao*) to be immanent in the world of everyday life. This is expressed in the opening statement of the Confucian classic, *The Doctrine of the Mean*, "The Way cannot be separated from us for a moment. What can be separated is not the *Way*." This would suggest that we have always lived in the *Way*. But on the other hand, the *Way* as transcendence must also be distinguished from the world of everyday life. Indeed, it would not be conceivable that the *Way* could have generated critical principles as it actually did without this transcendent dimension. However, it is an undeniably unique feature of the Chinese critical tradition that political and social criticism consists primarily in the interpretation of the *Way*, not in the discovery or invention of an alternative *Way*. In his *Interpretation and Social Criticism*, Michael Walzer, of the Institute for Advanced Study at Princeton, argues that since the moral world has long been in existence, neither discovery nor invention is necessary. It is rather in interpretation where the real possibility of

*Ying-shih Yü is Michael Henry Strater University Professor of East Asian Studies and Professor of History at Princeton University.*

125

social criticism lies. Moral principles and values are always unclear and uncertain in meaning; they require constant interpretation and reinterpretation on our part, particularly in time of crisis.[1] Walzer's emphasis on the importance of interpretation as a critical method fits in remarkably well with the Chinese critical tradition. But we must hasten to add that the very idea that an alternative *Way* can be discovered or invented to take the place of the one already in existence does not seem to have ever occurred to traditional Chinese critics.

Even popular radicalism in the Chinese tradition rarely, if ever, questioned the ultimate legitimacy of the *Way*. For example, the *Scripture of Great Peace* (*T'ai-p'ing ching* or *Taipingjing*),* a Taoist religious text datable to the second century, has been identified by many modern scholars as one of the earliest works containing "rebel ideologies."[2] The text advocates radical reforms and attacks social and economic inequalities of its time. But the critical method adopted in the text is clearly interpretation. By reinterpreting the *Way* in terms of Great Peace (or Great Equality), the author(s) of the text did not mean to demolish the Confucian order established since the beginning of the Han dynasty. On the contrary, there is every indication that the authors intended to cleanse the *Way* of its impurities. Little wonder that historians today, Marxist and non-Marxist alike, are often puzzled by the "Confucian model" they detect in the social structure represented in this text.[3] Rebel ideologies of later ages, even though sometimes inspired by religious ideas of non-Chinese origins, do not suggest an alternative social order substantially different from the traditional egalitarian model. In this respect, Chinese popular radicalism is probably not very dissimilar to its English counterpart as exemplified in London during the Restoration. There reformers "did not agitate merely to tear things down, but to restore to the community a customary order which the authorities themselves had allowed to come undone."[4]

REINTERPRETATION AND DISCOVERY

With this traditional picture as a contrast, let me now move on to the modern era. Radicalization of the Chinese mind at the turn of the

---

*This article was originally written using the Wade-Giles romanization system. For consistency throughout the volume, pinyin romanizations have been supplied.

century began with a strategic move from "interpretation" to "discovery" on the part of the Chinese intellectual elite. At the end of the nineteenth century, Chinese critics discovered that there was a new and better *Way* in the West which could displace and replace the old *Way*, not unlike Plato's philosopher who, having seen the sunlight, returned to the cave to tell his former fellow-prisoners what he discovered about truth. Antonio Gramsci, a leading Socialist theoretician, discussing the Russian Bolsheviks and their revolution, wrote:

> An *élite* consisting of some of the most active, energetic, enterprising and disciplined members of the society emigrates abroad and assimilates the culture and historical experiences of the most advanced countries of the West, without however losing the most essential characteristics of its own nationality, that is to say without breaking its sentimental and historical links with its own people. Having thus performed its intellectual apprenticeship it returns to its own country and compels the people to an enforced awakening, skipping historical stages in the process.[5]

This could be an equally accurate description of the Chinese intellectual elite in the late nineteenth and early twentieth centuries, except that we must also include Japan among "the most advanced countries." Yen Fu (Yan Fu, 1854–1921) was among the earliest "returned students" who, through his interpretive translation of Thomas H. Huxley's *Evolution and Ethics* and Herbert Spencer's *A Study of Sociology*, galvanized a whole generation of Chinese intellectuals into a fury of reform-related activity. It must be emphatically noted that when he was working on the translation of *Evolution and Ethics* from 1895 to 1896, Yen Fu was the foremost radical thinker in China. "Respect the people and rebel against the ruler; respect the present and rebel against antiquity" was the gospel he preached to everybody. Moreover, in a well-known essay, "In Refutation of Han Yü (Yu)" (1895), he dismissed as historically false the account of the origins of human culture given in Han Yü's "An Inquiry on the Way" ("Yuan Tao [Dao]"). Throughout the essay, Yen Fu not only explicitly questioned the legitimacy of the Confucian political order but also implied that the democratic system practiced in the modern West is much closer to the true *Way* as envisioned by ancient Chinese sages. Thus, Yen Fu began the process of radicalization, marked by the transition from interpretation to discovery as a critical method.

However, the transition was not easy. Generally speaking, from the 1890s to the Revolution of 1911, Chinese radicalism still took the form of interpretation, but it was, in fact, thinly disguised discovery. We can see clearly in the case of Yen Fu the earliest application of the method of discovery disguised as interpretation. He discovered in the West a much better alternative to the Confucian political order and he also discovered, much to his liking, social Darwinism and the ethic implicit in it. Interestingly, in his translator's commentaries on Thomas H. Huxley, John Stuart Mill, and Montesquieu, he often made laudatory references to the classical Taoist (Daoist) texts, *Lao-tzu* (*Laozi*) and *Chuang-tzu* (*Zhuangzi*). In his commentaries on *Lao-tzu* and *Chuang-tzu*, he pointed out that Western ideas like freedom, democracy, science, and evolution could be found in these two texts in their embryonic forms. Thus, following the Chinese commentarial tradition, Yen Fu appears to be merely reinterpreting the Chinese *Way* through a subtle shift in emphasis from Confucianism to Taoism. But, as his "In Refutation of Han Yü" makes clear, he was actually advocating a radical change in China from an authoritarian political system to a democratic one.[6]

If Yen Fu tempered his early radicalism with evolutionary gradualism, K'ang Yu-wei (Kang Youwei, 1858–1927) and T'an Ssu-t'ung (Tan Sitong, 1864–1898) boldly developed full-blown radicalism in modern China for the first time. Unlike Yen Fu, both K'ang and T'an as political reformers pushed for not only "whole-sale change" but "immediate change" as well. Of the two, T'an must be judged as the more radical because he was ready to break away from the Chinese tradition. There can be no doubt that both had been exposed to Western learning available in China before their reform program took its final shape. Current research shows that K'ang Yu-wei's theory of the three-stage social evolution, supposedly derived from his study of the *Kung-yang* (*Gongyang*) *Commentary* on the *Spring and Autumn Annals* of Confucius, was in part owed to Yen Fu's social Darwinism.[7] At any rate, it is now common knowledge that their reform program was formulated with a Western model in the background. However, both still found it necessary to disguise discovery as interpretation. In the case of K'ang, the disguise was more deceptive because his reinterpretation of Confucius as a reformer was inextricably entangled in a great variety of classical texts. By contrast, T'an did not pretend to build his radical vision on any particular classical text. However to the extent that he called his philosophical treatise *Jen-hsüeh* (*Renxue*, "A Study of Humanity"), he was certainly making no claim to discovery. On the contrary, it suggests that he was merely trying to reinterpret the Confucian ideal of *jen* (*ren*), even though his reinterpretation involved the idea of "ether" in nineteenth-century science. As the modern Chinese intellectual historian Chang Hao says, "the impact of T'an's discovery of the West was beyond gaining scientific knowledge. It opened his eyes in ways that inevitably had a bearing directly or indirectly on his moral outlook."[8] It is significant to note that the emphasis in the *Jen-hsüeh* is placed not on the discovery of the West but on the interpretation of the Confucian vision of humanity.

The last phase of discovery disguised as interpretation was well represented by the *Kuo-ts'ui* (*Guocui*, National Essence) movement organized around the journal *Kuo-ts'ui hsüeh-pao* (*Guocui xuebao*, Journal of National Essence, 1905–1911). Major contributors to the journal included Chang Ping-lin (Zhang Binglin, 1869–1935), Liu Shih-p'ei (Liu Shipei, 1884–1919), Huang Chieh (Huang Jie, 1874–1935), Teng Shih (Deng Shi, 1877–1941), Ch'en Ch'ü-ping (Chen Qubing, 1874–1933), and Ma Hsü-lun (Ma Xulun, 1884–1970). It is rather ironic that since the May Fourth period, the entire *kuo-ts'ui* group has been generally identified as cultural conservatives. In their own days, they were bona fide radical scholars. All were revolutionaries as opposed to the constitutionalists led by K'ang Yu-wei and his leading disciple Liang Ch'i-ch'ao (Liang Qichao, 1873–1929). They were intellectually more radicalized than either K'ang Yu-wei or T'an Ssu-t'ung in their attitude toward the Confucian tradition. It was due to their efforts that an iconoclastic undercurrent in the history of Chinese thought was rediscovered. Anarchists of the Wei-Chin (Jin) period (220–419) like Pao Chin-yen (Bao Jinyan) and left-wingers of the Wang Yang-ming (Wang Yangming) school like Li Chih (Li Zhi, 1527–1602), for example, were restored to grace for the first time. Additionally, several of the *kuo-ts'ui* scholars, notably Chang Ping-lin and Liu Shih-p'ei, sojourned in Tokyo during the first decade of the twentieth century and, as a result, were exposed to a variety of Western ideas and theories through Japanese translation. They not only went much further to discover the West but also were often intensely excited about their new discoveries.

If Yen Fu introduced Western ideas and theories to the Chinese reading public, *kuo-ts'ui* scholars set for themselves the central task of applying some of these ideas and theories to the study of the Chinese cultural heritage. As one of the editorial rules of the *Kuo-ts'ui Journal* makes abundantly clear, "With regard to Western learning, we shall also elucidate all those new theories and special insights that prove to be capable of illuminating Chinese learning."[9] It is undoubtedly true that the avowed purpose of the *kuo-ts'ui* movement was a quest for cultural identity in the face of the ever-growing Western influence. However, a general investigation of the writings of some of the leading *kuo-ts'ui* scholars will show, rather paradoxically, that what they identified as China's "national essence" turned out to be, more often than not, basic cultural values of the West such as democracy, equality, liberty, and human rights. This identification was justified on either of the following grounds: First, as Huang Chieh, an editor of the Journal of National Essence and a well-known classicist, put it, "*kuo-ts'ui* consists not only in what is indigenous and still suitable but also in what is borrowed but capable of being adapted to the needs of our nation." Second, they took these Western values as universal and insisted on their genesis in an early China completely independent of the West. A large part of the *kuo-ts'ui* historiography deals with these themes.[10] The theory of social evolution of the Spencerian variety together with its historical laws was now applied to interpret almost every aspect of Chinese history.

RADICALISM

Finally, during the May Fourth era beginning with the literary revolution in 1917, a paradigmatic change took place in the development of radicalism in modern China. From this time on, whether in criticizing the tradition or advocating changes, Chinese intellectuals would almost invariably invoke some Western ideas, values, or institutions as ultimate grounds for justification. It was now neither necessary nor possible to disguise discovery as interpretation.

The May Fourth Movement has been referred to by several other names, such as the "New Culture movement," the "Renaissance," and the "Enlightenment." Each name implies a particular historical interpretation regarding the nature and significance of the movement.

The two Western terms, "Renaissance" and "Enlightenment," require some observations. The application of these two Western historical terms to the May Fourth Movement is predicated on the assumption that the Chinese past can be reconstructed according to the historical model of the West. This assumption did not begin with the May Fourth era but is traceable to the *kuo-ts'ui* historiography as well as to Liang Ch'i-ch'ao's advocacy of New History. In the two essays on this topic, written in 1901 and 1902, Liang not only adopted the European scheme of periodization (ancient, medieval, and modern) as the model of universal validity but also accepted the Spencerian theory of social evolution as a self-evident truth.[11]

In recent years, however, it seems quite popular, in China as well as in the West, to interpret the May Fourth Movement as the Chinese Enlightenment.[12] I accept the term "enlightenment," however, only in a symbolic sense, not as a historical analogy. As mentioned earlier, the discovery of the West by modern Chinese critics reminds us of Plato's philosopher who returns to his cave after having discovered the sunlight in the outside world. This Platonic symbolism is particularly appropriate for the "returned" Chinese intellectuals of the May Fourth generation. So, too, is Gramsci's characterization of the Russian elite, as well as the following case about Hu Shih, a famous intellectual in the May Fourth Movement. In 1916, Hu Shih wrote a self-congratulatory poem in classical style on his birthday. In it he said that he dreamed that he made a trip to Heaven as an "immortal" where he discovered a few "magical drugs" unknown to other "immortals." He intended to return to the human world and use them to cure diseases. Obviously, his "Heaven" is America and his "human world" is China.[13] On March 8, 1917, just months away from his journey home, Hu Shih read a book about the Oxford Movement and was deeply touched by a quotation of John Henry Newman's, supposedly from the *Iliad:* "You shall know the difference now that we are back again." At the end of the entry in his diary, he remarked: "This sets the precedent for us returned-students."[14] Like the Russian elite in Gramsci's description, Hu Shih did not break his "sentimental and historical links with his own people." He returned to China and compelled the people to an "enforced awakening." For good or for bad, he did make a difference.

When Hu Shih arrived in Shanghai in July of 1917, he found to his dismay that his motherland was almost exactly the same as he had

left it in 1910. But China had not come to a standstill during his
absence. He had left an imperial China and had returned to a
republican one. A new storm of radicalization was gathering. His
explosive article on literary revolution, with a follow-up one by chief
editor Ch'en Tu-hsiu (Chen Duxiu, 1879–1942), had appeared in the
*New Youth* magazine early in the year. However, it would be unfair
to blame this new wave of radicalism, especially in its total rejection
of tradition, on a few May Fourth leaders including Hu Shih and
Ch'en Tu-hsiu. Contempt for tradition, a built-in feature of radicalism, had well begun with some of the *kuo-ts'ui* scholars. It continued
to grow after the Revolution of 1911, as R. F. Johnston, the British
teacher of the last emperor of China, observed:

> It is a bewildering phenomenon. . . that just when we Europeans were
> realizing with amazement the high value of China's social and political
> philosophy, her ethics, her art and literature, the Chinese themselves
> were learning to treat these great products of her own civilization with
> impatient contempt.[15]

We can ignore the European part of Johnston's statement, but the
Chinese part must be accepted as an eyewitness account of the
general Chinese mentality that made the May Fourth Movement
possible.

Since the end of the nineteenth century, radicalization of the
Chinese mind proceeded at an astonishingly accelerated speed. When
Hu Shih returned to China in 1917, most of the major radical
thinkers of the earlier generations were still alive, and some were still
politically and intellectually active. These included Yen Fu, K'ang
Yu-wei, Liang Ch'i-ch'ao, Chang Ping-lin, and Liu Shih-p'ei. But in
the eyes of Hu Shih and Ch'en Tu-hsiu, not to mention the younger
generation, they were already men of the past. All were conservatives; some were even reactionaries. How could this possibly be the
case? It becomes ever more puzzling if we consider the fact that by
Hu Shih's own admission, China did not make much progress
between 1910 and 1917. Ordinarily when we judge someone as
either ahead of or behind his time, our frame of reference is the status
quo or what the German sociologist Karl Mannheim calls "the
existing framework of life." With reference to the status quo in China
on the eve of the May Fourth Movement, none of the above thinkers
can be summarily dismissed as intellectually out-of-date. However,

this puzzle disappears once we realize that while intellectuals of the May Fourth generation regarded these early radical leaders as outdated, their frame of reference was not the status quo in China but some new truths they had recently discovered in the outside world, especially in the West. In this way, radical ideas in China rose and fell in quick succession according, by and large, to the inner logic of the world of thought and were virtually unrelated to the realities of society.[16]

In *The Conservative Mind from Burke to Eliot*, the American critic Russell Kirk points out that since 1790 at least five major schools of radical thought have emerged. They are the rationalism of the *philosophes*, the romantic emancipation of Rousseau and his allies, the utilitarianism of the Benthamites, the positivism of Comte's school, and the collectivistic materialism of Marx and other socialists. In addition, Kirk also mentions Darwinism as a force that has done much to undermine the first principles of a conservative order.[17] It is extraordinary that practically all these major schools of radical thought, as well as others, which have taken the West almost two centuries to absorb and digest, arrived in China within a short span of three or four decades. From hindsight, twentieth-century China has been so inundated with radicalisms from the West that thorough and rapid radicalization was hardly avoidable.

Mao Tse-tung (Mao Zedong) once characterized the intellectual climate of modern China as a "search for truth from the West." There has been more or less a consensus among historians that a profound sense of the crisis of national survival on the part of Chinese intellectuals was initially responsible for setting in motion this "search."

It is neither possible nor necessary here to examine every imported idea that helped to radicalize the Chinese mentality. For illustration, let us take only one or two examples. The idea of total demolition of tradition as a precondition for the building of a new society was wholly inconceivable to the traditional Chinese imagination, but it was one of the absolute presuppositions of the May Fourth iconoclastic antitraditionalism.[18] Many radical ideas undoubtedly helped but perhaps none more effectively than the Enlightenment notion of rationality and modernity, as Stephen Toulmin, a philosopher at Northwestern University, explains:

The belief that any new construction is truly *rational* only if it demolishes all that was there before and starts from scratch, has played a particular part in the intellectual and political history of France. . . but no one who enters the spirit of Modernity whole-heartedly can be immune to its influence. The most spectacular illustration of this is the French Revolution. . . . [19]

May Fourth intellectuals' early conversion to Marxism was certainly made much easier by their deep faith in "science" in its extreme positivistic sense. The very term "scientific socialism" carried with it a weight of authority which must have crushed many resisting wills. In this connection, mention may also be made of the enormous and long-enduring influence of social Darwinism.[20] It paved the way for the wholehearted acceptance by May Fourth intellectuals of the Marxist iron law of social evolution as self-evident truth.

However, not all the May Fourth intellectual leaders were radicals. Hu Shih, for example, must be recognized as a moderate liberal even though he did have his radical moments. Since radicalization sped up immeasurably after the May Fourth Movement of 1919, Hu Shih was soon to be dismissed as a conservative or, worse still, as a "counter-revolutionary" by radical Marxists and other revolutionaries. It is amazing that only one year after the May Fourth incident Ch'en Tu-hsiu was already converted to Marxism. Hu Shih's debate with the other May Fourth leader, Li Ta-chao (Li Dazhao, 1888–1927), over "Problems vs. Isms" (whether piecemeal solutions to concrete problems or holistic ideological choices ought to be the central concerns of the intellectuals) broke out as early as July or August of 1919.[21] It was the first ideological confrontation between liberalism and Marxism and it signaled the beginning of the final, highest stage of radicalization in twentieth-century China.

There can be no doubt that May Fourth Marxist radicals were always inclined to transform China totally by recourse to what Karl Mannheim calls a "systematic possibility," meaning that to deal with a single undesirable social fact, the whole system of society in which such a fact is possible ought to be transformed.[22] However, as their pursuit of the possible was always made in the abstract as opposed to the concrete, this possibility became forever out of reach. Scientific socialism turned out to be more utopian than utopian socialism. Moreover, from the very beginning, Chinese Marxism was cast in the negative mold of May Fourth iconoclastic antitraditionalism. Thus, it generated a radicalism of a highly destructive nature. I would like to suggest that Mao Tse-tung may well be interpreted as Chinese Marxist radicalism incarnate. He was a genius in destruction but wholly incapable of constructive work. Throughout his life he was in constant pursuit of an abstract possibility and unable to settle with anything concrete. In the 1940s, he designed a new democracy apparently in concrete terms, but never intended to put it into practice. He was the founding father of the People's Republic of China, yet his dissatisfaction with it was so deep that he never ceased to attack it by launching one campaign after another until his death. His destructive work culminated in the Cultural Revolution. It seems as if he deliberately worked against the actualization of the very possibility he himself had always pursued.

SOCIOLOGY OF KNOWLEDGE

It is sometimes said that ideas have lives of their own, but this is no more than a metaphor. In reality, it is the holders of ideas, especially the intellectuals, who give them lives. In order to understand why China since the turn of the century has been radicalized, I must now move from phenomenology of mind to sociology of knowledge.

Radicalization of the Chinese mind is an immensely complex topic deserving of a much fuller treatment. I would venture to suggest, however, that it grew first and foremost out of two interrelated historical developments which may be called, respectively, the marginalization of China in the world and the marginalization of intellectuals in Chinese society. I shall try to explain how this double marginalization helped to trigger the long process of radicalization in modern China.

By marginalization of China in the world I refer not to the historical reality itself, but the perception of it on the part of Chinese intellectuals. In reality, the replacement of the tributary system by the treaty system in the 1840s already marked the beginning of the end of the traditional Sinocentric world order. It would take Chinese intellectuals five more decades to see the full implications of this historic event. Their immediate response to the humiliating treaty of Nanking (Nanjing) of 1842 was rather a traditional one. Limited by experiences of barbarian invasions in the past, they interpreted China's defeat mainly in terms of the technological superiority of the

West. It did not occur to them that the Chinese political and social order as a whole was no longer adequate to cope with a barbarian threat of an altogether different nature. Discussing China's foreign policy toward the West in 1842, the reform-minded scholar Wei Yuan (1794–1856) came to the conclusion that China would be able to control the barbarians only if she were resolved to learn their superior techniques: warships, firearms, and methods of training soldiers.[23] On the other hand, his reformism was still very much in the Confucian *ching-shih* (*jingshi*, statecraft) tradition, showing not even the slightest trace of any Western influence. Two decades later the prophetic reformer Feng Kuei-fen (Feng Guifen) was among the earliest Chinese intellectuals to recognize the importance of Western learning to China's survival in the modern world. In his influential essay, "On the Adoption of Western Learning" (written in 1862), he advanced beyond Wei Yuan by pointing out that in order to learn the superior techniques of the barbarians, China must first grasp the fundamentals of Western leaning including mathematics, mechanics, optics, light, chemistry, and other branches of the natural sciences. His faith in the traditional political and social order, however, remained unshaken; Chinese ethics and Confucian teachings, he insisted, must continue to serve as the original foundation.[24] The prominent scholar-official Chang Chih-tung's (Zhang Zhidong) famous saying, "Chinese learning for the fundamental principles, Western learning for practical application" (1898), was clearly a crystallization of the ideas originally developed in Feng Kuei-fen's writings.[25]

In 1894–1895, Chinese intellectuals discovered for the first time the shocking truth about China being marginalized. Culturally, Japan had been borrowing from China since the T'ang (Tang) dynasty (618–907), if not earlier. In the eyes of many nineteenth-century Chinese intellectuals, Japan was one of China's cultural satellites in the East Asian world. When a Chinese scholar was told in the early 1870s that Japan had recently turned away from Chinese civilization and had begun to transform itself on the Western model ranging from legal institutions to social customs, he became so upset as to compare the Meiji Emperor to the First Emperor of Ch'in (Qin) who "committed books to flames and swept away all the Confucians."[26] Needless to say, no one in China could have possibly foreseen that precisely because of her success in westernization, Japan was able to defeat China decisively in the war of 1894–1895.

Criticizing the anachronism of the Sinocentric self-conception of the Chinese (*t'ien-hsia* or *tianxia* meaning "all beneath the sky"), the eminent translator of Chinese classics, James Legge, in 1872 made the following remarks:

> During the past forty years her (i.e., China's) position with regard to the more advanced nations of the world has entirely changed. She has entered into treaties with them upon equal terms; but I do not think her ministers and people have yet looked the truth fairly in the face, so as to realize the fact that China is only one of many independent nations in the world, and that the "beneath the sky," over which her emperor has ruled, is not *all* beneath the sky, but only a certain portion of it which is defined on the earth's surface and can be pointed out upon the map. But if they will not admit this, and strictly keep good faith according to the treaties which they have accepted, the result will be for them calamities greater than any that have yet befallen the empire.[27]

Legge's observation was not only accurate but startlingly prophetic. China's first war with Japan was a calamity. Even though by the 1890s Chinese ministers and her people no longer considered China as "all beneath the sky" vis-à-vis the West, they nevertheless continued to regard Japan with traditional arrogance. This is evident in the views expressed by advocates of war in the court as well as among the intellectuals during the period from 1894–1895. China may well have become only one of many nations in the world, but her central position in East Asia, however, was not open to challenge, especially from one of her cultural satellites. It is not without symbolic meaning that the war was fought, at least ostensibly, on account of China's claim of suzerainty over Korea, a claim that Japan refused to recognize.

From the above discussion it seems safe to say that as far as its perception was concerned, the marginalization of China did not fully manifest itself until the end of the first Sino-Japanese war. It was a catastrophe of this magnitude that finally awakened Chinese intellectuals to the painful truth that China had been marginalized not only in the world but in East Asia as well. As the Rutgers historian Michael Gasster pointed out in his study of origins of modern Chinese radicalism, "After 1894–95, the even more astonishing humiliation dealt to China by her hitherto lightly regarded neighbor, Japan, had almost immediate consequences in domestic politics and the intellectual world, as evidenced by the activities and ideas of K'ang Yu-wei, Yen Fu, and Sun Yat-sen."[28] The discovery of the marginalization of China led immediately to the radicalization of the Chinese mind. Within two weeks of the conclusion of the Treaty of Shimonoseki (April 17, 1895), ending the war, K'ang Yu-wei was joined by more than 1,200 examination candidates in Peking to present the famous "Ten Thousand Word Memorial" to the throne advocating comprehensive institutional reforms. Yen Fu's translation of *Evolution and Ethics* and T'an Ssu-t'ung's *A Study of Humanity* were both a psychological aftermath of the war. Psychologically speaking, Liang Ch'i-ch'ao was not exaggerating when he said that the war of 1894–1895 "awakened China from a slumber of four thousand years."[29] Never before had the Chinese intellectual world been radicalized on such an enormous scale and within such a short time.

From an exclusively political point of view, the post-1895 radicalization resulted directly from the intellectuals' sudden awareness of the crisis of national survival. There can be no question that the immediate goal of both K'ang Yu-wei's reform movement and Sun Yat-sen's more radical program of revolution was to "Save China" (*chiu-kuo* or *juiguo*) from being conquered by imperialist powers.

In culture, as in politics, the Middle Kingdom complex has been constantly at work since the end of the nineteenth century.[30] When Chinese intellectuals discovered the unpleasant truth about China being marginalized politically as well as culturally, they immediately confronted the difficult task of how to open China to Western influence without at the same time relinquishing her millennia-old status as a center of culture. The history of this bizarre intellectual enterprise can be divided into two distinct periods, corresponding exactly to "discovery disguised as interpretation" and "discovery undisguised."

During the period of discovery disguised as interpretation, the general strategy adopted by Chinese intellectuals was to interpret those Western ideas, values, and institutions particularly suited to the needs of China's modernization as long as they were discovered by ancient Chinese sages independently of the West. We can easily see where the ingenuity of this strategy lies: To the extent that it advocated changes on the Western model, its main thrust was clearly radical, not conservative; however, to the extent that it disguised "discovery" as "interpretation," the purpose of retaining China's status as a center of culture was also well served. For example, the theory of Chinese origins of Western learning meant that Western sciences, technologies, music, parliamentary system, economics, religion (Christianity), and law all had originated in classical China and somehow had found their ways to Europe. In this case, two points particularly deserve attention: First, although this theory had its early sporadic beginnings in the seventeenth and eighteenth centuries, it gained sudden but wide popularity from 1895 to 1900. Second, during these few years the theory was elaborately developed by scholars who were eagerly receptive rather than resistant to Western learning.[31] As a cultural phenomenon it lends considerable support to our observation that, since the end of the first Sino-Japanese war, the change-oriented mentality of Chinese intellectuals has been shaped, at the psychological level, by their discovery of the truth about China being marginalized to the periphery of human culture. The theory of "Chinese origins of Western learning" came into vogue at the beginning stage of radicalization because, perhaps, it functioned as a safe conduct to Chinese intellectuals assuring them, as it were, that to learn from the West was also the way to bring China back to the center.

My second example is the theory of the Western origin of the Chinese race proposed by the French scholar Terrien de LaCouperie (1844–1894) in the 1880s. Based on a highly dubious interpretation of Chinese etymology, he suggested that the Yellow Emperor (Huang-ti or Huangdi), supposedly the father of the Chinese race, was actually the generic title of the kings of Susiana (Nakhunti). The Yellow Emperor led a group of Chaldeans known as "Baks" from Mesopotamia to Central Asia and finally reached China in the third millennium B.C. The Baks under the leadership of the Yellow Emperor (Huang-ti or Nakhunti) eventually defeated the natives and conquered China. The Baks, whom LaCouperie identified as the ruling aristocracy known as *Pai-hsing* (*Baixing*, Hundred Surnames) in early Confucian texts, created the earliest civilization in China.[32] The theory is pure fantasy unworthy of even refutation. What is amazing about it, however, is the fact that in the first decade of the twentieth century, practically all Chinese historians of the *Kuo-ts'ui* school including Huang Chieh, Chang Ping-lin, and Liu Shih-p'ei accepted this theory without showing a slightest sense of embarrassment. In his "Foreword" to the inaugural issue of the *Journal of National Essence,* Huang Chieh repeatedly referred to the Han Chinese as "we, the race of the Baks."[33] Chang Ping-lin asserted that not only the Chinese race came from Chaldea but China in high antiquity also shared many cultural traits with the Greeks, Romans, Saxons, Franks, and Slavs.[34] Liu Shih-p'ei was even more explicit. He speculated that the Han Chinese and the Caucasians were originally of the same race but later migrated to China and Europe respectively as a result of a population explosion.[35] One cannot help wonder how such critical and learned scholars could possibly be so credulous and absurd. What mattered here was not historical scholarship but cultural psychology. Like the theory of the Chinese origin of Western learning, it happened to meet the deep psychological needs of Chinese revolutionary intellectuals at this particular juncture in history. On one hand, as anti-Manchu revolutionaries they wanted to distance themselves from the ruling ethnic group (Manchus) as far as possible, historically as well as culturally. On the other hand, as cultural radicals they took Western values as universal values and insisted on their genesis in early historic China. By invoking the theory of the Western origin of the Chinese race, they could thus conveniently kill two birds with one stone. Moreover, as historians they wanted Chinese history to retain its central place in world history, as in the past. If the Chinese race were of Western origin, then China would still be seen as in the very center of the West-dominated modern world, not on the periphery.

With the paradigmatic shift from interpretation to discovery, radicalization began to take a wholly new shape and relate to China's marginalization in a very different way. By the 1910s, as Chinese intellectuals had been increasingly gaining direct access to the West, the old strategy to defend the centrality of Chinese culture vis-à-vis the Western hegemony totally collapsed. Neither the theory of Chinese origins of Western learning nor the identification of values and ideas dominant in the modern West as China's national essence was acceptable to a new generation of intellectuals who came of age in the early years of the Republic. As Hu Shih wrote in the introduction of his doctoral dissertation in 1917,

How can we Chinese feel at ease in this new world which at first sight appears to be so much at variance with what we have long regarded as our own civilization? For it is perfectly natural and justifiable that a nation with a glorious past and a distinctive civilization of its own making should never feel quite at home in a new civilization, if that new civilization is looked upon as part and parcel imported from alien lands and forced upon it by external necessities of national existence. And it would surely be a great loss to mankind at large if the acceptance of this new civilization should take the form of abrupt displacement instead of organic assimilation, thereby causing the disappearance of the old civilization. The real problem, therefore, may be restated thus: How can we best assimilate modern civilization in such a manner as to make it congenial and congruous and continuous with the civilization of our own making?[36]

Hu Shih's theory sheds new light on the radicalization and marginalization of China. It is then its oldness, not Chineseness, that must be held accountable for the marginalization of Chinese culture to the periphery in the modern world. The real trouble with China was that due to her long isolation from the outside world, she had lagged behind the West in social evolution. Since Hu Shih regarded the universal and modern aspects of what he calls the "new civilization" of primary importance and its Westernness secondary, he could, therefore, advocate China's "complete acceptance of the civilization of the new world" without being troubled by the inferiority complex that had haunted Chinese intellectuals of earlier generations. This also explains why he later preferred "modernization" or "cosmopolitanization" to "Westernization" as descriptive terms for China's cultural borrowings from the West. In 1917, Hu Shih heralded a new approach to cope with China's marginalization and along with it a new way to radicalize.

From 1917 onward, efforts to repossess the center of culture for China on the part of Chinese intellectuals generally take the form of incessantly seeking to import the latest products in the cultural market from the West. As a result, a new frame of mind has been formed among the Chinese intellectual elite which may be called the neoterist mentality, a mentality obsessed with change, with what is new. This mentality is best described in the vivid words of the British political philosopher, Michael Oakeshott: "We are willing to try anything once, regardless of the consequences. One activity vies with another in being 'up-to-date': discarded motor-cars and television sets have their counter parts in discarded moral and religious beliefs: the eye is ever on the new model."[37] Since the radical would be nothing if not also a neoterist, China's marginalization and radicalization have thus grown, reinforcing each other at every turn. The tremendous overflow of radical ideas from the West and their rise and fall in quick succession in post-May Fourth China must be understood in this light.

As radicalization eventually led China to totalitarianism in 1949, the flow of ideas from the West came to an abrupt stop. However, China's drive toward the center of the world, recently intensified by revolutionary violence, continued to run its course. This is demonstrated in the so-called "Great Leap Forward" movement of 1958–1960 launched personally by Mao. On one hand, with iron and steel production, he announced that China would catch up with Britain in fifteen years and, on the other hand, with the "people's commune," he was very proud of the fact that China had actually beat the Soviet Union by entering into the Communist stage first.[38] Since he believed that spiritual regeneration must take precedence over economic development, he sensed no contradiction at all to say that a country still fifteen years behind Britain in production had already won the political contest against the Soviet Union. To a considerable extent it was also the same belief in the unfathomable power of the human spirit and will, especially his own, that drove him to the peak of a lifelong radicalism—the so-called Cultural Revolution.

## FROM THE CENTER TO THE PERIPHERY

Radicalization can be examined from a sociological point of view by linking it to the fact that the Chinese intelligentsia has been ever-increasingly marginalized from the center to the periphery in society since the end of the nineteenth century. This does not suggest, however, that the social marginalization of the Chinese intellectual began with the arrival of Western imperialism. As a matter of fact, historically the decline of the social position of the *shih* (*shi*, scholar) vis-à-vis the merchant had been going on slowly but steadily since the sixteenth century, if not earlier. As noted by the early nineteenth-century scholar Shen Yao (1798–1840), "While in the old days sons of scholars forever remained as scholars, in later times only sons of merchants could become scholars. . . . China's center of gravity has tilted towards commerce, and consequently heroes and men of intelligence mostly belong to the merchant class."[39] However, this process of social change suddenly accelerated toward the end of the century as the total collapse of the imperial system was drawing near. As a result, "China's center of gravity" moved further away from the *shih* who, according to the old Chinese system of social stratification, headed the list of the *ssu-min* (*simin*, four major functional orders), the other three being *nung* (*nong*, farmers), *chiang* (*jiang*, artisans and craftsmen), and *shang* (merchants and tradesmen).

As far as its bearing on radicalization was concerned, the social marginalization of the Chinese intellectual also reached a turning point in the early years of the twentieth century when the traditional *shih* was being rapidly transformed into what we now call *chih-shih-fen-tzu* (*zhishi fenzi*, intellectual). This transformation, ironically, went hand in hand with the educational reform that had been carried out with ever-increasing speed after the first Sino-Japanese war. From 1895 to the end of the Ch'ing (Qing) dynasty in 1911, new schools of various levels based on Western and Japanese models grew all over China. In the meantime, it also suddenly became fashionable for students to go abroad for education, especially to Japan. The net result of these developments was the replacement of the state examination system by a modern school system. When the examination system was finally abolished in 1905, a long Chinese tradition in education and learning which had produced the *shih* since 622 without interruption was brought to an end. Therefore, symbolically, the year 1905 serves well as a dividing line between the traditional "scholar" and the modern "intellectual."

There are, however, as many continuities between the traditional *shih* and the modern *chih-shih-fen-tzu* as discontinuities. But in one area of vital importance, the modern "intellectual" must be clearly distinguished from the traditional "scholar": The former is no longer directly linked to state power as the latter certainly was. Around the time of the abolition of the examination system, according to a rough official estimate, China had tens of thousands of *chü-jen* (*juren*), the intermediate degree, and several hundreds of thousands of *sheng-yuan* (*shengyuan*), the lowest degree holders, who were eager to improve their social status by earning the prestigious *chü-jen* and *chin-shih* (*jinshi*) degrees.[40] To these numbers, we must also add millions of degree aspirants who, having toiled for years in preparation, were ready to climb the ladder of success. Now, all of a sudden, the ladder was pulled away and they were thus deprived of the traditional status as *shih* which had made them an integral part of the ruling apparatus in late imperial China. This may well have been one of the unintended consequences of the educational reform of the Ch'ing court.

As the traditional *shih* turned into the modern *chih-shih-fen-tzu*, Chinese intellectuals also became politically marginalized in the sense that they now stood on the periphery of state power. Unlike *chin-shih* or *chü-jen* degrees, diplomas from new schools or even higher degrees from foreign colleges and universities did not automatically entitle their holders to state employments. As a result, modern intellectuals have been more readily susceptible to radicalization than the traditional *shih*. Captain James H. Reeves, the United States military attaché in Peking, made the following observation in 1912:

> The revolution has been largely effected through the work of Chinese who have gone to school in Japan during the last ten to fifteen years. . . . During the past few years the remark has been heard on all sides that the returned Japanese students [i.e., those Chinese who had returned from Japan] were revolutionary in spirit. . . . [they] returned to China republicans rather than monarchical reformers.[41]

At the same time, attention must also be called to the fact that in the imperial past, some *shih* turned into rebels only when they had repeatedly failed in examinations. Hung Hsiu-ch'üan (Hong Xiuchuan), the leader of the T'aiping Rebellion, is one example.

Discussing the interests of Asian intellectuals, Max Weber once characterized the Chinese *shih* (whom he calls "the Confucians") as "aesthetically cultivated *literati* and polished salon conversationalists rather than politicians."[42] Generally speaking, this is true. But we must hasten to add that the *shih* could also be highly politicized and radicalized in times of sustained national crisis, as amply illustrated by the students movements under the Han and Sung (Song) dynasties, the political protest of the Tung-lin (Tonglin) scholars in the late Ming dynasty, and the joint petition for reform by K'ang Yu-wei and 1,200 examination candidates in 1895. However, political radicalization of the *shih* had its prescribed limits. It was often expressed by way of internal criticism aiming primarily at restoration or modification of the imperial order; it did not question the legitimacy of the order itself. It invariably took the form of remonstrance or petition to the throne as if in the spirit of loyal opposition.

With the advent of the modern *chih-shih-fen-tzu*, the situation has been fundamentally altered. Marginalized to the periphery, they generally refuse to identify themselves with the political establishment against which they protest. Comparing K'ang Yu-wei's petition to the emperor in 1895 to the student movement of May Fourth will make this point clear. It may be argued that K'ang's movement is midway between tradition and modernity. The May Fourth Movement is decidedly a modern political action appealing to the patriotic feelings of the masses rather than petitioning to the government. To a considerable degree this radical mode of Chinese intellectuals can also be understood in terms of marginalization. Under a government dominated by warlords, intellectuals had no legitimate ways of seeking public office except, perhaps, through personal ties.

As in the case of China's marginalization, we can also conveniently divide the marginalization of intellectuals in Chinese society into two distinct periods with the abolition of the examination in 1905 as a symbolic though imprecise milepost. In the decade of 1895–1905, the last generation of *shih* still stood inside the power structure of the imperial state, even though they were considerably marginalized to the periphery. Nevertheless, the *shih* in the last years of imperial China continued to recognize, though not entirely without reluctance, the legitimacy of the Confucian order. They disguised discovery as interpretation and advocated changes within the limit of monarchical reform. By contrast, modern intellectuals, especially since 1905, stood outside the center of the imperial power. Armed with ideas imported from the West, they openly questioned the raison d'être of the imperial system.[43]

As much as I would like to distinguish the *shih* from the *chih-shih-fen-tzu*, I must point out that spiritually the latter has continued much of what had been cultivated by the former. For example, the idea that the intellectual must always be identified with public-mindedness is not a cultural borrowing from the modern West, but from Confucian heritage traceable ultimately to the sage himself. At any rate, the two most famous mottoes of the Confucian scholar and statesman, Fan Chung-yen (Fan Zhongyan, 989–1052), are still very much alive in the mind of practically every educated person in China even to this day: "The *shih* must take the whole world as his own responsibility"; "The *shih* is one who ought to be the first to worry about the troubles of the world but last to enjoy its pleasures." It was with this spirit that numerous modern intellectuals had plunged themselves into revolution after revolution until, more often than not, they were totally consumed by its flame. The real tragedy in the history of Chinese revolutions is that it was always the radicalized Chinese intellectuals who imported and sowed the seeds of revolution while the harvest was, without exception, reaped by those anti-intellectual elements who knew best how to manipulate the revolution in order to seize its power. For the intellectuals, the seeds of revolution turned out to be seeds of their own destruction.

CONCLUSION

This essay attempts to do two things: First, it tries to delineate the Chinese mind in the twentieth century primarily in terms of a process of radicalization. Attention is particularly drawn to the distinctive shape this radicalization takes, and the unique way in which it takes form. This is still very much an ongoing process in China today; a review of the past may therefore throw some light on the present. Second, radicalization is linked directly to the marginalization of China in the modern world and the marginalization of intellectuals in Chinese society. While some may link the first marginalization with the Middle Kingdom complex or simply nationalism, I consider "Middle Kingdom" too political and "nationalism" too general to serve my purposes. For Chinese intellectuals, the overriding concern has been to keep China from losing its status as a center of culture. Needless to say, this double marginalization does not wholly explain radicalization in twentieth-century China. It has been singled out because it seems to hold a key for unlocking one of the doors of the twentieth-century Chinese mind.

Radicalization is only one among the many faces of modern China. The term must not be taken to suggest that Chinese intellectuals of all levels have been radicalized since the turn of the century or the rise of the May Fourth Movement. In conclusion, if I may be permitted to indulge in a personal note, I also come from Anhui, the native province of both Ch'en Tu-hsiu and Hu Shih, and during the second Sino-Japanese war lived in a small village about sixty to seventy miles away from Ch'en's birthplace (Huai-ning or Huaining) for eight years (1937–1945). I heard of Ch'en's name only once when he was accused, falsely, as I later learned, of having changed the old Confucian dictum into "filial piety is the first of all evils and adultery the first of all virtues." I also spent a year (1945–1946) in the neighboring county, T'ung-ch'eng (Tongcheng), whose literary school had been singled out for abuse by the May Fourth leaders of new literature, especially Ch'ien Hsüan-t'ung (Qian Xuantong, 1887–1939). But there I was still encouraged to write prose and poetry in the classical style. It was only after I returned to the big cities such as Nanking, Shanghai, Peking (Beijing), and Shenyang in 1946 that I began to be exposed to the influence of radical ideas of Western origin. In those postwar years (1946–1949), as far as I can recall, neither Marxism nor iconoclastic antitraditionalism dominated the daily life of ordinary urban intellectuals. So, I have often been puzzled by the question as to how widespread and penetrating the May Fourth Movement or Marxism really was prior to 1949 in China as a whole.

If, however, we look at the campuses of major universities in post-May Fourth China, we see an entirely new face. The inevitable conclusion: though radicalization may have been confined only to scattered centers in a vast China, it did occur where it mattered most, both intellectually and politically.

ENDNOTES

[1] Michael Walzer, *Interpretation and Social Criticism* (Cambridge, Mass.: Harvard University Press, 1985).

[2] For a brief reference to this, see John K. Fairbank, Edwin O. Reischauer, and Albert M. Craig, *East Asia: Tradition and Transformation* (Boston, Mass.: Houghton Mifflin Company, 1989), 79.

[3] On the *Scripture of the Great Peace,* see Max Kaltenmark, "The Ideology of the T'ai-p'ing ching," in Holmes Welch and Anna Seidel, eds., *Facets of Taoism* (New Haven, Conn.: Yale University Press, 1979), 19–52.

[4] Margaret C. Jacob and James R. Jacob, eds., *The Origins of Anglo-American Radicalism* (New Jersey and London: Humanities Press International, Inc., paperback ed., 1991), 5.

[5] Antonio Gramsci, *Selections From the Prison Notes of Antonio Gramsci*, ed. and trans. Quintin Hoare and Geoffrey Nowell Smith (New York: International

Publishers, 1971), 19–20. Also quoted and discussed in Walzer, *Interpretation and Social Criticism*, 62–63.

[6]Benjamin I. Schwartz, *In Search of Wealth and Power: Yen Fu and the West* (Boston, Mass.: Belknap Press, 1964).

[7]T'ang Chih-chün, *K'ang Yu-wei yü Wu-hsü pien-fa* (*K'ang Yu-wei and the Reform of 1898*) (Peking: Chung-hua Book Company, 1984) and James Reeve Pusey, *China and Charles Darwin* (Cambridge, Mass.: Council on East Asian Studies, Harvard University, 1983), 89–91.

[8]Hao Chang, *Chinese Intellectuals in Crisis: Search for Order and Meaning, 1890–1911* (Berkeley, Calif.: University of California Press, 1990), 72.

[9]*Kuo-ts'ui hsüeh-pao* (*Journal of National Essence*) (1) (1905): 2.

[10]Hu Feng-hsiang, "Historiography of the National Essence School During the Revolution of 1911," *Li-shih Yen-chiu* (*Historical Research*) (5) (1985): 151–52.

[11]Liang Ch'i-ch'ao, *Yin-ping shih wen-chi* (*Literary Writings of Liang Ch'i-ch'ao*) (Peking: Chung-hua Book Company, 1989), vol. 6, 11–12; vol. 9, 3–4.

[12]Vera Schwarcz, *The Chinese Enlightenment: Intellectuals and the Legacy of the May Fourth Movement* (Berkeley, Calif.: University of California Press, 1986); Li Tse-hou, *Chung-kuo hsien-tai ssu-hsiang shih lun* (*On Contemporary Chinese Intellectual History*) (Peking: East Press, 1987), 7–49.

[13]Hu Shih, *Hu Shih liu-hsüeh jih-chi* (*Diary of Hu Shih as a Student in America*) (Taipei: Yuan-liu Publishing Company, 1988), vol. 4, 162–63.

[14]Ibid., 194–95.

[15]Quoted in Hsiao Kung-ch'uan, *Wen-hsüeh chien-wang lu* (*Memoirs of a Scholar*) (Taipei: Biographical Literature Press, 1972), 39. Johnston wrote this in 1913.

[16]Arif Dirlik, *Revolution and History: The Origins of Marxist Historiography in China, 1919–1927* (Berkeley, Calif.: University of California Press, 1978).

[17]Russell Kirk, *The Conservative Mind From Burke to Eliot* (Chicago, Ill. and Washington, D.C.: Regnery Books, 7th rev. ed., 1986), 9.

[18]Lin Yü-sheng, *The Crisis of Chinese Consciousness, Radical Antitraditionalism in the May Fourth Era* (Madison, Wis.: The University of Wisconsin Press, 1979).

[19]Stephen Toulmin, *Cosmopolis, The Hidden Agenda of Modernity* (New York: The Free Press, 1990), 175.

[20]Pusey, *China and Charles Darwin*, 57, 260–73.

[21]Jerome B. Grieder, *Hu Shih and the Chinese Renaissance, Liberalism and the Chinese Revolution, 1917–1937* (Cambridge, Mass.: Harvard University Press, 1970), 181–83.

[22]Karl Mannheim, *Conservatism, A Contribution to the Sociology of Knowledge*, ed. and trans. David Kettler, Volker Meja, and Nico Stehr (London and New York: Routledge & Kegan Paul, 1986), 88.

[23]Ssu-yü Teng and John K. Fairbank, *China's Response to the West, A Documentary Survey, 1839–1923* (Cambridge, Mass.: Harvard University Press, 1954), 34.

24Ibid., 51–52.

25Ying-shih Yü, "Sun Yat-sen's Doctrine and Traditional Chinese Culture," in Chu-yuan Cheng, ed., *Sun Yat-sen's Doctrine in the Modern World* (Boulder, Colo. and London: Westview Press, 1989), 90–91.

26Ch'en Ch'i-yuan, *Yung-hsien chai pi-chi (Jottings by Ch'en Ch'i-yuan)* (Peking: Chung-hua Book Company, 1989), 110.

27James Legge, *The Chinese Classics* (Hong Kong: Hong Kong University Press, 1960), vol. 5, 52.

28Michael Gasster, *Chinese Intellectuals & the Revolution of 1911, The Birth of Chinese Radicalism* (Seattle and London: University of Washington Press, 1969), 6.

29Ting Wen-jiang, *Liang Jen-kung hsien-sheng nien-p'u ch'ang-pian ch'u-kao (A Draft Chronological Biography of Liang Ch'i-ch'ao)* (Taipei: World Book Company, 1958), 24.

30The "Middle Kingdom" complex is a reference to China's sense of superiority as the center of the world. See Tu Wei-ming, "Cultural China: the Periphery as the Center," *Dædalus* 120 (2) (Spring 1991): 4.

31Ch'üan Han-sheng, "Ch'ing-mo te Hsi-hsüeh yuan ch'u Chung-kuo shuo" ("Theories of Chinese Origins of Western Learning in the Late Ch'ing"), collected in *Chung-kuo chin-tai shih lun-ts'ung (Studies on Modern Chinese History)* (Taipei: Cheng-chung Book Company, 1956), first series, vol. 5, 216–58.

32Martin Bernal, "Liu Shih-p'ei and National Essence," in Charlotte Furth, ed., *The Limits of Change, Essays on Conservative Alternatives in Republic China* (Cambridge, Mass.: Harvard University Press, 1976), 96–98.

33Huang Chieh, "Kuo-ts'ui hsü-pao hsü" ("Foreword to the Journal of National Essence"), *Kuo-ts'ui hsü-pao* (1) (1905): 1–4.

34Chang Ping-lin, *Ch'iu-shu (Chang Ping-lin's Essays)* (Shanghai: Classic Literature Press, 1958), 44–45.

35Liu Shih-p'ei, *Liu Shen-shu hsien-sheng i-shu (Collected Works of Liu Shih-p'ei)* (Taipei: Hua-shih Press, 1975), vol. 1, 721–22.

36Quoted in Grieder, *Hu Shih and the Chinese Renaissance,* 160.

37Michael Oakeshott, *Rationalism in Politics and Other Essays* (Indianapolis, Ind.: Liberty Press, 1991), 414.

38Fung Yu-lan, *San-sung T'ang tzu-tsü (Autobiography)* (Peking: San-lien Book Company, 1984), 166–69.

39Quoted in Yü Ying-shih, *Chung-kuo chin-shih tsung-chiao lun-li yü shang-jen ching-shen (Religious Ethic and the Mercantile Spirit in Early Modern China)* (Taipei: Linking Press, 1987), 97.

40Wang Teh-chao, *Ch'ing-tai k'o-chü chih-tu yen-chiu (Studies on the Examination System in Ch'ing China)* (Hong Kong: Chinese University of Hong Kong Press, 1982), 246.

41Quoted in Gasster, *Chinese Intellectuals & the Revolution of 1911,* 61.

⁴²W. G. Runciman, ed., *Max Weber: Selections in Translation* (Cambridge: Cambridge University Press, 1978), 200.

⁴³It is important to note that Chinese students in Japan kept themselves away from Sun Yat-sen and his revolution as late as 1903, but, in 1905, Sun found himself enthusiastically welcomed by hundreds of them. In the meantime, back in China, revolution also gained new momentum among radical intellectuals, such as in Shanghai and Chekiang. Gasster, *Chinese Intellectuals & the Revolution of 1911,* 50–51 and Mary Backus Rankin, *Early Chinese Revolutionaries, Radical Intellectuals in Shanghai and Chekiang, 1902–1911* (Cambridge, Mass.: Harvard University Press, 1971), 112, 146.

Myron L. Cohen

# Cultural and Political Inventions in Modern China: The Case of the Chinese "Peasant"

*The gods? Worship them by all means. But if you had only Lord Guan and the Goddess of Mercy and no peasant association, could you have overthrown the local tyrants and evil gentry? The gods and goddesses are indeed miserable objects. You have worshipped them for centuries, and they have not overthrown a single one of the local tyrants and or evil gentry for you! Now you want to have your rent reduced. Let me ask how will you go about it? Will you believe in the gods or in the peasant association?*

—Mao Zedong, 1927[1]

LIKE THE NOW-DEFUNCT LENINIST-STALINIST states of Central and Eastern Europe, the Chinese Communist government has sought to base its legitimacy on the creation of a "new" socialist society, one in which a pervasive and fundamental reorganization of the economy would, of Marxist necessity, lead to the emergence of a new culture, indeed to the emergence of a new kind of person. In order to create such a new society, and to supply the justification for its creation, it also required that the "old" society be defined in such a way as to provide the basis for its thorough rejection. All Communist states have thus faced the enormous burden

*Myron L. Cohen is Professor of Anthropology at Columbia University.*

of two major tasks of cultural construction: there must be both a totally objectionable "old regime" and a new liberated society. Furthermore, the characteristics of the old society have to be formulated in sufficiently convincing detail that they come to form a meaningful negative image assimilated into the consciousness and cultural outlook of the ordinary person. At the same time, the assertion that there is now a new society must be backed by cultural innovations that take firm and positive hold among the masses.

Communist states have taken upon themselves tasks of cultural creation so comprehensive that they comprise assertions of their cultural infallibility. Yet, it is precisely the enormity of Communist cultural ambitions, as backed by the politically enforced monopolization of cultural production and by the claim to be the sole legitimate source of cultural meaning, that in fact has led Communist states to be revealed as so culturally impotent. These states have been able to construct impressively well-organized arrangements of political and economic control, such that decades of Communist rule certainly have produced changes in many areas of social and cultural life, some linked to the severe disruption of the transmission of religious and other pre-Communist traditions. Therefore, it is all the more obvious and remarkable that their major cultural projects have been such failures. Although China's Communist government remains in power, cultural developments in that country, since decollectivization and other reforms were instituted more than a decade ago, bear some resemblance to those during the Soviet Union's terminal Gorbachev era and to the circumstances following the collapse of the other Communist regimes in Europe. The Communist states in Europe, China, and elsewhere in Asia demanded of their subjects both compliance and cultural change; for many observers of Communist societies it sometimes has been difficult to distinguish one from the other. If the energetic and frequently disastrous reemergence of long dormant ethnic and religious forces in ex-Communist Europe initially took many observers by surprise, so did the widespread and increasingly public revival of popular religion in much of China. Thus, the quotation at the beginning of this article can be compared with one describing circumstances after thirty years of Communist rule:

> At the time of Liberation there were many temples in the villages of northern Jiangsu, such as the Grandma Temple, Fire God Temple,

Guandi Temple, and Temple of the God of Wealth. At the time of land reform [ca. 1950] these were abolished and all superstitious sects and secret societies were banned. But ideas of ghosts and gods are deeply rooted among the people, and all kinds of superstitions are rampant.... The Yellow Stone Brigade once had a temple of the "Old Man Yellow Stone".... It was destroyed during the War of Liberation.... But the place where the temple had been is still considered to be sacred by the local peasants.... A myth suddenly surfaced in February and March 1979, saying that Old Man Yellow Stone had returned and would offer treatment to the sick. It is said that about thirty thousand people came from the local county, nearby counties, Shandong and Henan provinces, and even riding on motorcycles from Shanghai.[2]

But in China, the Communist state continues to assert its cultural dominance even though it remains unable to give it viable cultural expression. Furthermore, there had already emerged a major crisis of cultural integration and national identity during the century prior to the onset of Communist rule: the Western assault on and penetration of China, the collapse of the old dynasty, the emergence of new urban working and professional classes, and the rise of a new intelligentsia were among the developments linked to the construction of a particularly Chinese style of elite intellectual nationalism that was severely antitraditional and iconoclastic. By rejecting and condemning the traditional culture of the Chinese masses—even though this culture provided a strong albeit premodern awareness of national identity—the new elite lost an opportunity to participate in the construction of a modern popular nationalism that provided cultural linkages between the individual and the state.[3] In the absence of a successful effort to forge a meaningful and elaborated common cultural framework for the expression of Chinese identity, contemporary China is characterized by an obvious lack of cultural consensus: between city and countryside; state and society; intellectuals and the public; and between many intellectuals and the state.

During the early decades of this century, China's intellectual elites did indeed engage in cultural invention. Increasingly under the influence of Marxism and Marxist categories, both Communists and non-Communists began the construction precisely of an image of the old society that had to be rejected, an image that was to be refined and promoted to cultural orthodoxy after the Communist victory.

Key to this image was the redefinition of traditional Chinese culture and of the vast majority, especially in the countryside, who still adhered to it. For the elite, China's rural population was now "backward" and a major obstacle to national development and salvation. For them, rural China was still a "feudal society" of "peasants" who were intellectually and culturally crippled by "superstition."

Through the transformation of "farmers" into "peasants," "tradition" into "feudalism," and "customs" or "religion" into "superstition," there was invented not only the "old society" that had to be supplanted, but also the basic negative criteria designating a new status group, one held *by definition* to be incapable of creative and autonomous participation in China's reconstruction. There were variations in the depiction of the peasant condition: as noted by Charles W. Hayford, if in some of the new modern writings the "peasants" were "superstitious, ignorant, and inert," in others "they were no longer to be blamed for China's weakness, but to be pitied as a victim of soluble oppression."[4] Furthermore, a much smaller group of intellectuals had a somewhat more positive view of the cultural circumstances of China's rural inhabitants. Notable examples were the participants in the folklore studies movement of the 1920s, active organizers of rural reconstruction and development projects such as James Yen and Liang Shu-ming, and anthropologists and sociologists such as Fei Hsiao-t'ung, Lin Yue-hua, C. K. Yang, and Martin Yang.[5] For such intellectuals who had worked in villages, especially the anthropologists and sociologists, it was clear that the society, customs, and beliefs they investigated had positive meaning and considerable importance for the rural Chinese.

Except for the anthropologists and sociologists, again, even many of these intellectuals were hostile to village popular religion and encouraged the destruction or conversion of local temples and shrines; they, like the others, hardly appear to have been inclined to view the reconstruction of rural Chinese society and its reintegration into a renewed national cultural framework as a process that would draw upon the existing culture of the countryside. In any event, to the degree that they might sympathize with rural lifeways, theirs was the minority view, and the notion of the peasantry as a culturally distinct and alien "other," passive, helpless, unenlightened, in the grip of ugly and fundamentally useless customs, desperately in need of education and cultural reform, and for such improvements in their circumstances totally dependent on the leadership and efforts of rational and informed outsiders, became fixed in the outlook of China's modern intellectual and political elites. For the elites governing China, or seeking to assume power over it, this image of the peasant confirmed their own moral claim to an inherently superior, privileged position in national political life, and their conviction that populism or popular democracy were utterly unacceptable if China was to avoid chaos and achieve national strength.[6] Indeed, such elite sentiments have been aptly characterized as involving a strong strain of *antipopulism*.[7] Thus, Mao Zedong and other Communist intellectuals were hardly the only ones to believe that the physical, political, and economic liberation of the peasantry required its cultural destruction.

Key terms employed in the creation and negative perception of China's peasants were among the many loanwords from Japanese that entered China in especially great numbers during the late-nineteenth and early decades of the twentieth centuries, words which have played such an important role in shaping the modern Chinese vocabulary.[8] In addition to *fengjian* (feudal) and *mixin* (superstition), there is *nongmin*, precisely the term usually translated as "peasant." In some cases (i.e., *fengjian*, *nongmin*), the Meiji-era Japanese modernizers drew upon classical Chinese texts for the *kanji* terms they would use in their translations of works from the West, while in others they created their own neologisms (as with *mixin*). In all cases, however, these terms entered both written and spoken Chinese as "modern" words, inherently abstract and readily available for the assignment of new meaning precisely because they were largely unencumbered by any traditional cultural baggage that might interfere with their use in the context of visions of contemporary China. Although Hayford already has documented the transition from farmer to peasant in the English-language writings of both Chinese and Western observers of rural China,[9] there was a parallel change in Chinese, with a wide variety of words giving way, perhaps first in intellectual and political discourse, to the categorical *nongmin*.[10]

The conceptual transformation of the population of China's countryside from farmers into peasants was a reversal of the sequence of events involved in Western perceptions and scholarship concerning rural Europe, whose modernization was seen to turn peasants into farmers.[11] In Europe, the end of the peasantry was linked to the formation of modern nation-states, and to growing rural-urban ties in the context of industrialization, the modernization of communications and agriculture, and the spread of formal education. In China, however, Western influence and pre-Communist industrialization and modernization had their greatest impact in the cities, especially the major foreign-dominated "treaty ports"; the effect was the modern creation of the severe rural-urban contrasts which in the Western imagination, as formed by historical experience, are seen to be characteristic of Europe's premodern era. The different Western and Chinese experiences have been well summarized by the historian F. W. Mote:

> The idea that the city represents either a distinct style or, more important, a higher level of civilization than the countryside is a cliché of our Western cultural traditions. It has not been so in traditional China. . . . [The] sharp division into distinct urban and rural civilizations disappeared very early in China, although it remained characteristic of much of the rest of the world until recent times and produced distinct urban attitudes in other civilizations. The conditions allowing such attitudes in China seem to have vanished by the beginning of the imperial era [202 B.C.], so long ago that a sense of that kind of urban superiority has not remained.
>
> Chinese civilization may be unique in that its word for "peasant" has not been a term of contempt—even though the Chinese idea of a "rustic" may be that of a humorously unsophisticated person.[12]

Whatever the Chinese word for peasant that Mote may have had in mind, his observation underscores the significance of the adoption of the new term *nongmin,* precisely in the circumstances of the emergence and deepening of the cultural divide between the new urban-based intelligentsia and China's vast rural hinterland. This divide represented a radical departure from tradition: Mote and others have shown how, especially during the later imperial era (Ming and Qing dynasties, 1368–1911), China was notable for the cultural, social, political, and economic interpenetration of city and countryside.[13] But the term *nongmin* did enter China in association with Marxist and non-Marxist Western perceptions of the peasant, thereby putting the full weight of the Western heritage to use in the new and sometimes harshly negative representation of China's rural population. Likewise, with this development westerners found it all the more "natural" to apply their own historically-derived images of the peasant to what they observed or were told in China. The idea of the peasant remains powerfully entrenched in the Western perception of China to this very day; the term is commonly encountered both in journalism and in academic discourse, and even in reference to the contemporary rural scene, which in many areas of the country is characterized by rapidly mechanizing and increasingly prosperous family farms, growing economic diversification, and modernization. Yet, for many Chinese and westerners alike, peasant has been a purely cultural category since its first appearance in modern China. There were always many peasants who were not farmers; the fact that this is increasingly true does not yet appear to have altered perceptions of the countryside.

The staying power of this idea is at least in part attributable to the powerful reinforcement it has received since the establishment of the Communist government. Incorporated into its official and administrative classification of China's population is the distinction between peasants and other categories of persons, such as *gongren* (workers) or *jumin* (urban residents). Until a decade ago, there was the further differentiation of the peasantry into "classes," determined during the land-reform campaigns, first carried out in areas of the country under Communist control even before their final victory over the Nationalists. On the basis of their pre-Communist economic circumstances, villagers were classified as "poor," "middle," or "rich" peasants, or as "landlords," and among the various peasant classes there were further subdivisions. Once assigned, these class labels largely remained fixed until the end of the collective era. A person born after land reform inherited the class designation of his or her father. During the various political campaigns, those with "rich peasant" or "landlord" labels could be subject to public humiliation and condemnation, while the "poor and lower-middle peasants" were defined by the Communist state as the new rural political elite.[14]

Prior to the arrival of the Communists, there were wealthy landlords, and many if not most villagers were very poor. But the imposition of class categories on the basis of supposedly objective economic criteria was fundamentally an administrative act. Borderline cases sometimes had their class standing revised after appeal, and those with advantageous kinship or other social ties sometimes received a better class label than they might otherwise have expected. Even though the antilandlord "struggle" sessions encouraged by the land-reform cadres working in villages throughout China did in some cases lead to violence and to killings, the fact remains that with the elimination of these class labels, community, economic, and kinship ties once again came to form intricate social networks linking villagers of previously "good" and "bad" class backgrounds. This was quite evident in the Chinese villages where I conducted field-work: in 1986–1987 in a village in the North China Province of Hebei; in 1990 in an East China village near Shanghai; and in a village in Sichuan Province, West China. In all three villages, social reintegration was given public manifestation during occasions such as weddings, birthday celebrations for the aged, funerals, and death anniversaries. Both the rituals and banquets involved in such events were characterized by the easy participation of persons who, during the collective era, would not risk being seen to be involved with each other. What has been reported for a village in South China was equally true in the three villages where I have worked: "even the old landlords, now retired, could, for the first time since the land reform of the fifties, casually mingle with other villagers."[15] For most people, the old rural-class labels hardly had been productive of culturally deep and meaningful class consciousness, notwithstanding the fact that their imposition did lead to real resentments and antagonisms that have not been easy to forget. Yet these labels—a major factor in the practical affairs of daily life for over twenty-five years—did provide powerful reinforcement to the idea and reality of the peasantry as the overarching status group in which there were different kinds of peasants.

In terms of these labels, landlords were not peasants. But by 1959, landlords and the various classes of peasants were all peasants— *nongmin*—in contradistinction to *gongren* or *jumin*, the more inclu-sive term. This distinction between peasant and urban resident is inherited through the mother and was originally given legal standing in order to control migration from the countryside to the cities. But even in the far less restrictive social and economic environment of present-day China, it remains in force and is based purely upon household registration. Being an urban resident provides access to certain commodities at subsidized prices, employment with retire-ment and medical benefits, and a wide variety of other preferential treatments. Being a peasant, therefore, is to be disadvantaged, and the resentment felt by those so labeled, and their envy of urban residents, has been widely reported.[16] Peasants in modern China now have second-class citizenship, ironically, giving legal confirmation to the second-class culture they earlier had been identified with.

At the same time, the increasingly obvious and economically significant occupational diversity of these statutory peasants has led to some being labeled with what outside observers might take to be oxymora, such as peasant entrepreneurs, peasant merchants, or peasant businessmen.[17] Many of these peasants now live in the cities or in the smaller towns that have been rapidly developing since decollectivization and the other economic reforms of the past decade. In the course of my fieldwork, in the still overwhelmingly agricultural villages in the provinces of Hebei and Sichuan, I noted that most families with farms also had additional income in the form of wage labor or some kind of family enterprise, with the importance of such nonfarm earnings steadily increasing. Furthermore, with the expansion of China's cities, state-owned urban factories and other organizations have been acquiring farmland. With such a transfer of land, the organization involved sometimes must agree to hire a certain number of the people from the village providing it. This procedure represents one of the very few avenues for status change open to ordinary people and, in the village near Shanghai where I also did fieldwork, it involves entering on the household registration form of the person hired the notation *nongmin zhuan jumin* (peasant changed to urban resident) and the date of the change.[18] In that village, land transfers had reduced village-managed land to only a small fraction of what it had been twenty years earlier; by 1990, the majority of villagers had been reclassified as urban residents. Nevertheless, the demand for urban resident status and the associated employment has always been higher than the supply provided by any particular land transfer, so that with each new opportunity, care is taken by village leaders to distribute the status transfers on a one-per-family basis. As a result, most village families in 1990 had mixed memberships of peasants and urban residents, at the same time that the majority of those who were still peasants worked in village-run factories or ran their own nonagricultural enterprises.[19]

If the Western heritage played a role in the formation of the Chinese concept of the peasant, that concept in its developed form continues to impact on Western scholarship. In Western studies of contemporary rural China, the term peasant is commonly employed, as already noted, but rarely defined. While much of this scholarship resembles the Chinese usage in that the presence of a peasant category is assumed, it certainly does not usually involve any explicit expression of negative attitude. Nevertheless, such writings cannot avoid suggesting that there must be some special attributes making peasants different from other kinds of people, although they do not suggest what these are. Titles of books or articles certainly convey a very different impression if peasant is replaced by another word, such as farmer. The following, published during the past five years, serve as examples: "State and Farmer in Contemporary China," "China's Farmers," "The Re-emergence of the Chinese Farmer," "State Intervention and Farmer Opportunities," or "Farmer Household Individualism." Of course, farmer will not do. It hardly suggests the encounter with a primordial "other" that gives use of the term peasant such dramatic punch; it is even functionally inappropriate given precisely the occupational diversity that inevitably forces the peasant into a cultural mold, the subjective evaluation of which is by default left to others.

More firmly in the Western tradition of the comparative study of rural society is the effort to redefine the peasant in functional terms, free of the cultural associations provided by European history. In this context, the peasantry is seen to comprise the subsistence-oriented agriculturists of premodern societies, a portion of whose output is skimmed off by overlords in the form of rent, taxes, or tribute. Farmers, in contrast, are produced by modernization and characterized by their involvement in a commercialized, market-oriented economy.[20] The peasantry's production is based on survival requirements and the demands linked to their social and economic status; for farmers, it is based on economic rationality in response to market conditions. But such a distinction hardly does justice to the great variety of agrarian circumstances in the world both today and indeed in many premodern societies. Furthermore, it has not succeeded in placing the peasantry in a culturally neutral context, as the anthropologist Polly Hill describes:

> Despite the absurd waste of effort that has gone into attempts in the past fifteen years or more [as of 1986] to qualify *peasant* appropriately, its power to confirm our primitive ideas of an amorphous, undifferentiated mass of tillers of the soil, labouring against overwhelming odds to provide sufficient food for their families, remains undiminished.[21]

Yet the functional approach remains important as far as China is concerned. It is involved in the current controversy over whether there was growth or stagnation in the pre-Communist Chinese rural economy during the twentieth century and late imperial times. Those with a more optimistic view take the Chinese agriculturist to be a farmer, a rational economic optimizer in a market context. The pessimistic perspective, however, sees peasants trapped by economic stagnation and struggling to survive under increasingly harsh circumstances.[22] At issue in this debate is not the presence or absence of commercialized agriculture; all agree that by late imperial times it was widespread. The question, rather, is the extent to which this commercialization involved commodity markets fully open to the participation of the ordinary cultivator. Those involved in this controversy have shifted analysis from peasantry as a category to a focus on the real problems faced by rural Chinese and the means they employed to deal with them. In this sense all agree that those in the countryside were rational actors whose predicament was circumstantial rather than cultural.

Another tradition of analysis moves even further from the Chinese construction of peasant "backwardness" by focusing on those features of late imperial culture and society that may have been assets in China's later modernization. This focus restores a cultural approach, but it is the "economic culture" of late traditional society as a whole; it denies the salience of the peasant versus nonpeasant cultural and functional distinctions, thus placing the appraisal of China's heritage for modernization precisely in the late imperial context of rural-urban interpenetration and integration. This approach represents a refutation of the entire "peasant, feudalism, feudal superstition" bundle; it seeks to identify just those cultural advantages brought to bear by the many people of rural background who have made such important contributions to the rapid economic development of Taiwan, Hong Kong, and, more recently, mainland China.[23]

Key to my own approach to Chinese economic culture is the fact that family organization provided the common framework for the ownership, management, and exploitation of the enormous variety of income-producing assets present in what was indeed the highly commercialized economy of late traditional China (especially during the Qing dynasty, 1644–1911). The characteristics of the Chinese family system were such that personal and *fang* (conjugal-unit) property was clearly subordinate to that owned by the *jia* (family) as a unit. Brothers held basically equal rights to the family estate, which they would distribute among themselves during *fenjia* (family division)—the procedure whereby a large family with married brothers, their wives, and their children would form separate and independent smaller family units. Thus, it is safe to say that in China insofar as property was not held by corporations of one sort or another, it was overwhelmingly held by families. There was also a cultural distinction between the roles of *jiazhang* (family head), based on seniority and gender, and *dangjia* (family manager), based on competence and also—somewhat less uniformly—on gender. The family economy was characterized by the pooling of income from the earnings of family members and family property; families commonly adopted strategies of asset-diversification and personnel-diversification for purposes of sheer survival or, hopefully, to advance their fortunes. Such diversification commonly would involve farm-family investment in nonagricultural enterprises such as shops, and the assignment of family members to run them. These features of family organization are among those that served both to define the family as a corporate economic actor and to position it to deploy whatever resources it had available to be able to best succeed in the highly competitive economic environment of late imperial times. My own fieldwork in different areas of mainland China and in Taiwan confirms that historically this common pattern of family organization operated in very diverse geographic, environmental, and economic settings.

The extent to which agriculture was based upon subsistence crops as opposed to those mainly suitable for sale is thus far less relevant to family organization than the more general commoditization of assets of many kinds, including land or particular rights to land. It is important to make this distinction between commercialization and commoditization, because while the former refers to the extent that the economy in any particular region has gone beyond family self-sufficiency in the production and distribution of food and other necessary or desired goods, the latter relates more to economic culture itself. The issue is the degree to which economic life involves the cultural construction of things that can be bought and sold. In late imperial China, such construction went on at a high pitch. The fact that land itself could readily be negotiated through sale, rent, or mortgage is well-known. However, it is also a well documented fact that a single plot of farmland could be defined as two or even three commodities, especially in areas of central and southern China; most common was the distinction between subsoil rights and surface rights, each of which could be independently marketed. Linked to this commoditization and contributing to its expression was the availability of credit and the widespread use of contracts and other commercial papers. These were important in the formation of various kinds of corporations: some were based upon shareholding and in the countryside these included lineages, religious associations, and many others. Indeed, some of the corporations organized by ordinary villagers paid out per-share dividends, often annually, on the basis of profits realized from rental of corporation land. While the corporations might impose restrictions on the transfer of shares, or ban it entirely, the shares themselves were family property. In any event, some corporations did allow for the sale of shares, which therefore represented yet another kind of commodity. Thus, in some cases, a corporation's assets included shares in other corporations.[24]

Commercialization is a kind of buzzword in much of social science literature. As noted, it implies a movement away from a peasant subsistence-oriented economy to one where expanding market relationships tend to break down tight-knit rural communities and turn cultivators into rational managers of the farm enterprises. The term also conveys a sharp distinction between the worlds of agriculture and commerce, with the former largely comprised of intimate social relationships, and the sentiments reinforcing them, while in the latter dealings with strangers play an obviously important role. As far as late traditional China is concerned, the distinction between farming and market-dominated relationships breaks down even within this framework of commercialization, given how Chinese farmers indeed were widely involved in the commercial disposal of their crops. Nevertheless, the use of this term in effect assigns to particular cropping patterns what is really an arbitrary cultural significance, perhaps based upon assumed parallels with the Western experience. I suggest that commoditization far more accurately conveys the economic realities faced by Chinese in and out of farming, and helps explain their culturally easy movement from farming into commerce should other circumstances facilitate it.

An economic and cultural environment where assets were generally commoditized spans the divides between subsistence and commercial crops, farms and shops, and cities, towns, and the countryside. Likewise, the diversified activities of individual families could also span these divides; it was common for shops and firms to be run by families who also owned farms and had some of their members working them. The strategy of diversification of family economic roles and assets was common to both ordinary people and traditional elites.[25] There was structural equivalency between a very poor rural family where one brother might work a tiny plot of tenanted land and another be forced to hire himself out as a worker for other farmers, a somewhat better-off family where one brother worked the fields they owned or rented, while another managed the small family store, and a powerful elite family where one brother might be an imperial degree-holder, another the functional landlord in charge of the family's rural holdings, and yet another the merchant who ran the family's impressive urban commercial enterprises. The overall commoditization of assets provided the cultural context in which a common pattern of organization could characterize families sustaining or attempting to sustain themselves under a great variety of economic circumstances. Being generally commoditized, a wide variety of assets could take the form of family property, thus establishing one basic link between marked economic heterogeneity on the one hand, and uniformities in family organization on the other. Linked to this commoditization was the relative unimportance of hereditary economic and political statuses, such as those that might define serfdom or caste membership in other parts of the preindustrial world. Therefore, there was considerable social mobility in late traditional society; for an increasingly prosperous family, the almost inevitable occurrence of family division would commonly lead to the impoverishment of later generations, while in the generally risky economic environment of that time a great variety of factors could cause a family's economic ruin. Family strategy might lead to favorable occupational and economic mobility among the family's members, while a family's bad luck might have consequences that were functionally similar but economically disastrous or even fatal. In this context, the imposition of the historically burdened Western contrasts of town and country, peasant and shopkeeper, or merchant and landlord serves only to distort the realities of the Chinese economic tradition.

All families were enterprises insofar as they strove to obtain or preserve and manage assets that formed the basis of the family estate and to distribute among family members the product of these assets. A traditional focus in the Chinese family, therefore, was on flexible and entrepreneurial management geared to making the best use of available family resources and local economic opportunities, hence the importance of the family manager role. With collectivization imposed on the Chinese countryside by 1955, a period of approximately twenty-five years followed in which the rural population was in effect almost entirely transformed into wage earners for the communes, production brigades, and production teams. During this period, the rural family still retained its corporate character, but family property amounted to little more than housing and furnishings, and the scope of the economic activity of family members was almost entirely restricted to that assigned and managed by the collective organizations. Decollectivization and economic reforms in China during the past decade have paved the way for the reemergence of a variety of autonomous units in China's economic life. Most notable, especially but not exclusively in the countryside, has been the resurrection of the Chinese family as a major economic actor. China is now fed by the output of millions of family farms. These families, however, once again presented with what might be characterized as relatively open or unencumbered economic and social space, have rapidly expanded into other areas of entrepreneurial activity, contributing to the growing availability of goods and services and helping to give rise to the massive development of the new "small towns" that have received so much attention.[26]

An approach to Chinese economic culture emphasizing the family as a corporate unit creating, deploying, and managing its human resources and its property in a highly commoditized environment so as to provide for family survival or enhance family welfare better explains the continuity between the late traditional culture and modern economic trends than does focusing on the supposed inability of families to adapt to modernization due to their backward peasant status. The importance of the family as an enterprise in the modern economic development of Taiwan, Hong Kong, and, now, the China mainland is with respect to the capitalization and management of firms far different in function, organization, and technology from those characteristic of earlier times. But the attributes of these new economic units certainly are not incompatible either with the tradition of rational management or with that of commoditization.

In China, the invented peasant, associated with growing rural-urban differentiation, has given way to the statutory peasant, a result of administrative fiat. But this administrative peasant is now to be found in a context of rapid economic development, especially in some areas of the country, that is blurring the very rural-urban gap that encouraged the birth of the peasant idea in the first place. Nevertheless, in China the idea of the peasant as comprising a distinct and backward cultural category shows no sign of losing its force. That China's peasantry is for cultural reasons not fit to participate in political democracy is at least one point on which the country's Communist leaders agree with many of the students who were at Tiananmen, and with some of the established intellectuals who supported the students, including certain of those now in exile who are leading what they call a democracy movement. If, as I have suggested, the creation of the peasant in China was related less to the circumstances, potential, and culture of the country's rural inhabitants and more to an elite antitraditionalism that formed a moral claim to political privilege and power, then it is not at all surprising that Chinese elite attitudes remain consistent.[27] The peasants may do what they will, but the real issue is the elites' conceptions of their own role in China's polity and society.

ACKNOWLEDGMENTS

I am grateful to Charles W. Hayford and Arthur Waldron for their criticisms of earlier versions of this paper and to participants in the September 1992 *Dædalus* Authors' Conference for their many helpful comments.

ENDNOTES

[1]Quoted in Donald MacInnis, *Religious Policy and Practice in Communist China* (New York: Macmillan, 1972), 10.

[2]Quoted in Luo Zhufeng, ed., *Religion Under Socialism in China*, trans. Donald E. MacInnis and Zheng Xi'an (New York: M. E. Sharp, 1991), 164–65.

[3]These points are discussed in detail in Myron L. Cohen, "Being Chinese: The Peripheralization of Traditional Identity," *Dædalus* 120 (2) (Spring 1991): 113–34.

[4]Charles W. Hayford, *To the People: James Yen and Village China* (New York: Columbia University Press, 1990), 113; for more on the transformation of farmers into peasants, see Ibid., 62. Hayford's discussion in this book and in some later, unpublished writings is the stimulation for my own consideration of the role of the peasant in modern Chinese culture.

[5]James Yen is the subject of Hayford's book, and Liang Shu-ming's life and works are considered in Guy S. Alitto, *The Last Confucian: Liang Shu-ming and the Chinese Dilemma of Modernity* (Berkeley, Calif.: University of California Press, 1979). Representative works of the social scientists include Fei Hsiao-tung, *Peasant Life in China: A Field Study of Country Life in the Yangtze Valley* (London: Routledge and Kegan Paul, 1939); Lin Yueh-hwa, *The Golden Wing: A Sociological Study of Chinese Familism* (New York: Oxford University Press, 1947); C. K. Yang, *A Chinese Village in Early Communist Transition* (Cambridge, Mass.: MIT, 1959); and Martin C. Yang, *A Chinese Village: Taitou, Shantung Province* (New York: Columbia University Press, 1945).

[6]On such elite views see Andrew J. Nathan, *Chinese Democracy* (New York: Alfred A. Knopf, 1985).

[7]See Paul A. Cohen, "The Contested Path: The Boxers as History and Myth," *Journal of Asian Studies* 51 (1) (February 1992): 82–113.

[8]The significance of such terms will be evident from perusal of the partial but comprehensive listing provided in Li Yu-ning, *The Introduction of Socialism into China* (New York: Columbia University Press, 1971), 70–107.

[9]In Hayford, *To the People,* but especially in "The Storm Over the Peasant: Rhetoric and Representation in Modern China," paper presented at the 44th Annual Meeting, Association for Asian Studies (Washington, D.C.: Association for Asian Studies, 2–5 April 1992).

[10]Thus the term *nongmin* is nowhere to be found even in the second and final edition (Shanghai: 1912) of what for its time had been the definitive *Chinese-English Dictionary* of Herbert A. Giles. This large dictionary, representative of late nineteenth-century Mandarin, translates as "labourers; agriculturalists" the terms *nongfu, nongding, nongjia, nongren, zhuanghu,* and *zhuangjiahan.* Most of these terms, and several not in the Giles work, are translated as farmer in R. H. Mathews, *A Chinese-English Dictionary Compiled for the China Inland Mission* (Shanghai: 1931). Mathews translates *zhuangjiahan* and *zhuanghu* as "farmers; peasants" and the term *minfu* (which I have not found in Giles) as "coolies; peasants." *Nongmin* does make its appearance in his dictionary, in the totally Japanese-derived phrase *nongmin xiehui,* translated as "Peasants Union." Mathews' dictionary superseded Giles' product and in a slightly revised 1943 edition is still widely in use today. Cortenay H. Fenn's Chinese-English *The Five Thousand Dictionary,* first published in 1926, likewise has long served as a source of basic vocabulary; in its fifth and last edition with major revisions (Peking: 1940) there is still no entry for *nongmin,* with terms such as those listed by Giles and Mathews being translated as farmer, farm laborers, or husbandman. As far as I have seen, *nongmin,* translated as peasant or sometimes as "peasant; farmer," is a standard entry in all Chinese-English dictionaries of the modern language published during recent decades in China, Taiwan, Hong Kong, and elsewhere. According to

several knowledgeable Chinese with whom I have consulted, the most common prepeasant term for farmer probably was *nongfu*.

[11]For a classic study of the European transformation, see Eugen Weber, *Peasants Into Frenchmen: The Modernization of Rural France, 1870–1914* (Stanford: Stanford University Press, 1976).

[12]F. W. Mote, "The Transformation of Nanking, 1350–1400," in G. William Skinner, ed., *The City in Late Imperial China* (Stanford: Stanford University Press, 1977), 101–53. Quotation from Ibid., 102–103.

[13]On this also see the other essays in Skinner, *The City in Late Imperial China*.

[14]For good descriptions of land reform campaigns, see Yang, *A Chinese Village in Early Communist Transition*, which is based upon fieldwork observations, and Edward Friedman, Paul G. Pickowicz, and Mark Selden, *Chinese Village, Socialist State* (New Haven, Conn.: Yale University Press, 1991), which describes the process as reconstructed on the basis of later long-term fieldwork and interviewing. See Richard Curt Kraus, *Class Conflict in Chinese Socialism* (New York: Columbia University Press, 1981), for a general discussion of the role of class in China during the Maoist era.

[15]Anita Chan, Richard Madsen, and Jonathan Unger, *Chen Village: The Recent History of a Peasant Community in Mao's China* (Berkeley, Calif.: University of California Press, 1984), 283.

[16]For a comprehensive discussion of the origins and social implications of the distinction between peasants and workers or urban residents, see Sulamith Heins Potter and Jack M. Potter, *China's Peasants: The Anthropology of a Revolution* (Cambridge: Cambridge University Press, 1990), 296–312.

[17]On the use of these terms see Yia-ling Liu, "Reform From Below: The Private Economy and Local Politics in the Rural Industrialization of Wenzhou," *China Quarterly* 130 (June 1992): 293–316.

[18]In areas of North China, the notation is *nongmin zhuan feinongmin* (peasant changed into nonpeasant).

[19]In the entire village, with a population of about 650, there were only twenty-nine people (twenty-eight of them women) whose major employment was agriculture. They were all vegetable farmers working on what was left of village land. However, because they were assigned their own plots by the village-run vegetable farm, with their income based upon individual output, they were assisted during the busiest phases of work by other family members, be they workers or peasants.

[20]For classic studies in this tradition, see Eric R. Wolf, *Peasants* (Englewood Cliffs, N.J.: Prentice-Hall, 1966) and Theodore Shanin, ed., *Peasants and Peasant Societies* (Harmondsworth, England: Penguin, 1971; rev. and expan. ed., Oxford: Basil Blackwell, 1987).

[21]Polly Hill, *Development Economics on Trial: The Anthropological Case for the Prosecution* (Cambridge: Cambridge University Press, 1986), 9.

[22]For discussions of this controversy, and evaluations of some of the major writings involved, see Albert Feuerwerker, "An Old Question Revisited: Was the Glass Half-Full or Half-Empty for China's Agriculture Before 1949?," *Peasant Studies*

17 (3) (Spring 1990): 207–16; Ramon H. Myers, "How Did the Modern Chinese Economy Develop?—a Review Article," and Philip C. C. Huang, "A Reply to Ramon Myers," both in the *Journal of Asian Studies* 50 (3) (August 1991): 604–28, 629–33; and R. Bin Wong, "Chinese Economic History and Development: A Note on the Myers-Huang Exchange," *Journal of Asian Studies* 51 (3) (August 1992); 600–11. Some of the more recent relevant works include Loren Brandt, *Commercialization and Agricultural Development: Central and Eastern China, 1870–1937* (Cambridge: Cambridge University Press, 1989); David Faure, *The Rural Economy of Pre-Liberation China: Trade Increase and Peasant Livelihood in Jiangsu and Guangdong, 1870 to 1937* (Hong Kong: Oxford University Press, 1989); Philip C. C. Huang, *The Peasant Economy and Social Change in North China* (Stanford: Stanford University Press, 1985); Philip C. C. Huang, *The Peasant Family and Rural Development in the Yangzi Delta, 1350–1988* (Stanford: Stanford University Press, 1990); and Thomas G. Rawski, *Economic Growth in Prewar China* (Berkeley, Calif.: University of California Press, 1989).

[23]For a discussion of the development of the economic culture approach and an example of its application to present-day rural China, see Myron L. Cohen, "Family Management and Family Division in Contemporary Rural China," *China Quarterly* 130 (June 1992): 357–78.

[24]For more on contracts, corporations, and credit in Chinese economic culture, see Fu-mei Chang Chen and Ramon H. Myers, "Customary Law and the Economic Growth of China During the Ch'ing Period," parts one and two, *Ch'ing-shih wen-t'i* 3 (5) (November 1976): 1–32 and *Ch'ing-shih wen-t'i* 3 (10) (December 1978): 4–27. Also see Myron L. Cohen, "The Role of Contract in Traditional Chinese Social Organization," *Proceedings VIIIth International Congress of Anthropological and Ethnological Sciences, 1968, Tokyo and Kyoto, Ethnology*, vol. 2 (Tokyo: Science Council of Japan, 1969), 130–32; Maurice Freedman, "The Handling of Money: A Note on the Background to the Economic Sophistication of Overseas Chinese," in G. William Skinner, ed., *The study of Chinese society: essays by Maurice Freedman* (Stanford: Stanford University Press, 1979), 22–26; Evelyn S. Rawski, "Property Rights in Land in Ching China," *Proceedings of the Second International Conference on Sinology, Section on Ming, Ching and Modern History* (Taipei: Academia Sinica, 1989), 357–81; and P. Steven Sangren, "Traditional Chinese Corporations: Beyond Kinship," *Journal of Asian Studies* 43 (3) (May 1984): 391–415.

[25]For discussions of family diversification strategies and consequences in both late traditional China and in more modern contexts, see Cohen, "Family Management and Family Division," and Myron L. Cohen, *House United, House Divided: The Chinese Family in Taiwan* (New York: Columbia University Press, 1976).

[26]See Fei Hsiao Tung et al., *Small Towns in China: Functions, Problems, and Prospects* (Beijing: New World Press, 1986).

[27]For discussions of such attitudes among both power-holding and opposition intellectual and political elites in contemporary China, see Ernest P. Young, "Imagining the Ancien Régime in the Deng Era," and Elizabeth J. Perry, "Casting a Chinese 'Democracy' Movement: The Roles of Students, Workers, and Entrepreneurs," both in Jeffrey N. Wasserstrom and Elizabeth J. Perry, eds., *Popular*

*Protest and Political Culture in Modern China: Learning from 1989* (Boulder, Colo.: Westview Press, 1992), 14–27, 146–64.

*Tongqi Lin*

# A Search for China's Soul[1]

O N THE MORNING OF APRIL 18, 1989, thousands of college students in Beijing filed silently into Tiananmen Square. Many laid wreaths around the Monument to the People's Heroes in memory of Hu Yaobang, Secretary General of the Chinese Communist Party, whose death three days earlier would ignite the Protest Movement in May and June.[2] One group from Beijing University spread a banner across the ground on which the following characters were inscribed: *Zhong-Guo-Hun*—the Soul of China.

## CHINA'S SOUL: A CHANGING, CONFLICTING, MULTILAYERED STRUCTURE

*In accordance with* [Lionel Trilling's] *dialectical view of culture* [as a struggle, or at least a debate], *the outlook of any individual also may be said to consist of several overlapping, partly conflicting belief systems: religious, class (socio-economic), political, regional, racial, ethnic, gender, vocational, or generational.*

—Leo Marx
*The Pilot and the Passenger*[3]

China's soul was first raised as a national conundrum at the turn of the last century. A small group of intellectuals, disillusioned by the Tongzhi Restoration (1861–1874) and the Self-Strengthening Movement (1875–1894) and shocked by China's humiliating defeat in the Sino-Japanese War (1894–1895), began to realize the need to change the Chinese mind and character as well as its sociopolitical institutions. Yan Fu (1853–1921), a famous translator of Western social

*Tongqi Lin is a research associate in the Department of East Asian Languages and Civilizations at Harvard University.*

171

and political thought, called on the nation to "boost up the people's strength, cultivate the people's mind, renovate the people's morality."[4] Yan's call marked the inception of a sometimes frustrated but sustained effort to invigorate China's soul—physically, intellectually, and morally. In a tone characteristic of the grievance of the day, reformer and publicist Liang Qichiao (1873–1929) expressed this agonized concern in the title of one of his articles: "Oh, Where Now is the Soul of China?"[5] For two millennia, China's soul was preserved proudly and safely in the sanctuary of an entrenched and self-sufficient ethico-religious world. Liang's question alerted his countrymen that China's soul was now nowhere to be found. It was wandering homelessly around the world. Yet Liang rejected as a remedy the option of recalling the wandering soul. He opted instead for the construction of a new one. "What is of paramount importance today," he maintained, "is nothing less than the remaking of China's soul."[6] Since then, the search for a new national soul has been a recurrent theme haunting generations of Chinese intellectuals—conservative, liberal, and radical.

The issue became a central theme of the May Fourth Movement (1919–1927) under the battle cry of "Down with Confucius and Sons!" The same theme reappeared during the 1930s and 1940s when nationalism was the rage of the day. When Lu Xun (1881–1936), one of China's foremost literary figures, died in 1936, his body was covered with a banner bearing a similar inscription dedicated to Hu Yaobang: *Ming-Zhu-Hun* (the National Soul).

The protracted and massive "thought reform movement" that spanned most of the Mao Zedong era (1949–1976), despite its ideological indoctrination, can be seen as a peculiar variation on the same theme. For a time, the wandering soul of China seemed to have found its incarnation in the "proletarian sage." But the "reign of virtue," as Benjamin Schwartz calls it, proved to be only a short-lived dream. As soon as the reform and opening-up era began in 1978, the "fission" of China's soul erupted on a scale unparalleled in Chinese history. The heated debate on China's "national character" and its relation to modernization in the mid-1980s resonated with the parallel theme of the "reformation of the national character" of the May Fourth Movement seventy years earlier. The tragic end of the Protest Movement of 1989 served only to intensify and accelerate the soul-searching process as Julia Ching's recent book, *Probing China's*

*Soul: Religion, Politics, and Protest in the People's Republic,*[7] and Xiao Jefu,[8] a leading intellectual historian in the mainland, suggest. These examples, among others, reflect a century-long effort to search for a new soul, for the "changing meaning of being Chinese."[9]

## CONFESSIONS: SELF-SEARCHING FOR CHINA'S SOUL

> *I have displayed myself as I was, as vile and despicable when my behavior was such, as good, generous, and noble when I was so. I have bared my secret soul as Thou thyself hast seen it, Eternal Being!*
>
> —Jean-Jacques Rousseau
> *The Confessions*[10]

Confession, whether in the Augustinian sense of "sighing for [God] when pouring out my soul"[11] or in the Rousseauean sense of intending to be "in every way true to nature,"[12] is not a tradition for Chinese intellectuals. Perhaps influenced by Václav Havel, in 1986, Liu Zaifu, a leading literary critic now in exile, called on Chinese writers to "repent (or confess) with the whole nation" for their "complicity" in the catastrophe of the Cultural Revolution.[13] Confession on that scale has not happened. Yet, in the past decade, Chinese intellectuals "have been searching their own souls" while searching history.[14] A series of conferences were held and articles appeared that discussed the important but tragic role of Chinese intellectuals and the merits and demerits of their character. After 1989, self-examination was intensified. Two confessions, Ba Jin's *Random Reflections* (1987) and Liu Xiaobo's *The Monologue of a Doomsday's Survivor* (1992), exemplify this trend revealing the moral and spiritual distress of Chinese intellectuals and their soul-searching.

Ba Jin (1904– ), one of China's most venerated writers, calls himself a "son of the May 4th movement"[15] and remains to this date true to its tradition. He is deeply imbued with Western individualism and humanism represented by Rousseau, Herzen, Tolstoy, Kropotkin, and Bakunin. His famous trilogy, *The Family, Spring, and Autumn,* published in the 1930s, exposed the hypocrisy and oppression of the patriarchal Confucian family. His new book, written half a century later, sounds a different note. It is a soul-confession of his experience during the Cultural Revolution (1966–1976), the loss of personal integrity, moral courage, and the ability to think independently which he had treasured so much as a young writer. Calling himself "a sickly and decrepit old man," he took eight years to finish his confession, or rather, his "final will."[16]

> It's really hard for me to write. I can't move (yes, move) even a ballpoint pen. But my thought refuses to stop and waits for my pen to move. I sit at the desk, helpless and desperate. I move the pen forward and backward. Sometimes no trace appears on the paper and I have to press harder. In this way I produce one sheet of manuscript after another. Sometimes I can't even write two hundred characters the whole day. I feel I am on the verge of utter exhaustion, both physically and mentally.[17]

What, one may ask, is it that urges this "sickly and decrepit old man" to keep on writing? Ba Jin has this to say: "When I am writing, I am actually digging, digging into my own soul. I must dig deeper so that I can understand more, and see more clearly."[18]

Ba Jin's confession is not only a search for his own soul, but a search for the soul of the nation. Those who died in the Cultural Revolution, he stresses, "were much better than us who have survived," because while they did not succumb to the oppressive power of the day, we did. "Doesn't an ancient nation need new blood?," he asked.[19] This was why he called earnestly and repeatedly for the establishment of a Cultural Revolution Museum, saying "I use the blood and tears of the victims to build my 'Cultural revolution Museum.'"[20] "His repentance," as Liu Zaifu puts it, "expresses the feelings of a whole generation of upright intellectuals. He is repenting with the whole nation. His self-interrogation is an inner mechanism by which the goal of the betterment of the nation is to be achieved."[21]

Ba Jin's confessions can be seen essentially as a revolt of the humanistic and individualistic ideas and values he inherited from the Movement against the tyranny of a superimposed ideology. Although he had condemned submission vehemently, he succumbed to it during the Cultural Revolution. For him the struggle between the two is not a theoretical debate. It is, to use his own words, "the pus flowing from unhealed wounds,"[22] wounds that had been gnawing at his heart, vaguely or acutely, for years. His confession came as a resolution to the conflict, a healing of the wounds. It came as a reassertion of his authentic self; his moral courage was regained. Two years later when the Protest Movement of 1989 was entering its height, Ba Jin wrote a letter which openly supported the student hunger strike. Referring back to the May Fourth Movement, he declared: "What [the students] are doing today is completing the task we were unable to finish at that time. They are the hope of China."[23]

Ba Jin's critics, while paying homage to his "relentless lashing of his own soul," are not satisfied. They think his confessions betray a sense of helplessness when faced with a harsh reality and a disposition to retreat to one's inner world for salvation. They maintain that he has not been able to rid himself of the inherent weaknesses of Confucian literati.[24] Yet, Ba Jin's undaunted courage draws its strength from a deep Chinese faith in the existence of *tianli liangxin* (Heaven's Principle and Man's Conscience), an integral part of the soul of Confucian literati. He said, "One sound constantly urges me on. . . . "[25] This sound can be seen as a Chinese type of "imperative command," the voice of the "heavenly endowed conscience." Ba Jin continues: "*Random Reflections* is a witness to my art's conscience."[26] It may not be farfetched to say that the "far tradition," nurtured by Confucianism, has played an indispensable, if not a decisive role in the resolution of the tension between the May Fourth tradition and the Marxist tradition. Ba Jin's confessions are a uniquely Chinese form of confession, not just a reflection of Western humanism.

Another noteworthy confession is that of Liu Xiaobo, in his newly published book, *The Monologue of a Doomsday's Survivor*. Liu, born in 1955, received no formal education as a teenager because of the Cultural Revolution. In 1978, he entered college and later earned a doctorate in comparative literature and became a prolific literary critic. Liu's confession is criticized as "overly self-centered."[27] It contains pungent attacks on the Chinese national character, especially the character of Chinese intellectuals with whom he openly identifies. His soul, like Ba Jin's, is a mirror of the nation's soul.

Liu is perhaps the most trenchant "rebel's voice" from China.[28] Traditional culture "gives me nothing but utter despair and illusion," he says, "I reject it totally. The May Fourth tradition was also a 'tragic failure,' because it was an enlightenment with 'no inner awakening,' 'no emancipation,' an enlightenment that 'looked for a savior,' 'new idols,' 'an absolute truth.'"[29] In 1986, Liu fired a broadside against the "new literature" that had flourished since 1978, denouncing it as "backward-looking" and "lacking individual consciousness."[30] In 1988 he created a sensation by launching a vehement attack on Li Zehou, perhaps the most original and influential thinker in post-Mao China, for "retreating back to the tradition," and "reflecting the weaknesses imbedded in the character of Chinese intellectuals."[31]

Historically, the rebuilding of China's soul was composed of two complementary traditions: the rebuilding of the rational spirit of humanity, which stresses the social, moral, and universal aspect of human life, and the rebuilding of the sensual vital force of humanity, which stresses the individual, aesthetic, and unique aspect of human life.[32] Liu's thinking is an extreme expression of the latter tradition. It attempts to demolish the Marxist orthodoxy with dynamite from the arsenal of contemporary Western thought. Broadly speaking, it is a hasty but efficient integration of Sartre, Nietzsche, and Freud, the three most stimulating and influential Western thinkers in the early and mid-1980s.[33] His confession is a concentrated expression of the theoretical yearnings of his generation.

When the student movement was at its height in 1989, Liu was in the United States as a visiting scholar at Columbia University. He decided to return to China and soon began to play a prominent, even crucial role. Following the June 4th crackdown, he was placed under arrest until his release in January of 1991. He felt guilty because in order to get himself released, he had to plead guilty and write a "confession," denouncing himself for what he had done during the movement. His subsequent *Monologue* is a confession of this earlier "confession," a record of "an incurable wound at my soul":

> The book can also help me to redress the psychological imbalance caused by my confession, to free myself from the haunting guilty sense and achieve peace with my conscience. Confession is indeed self-salvation. . . .
> Mankind can only choose between two realities: either a world with God and evil and confession too or a world with only evil but neither God nor confession.
> I chose the former. Therefore, I wrote *The Monologue of a Dooms-day's Survivor.*[34]

Liu's choice contradicts some of the central ideas he advocated before the ordeal of 1989. In 1988, for example, he declared in a Nietzschean vein that "for the masses, God is gospel, paradise, light, happiness and spiritual solace; but for the genius he is the devil, hell, darkness, suffering, and the blasting of inner balance."[35] "If aesthetic experience has any moral significance at all, it is 'evil.'" "What is called evil is actually not evil, because the world as such is evil." "Conscience and sense of guilt and responsibility" are nothing but the "internalization of external social restrains" imposed coercively on the dynamic system of human desires and instincts.[36] "Kafka is stronger than Rousseau and Nietzsche, because in his eyes. . . there is no salvation for human life."[37] Liu's glorification of *evil* and *nonsalvation* and his depreciation of *God, conscience, sense of guilt,* and *psychological balance* seem all in sharp contrast with, if not in direct contradiction to, the position he adopted when he decided to write his new book, as the above quotation amply shows. Liu chose a world that he had explicitly despised two years before.

The issue, however, is not to blame a soul already burdened with painful conflicts and unresolved tensions. It is, rather, to explore the cultural-intellectual sources of these conflicts and tensions: If Liu had drawn upon Nietzsche and Freud for intellectual and spiritual aspiration, what then was the moral and spiritual force that enabled him to break away from them, if only temporarily? It is true that this time Liu "chose a world with God," which may have given him the strength. But Liu's God is certainly neither St. Augustine's God nor even Rousseau's God. He openly declares that "God exists for man's evils" and that God is only a "garbage can," and "confession is the janitor." In the triadic chord of God, evil, and confession, it is evil, not God, that is the primordial Being. God is, here, more like a makeshift whose function is to provide a "retreat" for man the evildoer.[38] Although Liu repeatedly expressed his admiration for the religious and martyr spirit of Jesus Christ, a Christian God can only supply limited moral strength to an atheist. I would like to argue that as with Ba Jin, it is *liangxin* or *liangzhi* (Confucian Chinese conscience) that constitutes the mainspring of his moral-spiritual courage to confess. "To be responsible to my own conscience" or *wen xin wu kui* (to have a clear conscience in self-examination) is the moral-spiritual bedrock in the psychological quicksand or labyrinth that Liu tries to probe for himself in the book. For Liu, the truly resonant triadic chord is not God, evil, and confession, but conscience, evil, and confession. It is a conscience with some sort of transcendental anchorage, rather than God with his grace for redemption, that gave Liu the strength to write his confessions. Moreover, Liu's love for his parents, exemplified in his moving account of how his "father's tears crashed his last resistance (to pleading guilty),"[39] for his wife, his friends, and his comrades-in-arms, especially those who had died for the cause, constitutes the very essence of some of the most touching passages in his book. This interpersonal love betrays a *renqinwei* (human warmth) which can hardly be called Nietzschean or Freudian, but is typically Chinese. Both the ethos of Liu's confessions and the ethical standards reflected in his moral judgments are much closer to the Chinese than to the Nietzschean-Freudian tradition. Liu is much more conventional than he and his friends believe him to be.

Recently Liu Zaifu stressed the urgency of "reconstructing the *liangzhi xitong* (conscience-system)" in mainland China. Conscience, according to him, is an "unconditional commitment to moral responsibility." "Conscience as a system" consists of external commitment, which is love, and internal commitment, which is confession or repentance.[40] Even two confessors so widely separated in character, philosophy, and generation as Ba Jin and Liu link *confession* and *love* to *conscience*. Is not the "reconstruction of the conscience-system" the very essence of the rebuilding of China's soul? Confessions like those of Ba Jin and Liu are rare among Chinese intellectuals. But they are part of a growing trend of *ziwofansi* (self-examination) in the post-Mao era among intellectuals. It is important, however, to note that this trend of self-examination is, in turn, only part of a new-born intellectual discourse, which provides not only the standard of reference for self-examination but also its moral and intellectual strength. The main thread running through the new discourse is a "humanist quest"[41] that reorients the search for China's soul.

THE HUMANIST QUEST: REORIENTATION OF CHINA'S SOUL

*I believe that the salutary side of the tradition of Chinese intellectuals is that it not only requires a rich professional knowledge but also a profound "concerned-consciousness" (yuhuanyishi) for human life—a consciousness that has become the driving force for exploring the secret of knowledge and makes me feel spiritually sublimated.*

—Wang Yuanhua
*Tradition and Anti-Tradition*[42]

Wang, a venerated literary critic, is representative of Chinese intellectuals today. Despite growing commercialization and secularization, younger scholars' recent critiques of the traditional sense of mission and social responsibility, the "concerned-consciousness" Wang advocates, remain a prominent feature of most Chinese intellectuals. Unlike most Western countries, where the political and moral order is relatively stable, China is undergoing momentous social and spiritual transformation. Broad and fundamental social and cultural issues loom in the minds of Chinese intellectuals. These issues are their souls' concerns and the "driving force" behind their "exploration of the secret of knowledge." The theoretical exploration of these issues is not a highly professionalized and impersonal enterprise. Nor is the new intellectual discourse a new ideology completely dictated by political needs or a product of disinterested, academic scholarship. It is essentially the voice of Chinese intellectuals searching for the soul of their nation.

"Intellectual discourse" refers to a sharing and exchange of ideas aimed at theoretical validity. This concept of intellectual discourse does not necessarily exclude the Foucaultian notion of discourse as power or social-political control, but it does imply that the discourse will focus on its logical structure rather than on its social and historical formation process. This logical structure consists of three elements: *1)* concerns common to the participants of the discourse; *2)* some widely shared theoretical assumptions or value judgments; and *3)* a set of debated issues.

From 1949 to 1978, China's intellectuals were dominated by a strong ideology whose central concern was the theoretical justification of the shifting political needs of the Party.[43] The theoretical assumptions shared by, or imposed on, the participants were strict and pervasive. One could find in almost every field of study a number of theoretical assumptions known as *tifa* (proposition). *Tifa* refers to a succinct way of couching a thesis that has been carefully worked out by authoritative theoreticians and endorsed by the Party, to serve as unifying guidelines for theoretical discussions. With this tight theoretical control, the debated issues were trivial. The language involved was known as *ja da kong* (false, bragging, empty) and was exemplified in the mass criticism during the Cultural Revolution.

When the era of "reform and opening-up" began in 1978, a new discourse took shape. The emergence of the discourse was perhaps the most important event in the intellectual history of the post-Mao era. Its structure possessed its own central concerns, shared assumptions, interrelated issues, and even some linguistic features. The central concern of the discourse was China's modernization. Two concepts preoccupied the participants: self and culture. While the deep concern for self was a reaction to the painful experience of what might be called the prior "dissolution of man,"[44] the intense interest in culture was a reaction to the long reign of economic determinism and cultural vandalism. The interplay spearheaded the development of a discourse in which self returned to culture. The urge for self-realization merged with a quest for cultural identity, foreshadowing a long process of the rebirth of China's soul.

What gives the rebirth of China's soul its new orientation are its shared assumptions and values—a humanist quest that has manifested itself in three overlapping phases: *1)* a quest for the independent existence of man (humanity) with inherent value, dignity, and rights, namely a quest for the "rediscovery of man"; *2)* a quest for the essence and strength, the distinguishing features and inner structure of man in which man seeks to *know* himself, the "reexploration of man"; and *3)* a quest for the ultimate meaningfulness and fulfillment of life as man seeks to *realize* himself, a quest which may be called the "rebuilding of man." This humanist quest joins the rediscovery, reexploration, and rebuilding of man. Faith in the value of the quest underlies the shared assumptions, the main thread which runs through five major intellectual encounters and reverses an ideology that has dominated China for three decades, opening up a new vista for the building of China's soul.

Many Chinese intellectuals have had to face the agonizing fact that for almost three decades they have "dissolved" into the ocean of the masses. Man as an independent existence completely vanished. He had become a cog in the machine, a so-called "servile tool of the Party." Dai Houying, author of the novel *Man, Oh Man!* which triggered a heated discussion in 1980, expressed this feeling:

> What motivated me to write was a strong desire to find out the cause behind the Cultural Revolution and I discovered it was the distortion of man, of human nature, human affection and humanism. I must use my pen to restore the dignity of man, to treasure the value of man, and eulogize humanism.[45]
>
> What I write is the blood and tears of man, the painful moaning of a distorted soul, the spiritual sparks that erupt in darkness. I raised a loud cry: "Oh, my soul, may you come back again!" With infinite joy I recorded the revival of human nature.[46]

"The revival of human nature" or "the humanist quest" started with the awakening of human reason. The first signs of the awakening appeared in the late 1960s. It became a national movement with the "discussions on the criteria of truth," the first major intellectual event since 1978. The discussions were used by Deng Xiaoping to dislodge his political opponents, who insisted that the words and actions of Mao exclusively constituted the criteria of truth. The conclusion of the discussions, which helped pave the way for Deng's drastic reform, was straightforward: "Practice is the sole criterion of truth." Although the discussions yielded practically nothing of theoretical value, they marked a decisive step toward the rediscovery of man in contemporary China by triggering a "Thought Emancipation Movement" that spread the message of independent thinking across the entire country. This message was communicated by Hu Jiwei, former chief-editor of the Communist Party's organ, "The People's Daily," in an article entitled, "Tinghua? Butinghua?" ("Listen to the Party's Words or not?"). Hu confessed: "As one accustomed to listening to the Party's words, I began to awaken gradually after experiencing ten years [of] painful internal Party strife. But it was not until the discussions of the criteria of truth that I was awakened and began to question the truth of this principle."[47]

The Chinese term *tinghua* carries the connotation of children conforming unquestioningly to their parents' bidding. It corresponds precisely to what Kant termed "self-inflicted immaturity" or the "incapacity to use one's own understanding without the guidance of others," terms Kant used in his famous definition of the Enlightenment. While Chinese scholars ritualistically claimed "great breakthroughs" as a result of the discussions,[48] what was more significant was the further reawakening of reason.

The humanist quest pressed on. Wang Ruoshui, standard bearer of "Marxist humanism" in China, asked: "If practice is the sole criterion of truth, what then is the criterion of successful practice?"[49] His answer, "the needs of man," was as simple as the question itself, and in turn encouraged "discussions on humanism and alienation." The major issues of this debate were: does human nature have an independent existence of its own apart from its "class nature"? Does "alienation" exist in socialist society, and how do these issues relate to Marxism? In sum, does man exist apart from being a tool of the

Party? Whereas the discussions on the criteria of truth marked the emancipation of man's intellect or ability to think independently, the humanism discussions marked the emancipation of man himself, man with his own intellect, his own will, emotion, dignity, and value. Man, denied his own independent existence, now reemerged. To quote Dai Houying again:

> I finally walked out from my role and discovered myself. I am indeed a human with flesh and blood, love and hate, with various kinds of desires and emotions, a human with an ability to think. I should have my own value as a human being and should not be deprecated and denigrated willingly into a "servile tool [of the Party]."[50]

Wang Ruoshui ended his famous article, *In Defense of Humanism,* on an optimistic, confident note:

> A specter stalks the earth of China.
> "Who are you?"
> "I am Man."[51]

With the establishment of Man, the next question was: What is his essence? What is the structure of his inner world? What are his moral sense, his aesthetic sensibilities, his quest for the transcendent, and his ultimate concern? Where do all these come from? These were the major issues of the "subjectivity trend" dating from 1980 forward, the third major intellectual engagement in the post-Mao era. The discussions on subjectivity were a logical development of the discussions on humanism. Li Zehou, the trend's undisputed initiator, asked: "Now that most people have agreed that human nature is different from class nature, what then is human nature?"[52]

Li defines subjectivity as "the existence, strength, and structure of humans as a supra-biological species with special emphasis on the psychological structure of man's intellect, emotion and volition."[53] The subjectivity trend explored the inner strength and structure of man. This approach took the subjective initiative and autonomy of man as its point of departure, and aimed at the full realization of the infinite strength and creativity of man. The exploration of subjectivity constituted the bulk of the philosophical discussions in mainland China during the 1980s. Discussions of how we know, what is beautiful, what is ethical, what is creative all led to a quest for the transcendent that could be roughly charted as follows:

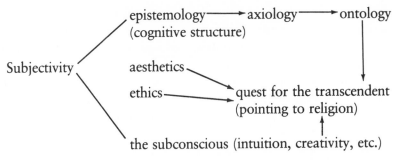

A large number of articles exploring each of these subjects appeared, testifying to the vigor and zest with which Chinese intellectuals explored the vast inner universe of man. Perhaps because the issues were shrouded in Marxist terminology, they were ignored by most foreign scholars.[54] Few were aware that a fundamental shift had occurred in Chinese consciousness. By 1986, the humanist quest manifested in the form of the subjectivity trend had invaded literary criticism and then spread to history and the social sciences. One scholar rightly noted in 1987: "In the last few years, you can hardly open a philosophical or theoretical journal without finding some discussion of subjectivity."[55]

The fourth and perhaps the most spectacular intellectual event in this redefinition or reconstruction of Chinese consciousness was a great debate on culture from 1984–1989.[56] The "culture fever," as it is popularly referred to in China, started with a revival of the study of premodern Chinese traditional culture. It spread quickly to a comparative study of Chinese and Western cultures and of the theories and methods of cultural analysis. In 1985, the focus turned to the modernization of the Chinese culture. "Whither Chinese culture" became the central theme. Over 1,500 articles were published; several new journals were founded; and over twenty centers for cultural study were established across the country. The "fever" spread from the academic to the official world and finally to the general public. The debate was revitalized by the controversial miniseries *River Elegy (Heshang)* in 1988[57] and then fed into the Protest Movement of 1989.

Although culture constituted the central theme of the debate, it was man's subjective world that engaged the major attention of the participants. What preoccupied the debaters' minds were the subjective structures of ideas and values, which inform and shape the intellect, affection, and volition of man. The key topics of the debate included world views, modes of thinking, value systems, moral judgments, aesthetic sensibilities, and "ultimate concern." Culture was primarily seen as "sources of the self."[58] The debate took the rebuilding of man and the rebirth of the national soul as its focal issue. If the discussions on humanism rescued man from the tyranny of personality cult and the subjectivity trend explored the structure of man, the debate on culture breathed life into the Chinese soul with ideas and values derived from various cultures, ancient and modern, Eastern and Western. Through self-assertion, self-exploration, and self-fulfillment (the humanist quest of the new intellectual discourse), a new soul was nurtured by a new culture. The goal reemerged in the long search for China's soul.

There are, of course, other intellectual trends in the new discourse apart from that represented by the humanist quest. The most influential among them is what has been called the scientific trend. The discussions of the feasibility of applying natural scientific methodology to the study of humanities constituted the fifth major intellectual event in the post-Mao era. Many Chinese scholars saw a dichotomy of scientism versus humanism.[59] This dichotomy, however, is largely a methodological one. Jin Guantao, for example, the most influential initiator of the scientistic trend, explained that in the past twenty years of his philosophical exploration, epistemology and methodology were only "the beginning of the reconstruction of the edifice of rational philosophy," the peak of which is "the value, the meaningfulness, the ultimate concern of human life."[60] Jin warmly "welcomes the awakening of humanism in the whole nation as a sign of the emergence of a new culture."[61] He stresses the importance of the modernization of man. He does not object to the principle of subjectivity. Rather, he insists that "the specific subjectivity of modern man should express itself" in "scientific rationality."[62]

The tortuous search for China's soul involves nothing less than the exploration for the destiny of man. This quest has momentum and cannot be easily stopped, even by tanks and guns. Despite its large and political implications, it will try to maintain its autonomy as an intellectual discourse.[63] The focus of the quest may change, the approaches to it may differ, the attention it draws may vary. But the quest will go on, simply because the destiny of man, the probing of his soul, will be a perennial concern for mankind. Put in a historical perspective, could the humanist quest in post-Mao China, together with the new intellectual discourse that has emerged, be seen as a harbinger heralding the advent of the transformation of China's soul?

## ACKNOWLEDGMENT

I am indebted to Edward Friedman for his help in putting this article in its final form.

## ENDNOTES

1 "Soul" is used here to mean the vast inner universe of man (used in its gender neutral sense of humanity), including the functions of thinking (intellect), willing (volition), and feeling (affection).

2 For calling the event the Protest Movement rather than the Student Movement or the Democratic Movement, see Geremie Barmé and Linda Jaivin, ed., *New Ghosts, Old Dreams* (New York: Times Books, 1992), xvii.

3 Leo Marx, *The Pilot and the Passenger* (New York: Oxford University Press, 1988), x.

4 Yan Fu, *Yan Jidao shiwenchao* (*Selected essays and poems by Yan Jidao*) (Wenhai chubanshe), 52.

5 Liang Qichao, "Zongguohun an zai hu?"("Oh, Where Now is the Soul of China?"), *Qingyi Bao*, vol. 5 (Yukohama: Qingyi Baoguan, 1899), 2138.

6 Ibid., 2139.

7 Julia Ching, *Probing China's Soul: Religion, Politics, and Protest in the People's Republic* (New York: Harpers and Row Publishers, 1990).

8 Xiao Jefu, "Renwenyi yu minzuhun" ("The humanistic *I* and the national soul"), *Xinhua wenzhai* (Beijing) (5) (1992): 168.

9 "The Living Tree: The Changing Meaning of Being Chinese Today," *Dædalus* 120 (2) (Spring 1991).

10 Jean-Jacques Rousseau, *The Confessions* (New York: Penguin Books, 1953), 17.

11 St. Augustine, *Confessions* (New York: Oxford University Press, 1991), 281.

12 Rousseau, *The Confessions*, 17.

13 Liu Zaifu, "Xinshiqi wenxue de zhuchao" ("The mainstream of New Time literature"), *Wenhui Bao* (Shanghai), 10 September 1986.

14 Julia Ching, *Probing China's Soul*, 51.

15 Ba Jin, *Suixiang lu* (*Random Reflections*) (Beijing: Renmin wenxue chubanshe, 1991), 727.

16 Ibid., 273.

17 Ibid., 756–57.

18 Ibid., 366.

[19]Ibid., 731.

[20]Ibid., viii.

[21]Ibid., 315, 313, 323.

[22]Ibid., iii.

[23]Barmé and Jaivin, *New Ghosts, Old Dreams,* 64.

[24]Sun Yu, "Cong *Suixiang lu* kan zhongguo wenren jingshen" ("The mentality of Chinese literati as reflected in *Random Reflections*"), *Xinhua wenzhai* (November 1991): 210–11.

[25]Ba Jin, *Suixiang lu,* iii.

[26]Ibid., 366.

[27]Gong penchen, "Pin Liu Xiaobo *Mori xingcunzhe de dubai*" ("Comments on Liu Xiaobo's *The Monologue of a Doomsday's Survivor*"), *Shibao zhukan* (Taibei) (42) (1992): 82–83.

[28]Liu Xiaobo, *Xuanze de pipan: yu Li Zehou duihua (The critique of choice: a dialogue with Li Zehou)* (Shanghai: Shanghai renmin chubanshe, 1988), 13.

[29]Liu Xiaobo, "Qimeng de beiju: 'wusi yundong' pipan" ("The tragedy of Enlightenment: a critique of the 'May 4 Movement'"), *Wenhua yanjui* (Beijing) (2) (1989): 80–83.

[30]"Guanyu xinshiqi wenxue pingjia de taolun" ("Discussions on evaluations of New Time literature"), *Feitian* (3) (1987).

[31]Liu Xiaobo, *Xuanze de pipan,* 9, 2.

[32]See Guo Guocan, "Jindai shanli sichao shulun" ("An analytical survey of the 'pro-vital force' trend in modern China"), *Ershiyi shiji,* June 1992.

[33]Wang Junren, "Shixi xiandai xifang lunli sichao dui woguo qingnian daode guannian de chongji" ("A preliminary analysis of the impact of contemporary Western ethical thought upon the moral ideas of the youth of our country"), *Zhongguo shehui kexue* (2) (1989): 14–15.

[34]Liu Xiaobo, *Mori xingcunzhe de dubai (The Monologue of a Doomsday's Survivor)* (Taibei: Shibao wenhua chuban gongsi, 1992), 8–10.

[35]Liu Xiaobo, "Xingershangxue yu zhongguo wenhua" ("Metaphysics and Chinese culture"), *Xinqimeng* (Shanghai) (1) (1988): 72.

[36]Liu Xiaobo, "Wo kan shenmei" ("Aesthetic experience as I see it"), *Wenyi zhengming* (5) (1988): 4–5.

[37]Liu Xiaobo, "Xingershangxue yu zhongguo wenhua," 72.

[38]Liu Xiaobo, *Monologue,* 9. All this, of course, does not deny the continuity between Liu's earlier thinking and the thinking expressed in his new book. One can still see much of Nietzsche's image in his new book, although it is now a broken one. Besides, Liu never totally rejected confession. Once he even praised the "unreserved pouring of one's inner world with the upmost piety under God's watching eye. No matter how evil a man's soul may be, a sincere confession is always pure." See Liu Xiaobo, *Xuanze de pipan,* 201. As a disciple of Kafka, Liu

may well regard his confessions as only one of the endless Sisyphean efforts to transcend oneself, an example of the absurdity and cruelty of life itself. Liu's philosophizing is sometimes self-expressive, more emotional than logic. "I am destined to be nailed by puzzlement on broken painfulness and even madness," he declares in his new book. See Liu Xiaobo, *Monologue*, 67.

[39]Ibid., 36–38.

[40]Liu Zaifu and Lingang, "Chanhui yu daode liangzhi: wenxue yu chanhui yishi (diyi zhang)" ("Confession and moral conscience: literature and consciousness of confession, Chapter One"), *Zhishifenzi* (New York) (Winter 1992): 66–80.

[41]Paul A. Cohen suggested the term "humanist quest" rather than "humanism" to cover the shared assumptions of the discourse. The former is an intellectual and moral aspiration that involves a set of unresolved issues on the destiny of man, whereas the latter refers to a variety of more or less well-defined theories that stress the priority of man. I am also indebted to him for "self and culture" in the title of my forthcoming book, *Self and Culture: An Interpretive Survey of the New Intellectual Discourse in Post-Mao China, 1978–89*.

[42]Wang Yuanhua, *Chuantong yu fanchuantong* (*Tradition and Anti-Tradition*) (Shanghai: Shanghai wenyi chubansche, 1990), 174.

[43]There were some minor exceptions, such as the well-known debate on aesthetics in the 1950s and 1960s.

[44]I am indebted to Benjamin Schwartz for this term. It refers to the gradual and mostly unconscious erosion of the individual as an independent existence. For an analysis of the process see Liu Zaifu, "Lishi jiaose de bianxing: zhongguo xiandai zhishifenji de ziwo mishi" ("The metamorphosis of historical roles: the self-dissolution of intellectuals in modern China"), *Zhishifenzi* (New York) (Autumn 1991); and Jin Guantao and Liu Qinfeng, *Xin shiritan* (*The new Decameron*) (Taibei: Fengyung shidai chuban gongsi, 1989), 109–34, 231–332.

[45]Lu Keng, "Ren a, ren! Zhai tianya—Dai Houying yinxiang ji" ("Man! Oh, Man! at the end of the world: an impression of Dai Houying"), *Wenxing* (Taibei) (4) (1988): 37.

[46]Wang Ruoshui, "Ren de nanchan" ("The 'dystocia' of Man"), *Tansuo zazhi* (5) (1992): 26.

[47]Hu Jiwei, "Tinghua? Butinghua?" ("Listen to the Party's Words or not?") in Yu Guangyuan and Hu Jiwei, eds., *Mengxing de shike* (*The moment of sudden awakening*) (Beijing: Zhongwai chuban googsi, 1989), 253.

[48]Feng Peiwen, "cong luxian de da zhuanzhe dao lilun de dai tupo" ("From a sharp turn in [the Party's] line to a great breakthrough in theories") in Yu Guanyuan and Hu Jiwei, eds., *Mengxing de shike*, 32–70.

[49]The question was raised by Wang as early as May 1980 at a meeting sponsored by *Guangming ribiao*. See Wang Ruoshui, *Wei rendaozhuyi bianhu* (*In defense of humanism*) (Beijing: Sannian shudian, 1986), 74.

[50]Lu Keng, "Ren a, ren! zhai tianya—Dai Houying yinxiang ji," 37.

[51]Wang Ruoshui, *Wei rendaozhuyi bianhu*, 233.

# 188  *Tongqi Lin*

52Li Zehou, *Pipan zhexue de pipan* (*The critique of the philosophy of critique*) (Beijing: Renmin chubanshe, 1984), 422.

53Ibid., 429, 422, 424.

54An exception is Bill Brugger and David Kelly, *Chinese Marxism in Post-Mao Era* (Stanford: Stanford University Press, 1990).

55Wang Pengling, "Mianxiang zhuti yu kexue" ("Facing subjectivity and science"), *Zhongguo shehuikexue* (Beijing) (3) (1987): 68.

56The beginning of the debate was variously placed at 1982, 1984, and 1986. See Guo Qiyung, "Guan yu jinglai zhongguo wenhua he zhongxi wenhua bijiao yanjiu de pinjie" ("A review of a recent study of Chinese culture and a comparative study of Chinese and Western culture"), *Renmin ribao*, 13 January 1987; Chen Lai, "Bashi niandai 'wenhuare' de huigu yu fansi" ("A review and reflection on the 'cultural fever' in the 1980s"), (forthcoming); and Chen Kuide, "Wenhuare: beijin, shichao ji nianzhong quingxiang" ("Cultural fever: its background, intellectual trends, and two tendencies") in Chen, ed., *Zhongguo dalu dangdai wenhua bianqian* (*Cultural change in contemporary China mainland*) (Taibei: Guiguan tushu gongsi, 1991), 39–40.

57A radically antitraditionalist television miniseries. It is probably the most popular and controversial one in the short television history of China.

58For an example of the study of the interaction between cultural-intellectual strands and the shaping of the ideals and interdicts of the self, see Charles Taylor, *Sources of the Self* (Cambridge, Mass.: Harvard University Press, 1989).

59See, for example, Wang Pengling, "Mianxiang zhuti yu kexue"; and Chen Lai, "Sixiang chaoliu de san dongxiang" ("The three new orientations in currents of thought") in Gan Yang, ed., *Zhongguo dangdai wenhua yishi* (*The cultural consciousness in contemporary China*) (Hong Kong: Sanlian shudian, 1989), 581–87.

60Jin Guantao, *Wede zhexue tansuo* (*My philosophical explorations*) (Shanghai: Renmin chubanshe, 1988), 49–51.

61Zhang Yaohung, "Heshang yu dongxifang mianlin de tiaozhan: Jin Guantao yu Richard Madisen de duihua" ("River Elegy and the challenge for East and West: a dialogue between Jin Guantao and Richard Madison") in Sanlian Shudian, ed., *Lunnian de beicang* (*The pathos of the Year of the Dragon*) (Hong Kong: 1989), 147.

62Jin Guantao and Liu Qingfeng, *Xin shiritan*, 351.

63For a balanced view of the distinction and relation between ideology and *xueshu shixiang* (i.e., intellectual discourse as it is used here), see Yu Yingshi, "Yishixingtai yu xueshu shixiang" ("Ideology and intellectual discourse") and "Zailun yishixingtai yu xueshu shixiang" ("Additional comments on ideology and intellectual discourse") in Yu Yingshi, *Zhongguo sixiang chuantong de xiandai quanshi* (*Modern interpretation of Chinese intellectual tradition*) (Taibei: Lianjing chuban gongsi, 1987). For a personal reflection on how to achieve the difficult task of striking a balance between academic detachment and personal involvement, see Tu Wei-ming, "Wang Yang-ming's Youth: A Personal Reflection on the Method of My Research," *Ming Studies* (Fall 1976): 11–18.

*Perry Link*

# China's "Core" Problem

C HINA HAS BEEN EXPERIENCING an economic boom in recent years. During most of the 1980s, as markets advanced and central planning retreated, the gross national product grew 9 to 10 percent annually.[1] It grew 12 percent in 1992.[2] Foreign trade has grown even faster; by 1991, China's foreign exchange reserves equaled those of the United States.[3] The economy's nonstate sector (including cooperatives, family and individual enterprises, and joint ventures with foreigners) has come to produce about half the country's industrial product, and it continues to grow rapidly.[4]

Since 1989, when protest movements were violently suppressed, these economic trends have continued alongside a major political clampdown that has stifled overt dissent. But the repression today is very different from the repression during the Maoist period. Central authority then was strong enough to have its way in nearly every corner of the country; dissent, even in private, was extremely dangerous. Now, with the moral authority and political power of the center much diminished, local work units and governments are far more independent than before. Ideological pronouncements from the center are commonly accepted at a rhetorical level but ignored in practice. As the economy has moved increasingly into private markets, so, in fact, have any number of political arrangements. Burgeoning corruption accompanies the barter of power at every level. At the highest level, the grand bargain that Deng Xiaoping has temporarily forged between himself and the Chinese people can be seen as the ultimate example of power brokering. Deng's message is clear: economic reform, yes; political reform, no. So long as you make no move that could threaten the highest level of leadership, you are free to make money.

*Perry Link is Professor of East Asian Studies at Princeton University.*

Some Western analysts, especially those who defend Western business interests and the policies of the former Bush administration, have argued that Deng's economic policies have put China on the right track, and in more than just the economic sense. They predict that wealth in China will lead, as in other societies, to the creation of a middle class, a modern "civil society," and hence to political liberalization as well. This prediction cannot be faulted so long as it is understood as pointing to certain effects that will weigh among many others. But to press the case more strongly than that reflects an optimism that is either ill-informed or—in the case of business interests—sometimes self-serving. The prospects for an early transition to a modern civil society in China are far from clear.

The same release of controls that has allowed the Chinese economy to grow has also made space for a variety of serious problems: corruption is practically taken for granted; crime rates, including those for robbery and murder, have risen sharply; prostitution has returned and is flourishing again; in some areas a market has developed in kidnapped peasant women and children; and fraudulent products and services have appeared in the marketplace.[5] School dropout rates have risen as state investment in education has continued to decline. Young people have become *liumang* (hoodlums) in increasing numbers. A "floating population" of people from the countryside who have flocked to major cities in search of work now number about fifty to seventy million nationwide. Unplanned and unchecked development in some areas is rapidly pushing China's already strained natural environment toward the brink of disaster.[6] Reflecting on all this, Liu Binyan, China's famous investigative journalist, uses the Chinese word *xie* (bedeviled, irregular) to characterize much of Chinese life today.

Many of these mushrooming problems can be understood as the filling of a vacuum left by the retreat of Communist power. At its Maoist height, that power reached everywhere in Chinese society, structuring all public values, meting out severe punishment to those who did not conform, and destroying many of the values and nearly all the institutions that had formerly filled the space between the state and the individual. People conformed under a pervasive pressure that emanated from the top. The longer this great pressure lasted, the less necessary were family, clan, and religious values in shaping social behavior. Consequently, those values and institutions withered.

Eventually, even personal integrity suffered. Now, as state power retreats and people leap toward "freedom," the distinction between freedom and license is sometimes lost. In celebrating their escape from authoritarian controls, people sometimes assume that whatever they do beyond those controls must be all right. This is not only a Chinese problem. The same kind of morality-vacuum is visible in Eastern Europe and in the former Soviet Union where the collapse of Communist authority has been even more abrupt than in China. Thus Václav Havel, looking at the Czechoslovak society emerging from decades of oppression, speaks of "an enormous and dazzling explosion of every imaginable human vice."[7] And, in Russia, *The New York Times* reporter Craig Whitney finds that ". . . values, as well as buildings, fall into decay. A year after the end of the Soviet Union, anything goes in Moscow."[8]

A fundamental question for China today is: What values and institutions can help to restructure a civil society within the current vacuum? A revival of family, clan, and religious practices as they existed in the early twentieth century? More modern associations, perhaps based on specific occupation? Certainly a modern legal system could help, but neither China's current legal system nor the level of understanding of modern civil law among the populace is anywhere near sufficient for law by itself to answer the tremendous need.

The most "Chinese" answer—originally a Confucian one, but after centuries of custom now so deeply rooted in Chinese culture that it tends to appear almost reflexively—would be to pursue some kind of moral education. People should be taught to behave properly and be subject to moral criticism if they do not. In imperial China, when the system worked properly, state officials were chosen for their learning and had a special obligation to behave correctly. Although China developed a considerable history of corruption among officials, this history was paralleled by an equally long history of popular moral condemnation of corruption. The eighteenth-century novel *Rulin waishi* (*Unofficial History of the Scholars*) spiritedly satirizes the corruption and hypocrisy that began to appear in the officialdom of the Qing dynasty at its height. In the early twentieth century, when the Qing was tottering, the novels *Guanchang xianxingji* (*Panorama of officialdom*) and *Ershi nian mudu zhi guai xianzhuang* (*Strange scenes witnessed over twenty years*) were even more cutting in their indictment of official corruption. There were other such novels in the Republican period. Post-Mao "scar" literature in the early 1980s was in many ways a similar outpouring of criticism of officials who betrayed their duty to act morally. At Tiananmen in 1989, official corruption was the most broad-based issue. No slogan was more popular than "Sell the Benzes to Pay the National Debt."

In the money-first ethos that has prevailed recently in China, the underlying cultural values of education and proper behavior have seemed to recede. But it would be naïve to suppose that such a long tradition has suddenly disappeared. Moreover, the continuing satire on official corruption, which remains lively and common in China's oral network of gossip called *xiaodao xiaoxi* (alleyway news), confirms the persistence of popular moral indignation. But indignation, of course, must rest on positive values. In order to judge certain behavior to be improper, one needs at least a hazy concept of what proper behavior is. The problem in China today is that there is no publicly accepted set of moral values to define proper behavior. Intellectuals speak today of a *sixiang weiji* (crisis of ideology) and even a *jingshen weiji* (spiritual crisis). The gap is especially discomfiting because of the traditional role that moral ideology enjoyed in China.

## THE TRADITION OF AN ETHICAL-IDEOLOGICAL CORE

During most of China's imperial history of the last thousand years, explicit Confucian guidelines were available. Set down in writing and widely accepted, they were assumed to be valid all the way from the personal level to affairs of the empire. *The Great Learning*, a seminal Confucian classic used in civil service examinations beginning in Song times (960–1279), explained how a person's moral power, rooted in learning, could benefit the rest of society. The success of ancient rulers, according to this classic work, originated in their "investigation of things," which led, in orderly sequence, to "thoroughness of understanding," "sincerity of will," and "personal cultivation." Cultivation, once it had taken root in character, led to a power that could, in turn, "regulate the family," "properly govern the state," and finally "bring peace under all of heaven." This theory—understood as true not only of ancient rulers but of all civilized human beings—found institutional expression in the civil service examination system, where scholars were tested for their mastery of classic texts and literary skills as a measure of whether their cultivation warranted appointment to public office.[9] Scholars began their study of the classics by internalizing them in the most blunt manner—rote memorization. Their highest aspiration was to reach the level of giving advice to the emperor.

Tersely put, the basic tenets of this outlook were that morality was inscribed in publicly venerated texts, could be absorbed by individuals through study, and could then take root in personal character and radiate outward—to family and community—eventually to reach "all under heaven" via service to the Son of Heaven, the highest ruling authority. When working properly, the system defined what it meant to be Chinese, and justified the individual's pride in being so. These several notions comprised a seamless continuum, without the "disciplinary" boundaries taken for granted in the modern West. Were modern scholars of literature, ethics, sociology, and political science to travel to the China of four hundred years ago, they would be viewed as quaintly narrow specialists working on different aspects of the same thing.

The Confucian notion of proper behavior is, moreover, essentially a human ideal, not just a Chinese one. People other than the Han Chinese can learn it. In popular conceptions of their own history, Chinese see themselves as conquering barbarian invaders by civilizing them. Caucasians who study Chinese have noticed that the more they speak and act in a Chinese manner, the closer they come to being accepted as Chinese (even if it remains impossible to go the whole way).

During the twentieth century, Confucianism lost its place as China's state ideology and became the target of deliberate attack.[10] Nevertheless, scholars of twentieth-century China have often noted the persistence, under both the Nationalists and the Communists, of cultural assumptions about the proper place of ideology. Even Maoism, while vastly different from Confucianism in content, and although pressed into every corner of Chinese society with a non-Confucian virulence, inherited many assumptions about what an ideology should do. Ironically, these parallels to tradition were clearest during the Cultural Revolution when Mao was trying to be most radical. Maoism was, first of all, written down in authoritative texts: *The Complete Works of Chairman Mao*, the shorter *Selected*

*Works of Chairman Mao,* and the pithy *Quotations from Chairman Mao.* The texts were publicly venerated, memorized by the young, and assumed to contain a morality that could transform personal character (producing "new Socialist Man"), be a guide to practical behavior, conduce to service of the larger society, and associate the disciple with the highest ruling authority. The whole result also stood as a claim about what is distinctive and exemplary in being Chinese. Even Mao Zedong's presentation of a "revolutionary model" to the Third World, and his eagerness to distinguish this model from the errant example of the Soviet revisionists, may be seen as a reassertion of the claim that China should be the place where the best way to conduct human affairs (not just Chinese affairs) can be observed and emulated. Many Chinese intellectuals today, while repudiating Mao completely, continue to feel vaguely but profoundly that something is askew if China cannot be a good example.

Since the mid-1970s, Maoism has declined steadily. But underlying notions that Chineseness should entail a moral aspect, and that this aspect ought to color a broad range of social life, continue to appear in claims from the political center. When the Deng Xiaoping regime mounted campaigns against "spiritual pollution" in 1983 and "bourgeois liberalization" in 1987, it painted a wide spectrum of behavior with a single brush. To question party leadership, to expose social problems, to write modernist poetry, to wear bell-bottom trousers, to watch pornographic videotapes, and to murder taxi drivers were all, in the rhetoric of these two campaigns, presented basically as mutations of a single problem: improper behavior. Wang Zhen and other conservative ideologues actually used the phrase "un-Chinese" to cover this wide variety of transgressions.

Chinese intellectuals, despite their profound alienation from the regime and its rhetoric, continue to share with the regime certain fundamental assumptions about China: that it is a unique place, worthy of special respect, where—if everything were right—propriety would be exemplified. Such assumptions are held so deeply that neither side, that of the regime nor that of the intellectuals, normally takes much notice of this rare area of agreement. The same notions of China's primacy extend deeply into the popular culture as well. What sustains these views so powerfully? They certainly grow in part from an awareness, preserved both in written and oral tradition, of the glories of China's past. Chinese who live in the physical settings of ancient events often speak of them as if they happened not very long ago, and as if they obviously still have relevance. The poet Qu Yuan, who drowned himself in the river Miluo in 289 B.C. after vainly remonstrating with his king, is still a model of integrity for contemporary Chinese intellectuals. In Hangzhou, people still spit on a statue of the traitorous minister Qin Kui, who died in 1155. In a vaguer and much more general sense, people seem to bear in mind that the dust in which Confucius and Mencius trod—together with Laozi, Zhuangzi, the first emperor of Qin, Liu Bang, Zhuo Wenjun, Sima Xiangru, Zhuge Liang, Wang Xizhi, Tao Qian, Wang Wei, Li Bai, An Lushan, Wang Anshi, Mi Fei, Zhu Xi, Wang Yangming, Cao Xueqin, and countless other singular thinkers, poets, artists, calligraphers, statesmen, rebels, courtesans, and warriors—is, whatever else happens, *this* dust, which cannot be the same as any other.

In addition to consciousness of history, the Chinese language itself provides another, even more constant, reinforcement of deeply-embedded notions of propriety, dignity, and Chineseness. Some of the most common phrases in ordinary Chinese prompt people to judge the morality or propriety of behavior according to a public standard set in language. For example, outlandish behavior can be described as *buxiangyang* (not resembling the pattern) or *buxianghua* (not resembling [proper] words). The simple phrase *ni shuo de hen hao* can mean either "what you said is good" or "you said it well." (Chinese people have no trouble distinguishing these two meanings when they want to, but in common use the phrase means both, without the question of a distinction ever arising.) To correct a false statement, ordinary Chinese allows *bushi neme shuo de* (that is not the way you say it). The word *xue*, often translated as "study" or "learn," originally means "imitate" or "emulate," and is still often used in that sense; to learn something, at least at the beginning stages, is to train oneself to conform to a proper pattern. Communist jargon has drawn heavily upon the moral-performative underpinnings of ordinary Chinese language, for example in the use of *biaoxian* (performance, literally surface-showing) in measuring the political correctness of a person's overt speech and behavior.

In short, habits of language, memories of history, and other cultural tendencies continue to ask that a publicly-accepted moral ideology play a role in Chinese life. But what is that ideology today? Confucianism was explicitly repudiated in the early twentieth century. By the 1990s, Marxism-Maoism has fallen even lower than Confucianism in popular acceptance. Yet, while ideologies have slipped out of daily life, the space they have left remains and begs to be filled. Here and there one can observe signs of continued Chinese yearning for a distinctive moral-social-political core.

### SHADOWS OF A CORE TODAY

In recent years there has been very little direct address of the "core" problem in Chinese political or intellectual life. It can be embarrassing, even painful, to admit that the problem exists. But if one listens for the assumptions that undergird discussion of more discussible topics, it is fairly easy to see that this large question animates a wide variety of other concerns, and is at work among a broad spectrum of men and women in Chinese society. Both the highly educated and the barely educated—both the regime and its critics—show clear signs of worry about it. I offer below six examples, chosen to illustrate the wide variety of contexts in which the core problem arises indirectly.

*An Old Method.* In early 1989, a distinguished Chinese historian in Beijing told a story about how his parents had fled the Japanese during World War II. In the fall of 1944, the fighting had approached to within two days of Chongqing, their temporary home.

> I asked my parents what they would do if the Japanese really arrived. My father just looked out the window at the Yangzi River and said, "We Chinese have an old method." I panicked when I realized what he meant. "But what about *me*?," I asked. I was in high school then. My father answered, "If such a day really comes, can we still care for you?"[11]

Although the historian went back forty-five years into the past for his anecdote, his point was to illustrate the timeless and exalted nature of Chinese patriotism and to signal his own loyalty to it. He felt that, with the dramatic decline in the moral prestige of the Communist movement, the younger generation of Chinese was in danger of not properly grasping this important cultural value.

*Four Little Dragons.* Shortly after China opened to the world in the late 1970s, many Chinese—especially along the southeastern coast and in the major cities, but elsewhere as well—became strongly attracted by the economic and technological development they saw outside. They felt that China had fallen terribly behind, and their admiration of foreign places was tinged with envy. On the fringes of China they observed the rise of the so-called "Four Little Dragons" of South Korea, Taiwan, Hong Kong, and Singapore. These three words ("four," "little," and "dragons"), while at one level comprising a mere catchphrase, have deeper connotations.

"Dragon" implies China. The populations of Taiwan, Hong Kong, and Singapore are predominantly Han Chinese; South Korea, although not Han, clearly falls within the China-centered, originally Confucian, culture of East Asia. "Dragon" further suggests not only China but august China, spiritually worthy China. Even the young rebels at Tiananmen in 1989 called themselves (after the lyrics of a Hou Dejian song) "children of the dragon."

But the four dragons are "little"—or, as the word *xiao* can also mean, "young." However advanced South Korea, Taiwan, Hong Kong, and Singapore may be in certain ways—however able to help China in such matters as technology, expertise, and capital—none of them is, or ever could be, a replacement for China proper. However decrepit and problem-ridden by comparison, China proper is still the principal dragon. Its superiority is not only in size but, ultimately, in nature—even if the only ground for this claim is an abiding confidence that this *ought* to be the case. In the end, there is something absurd about even comparing a place like Singapore with China. The two exist on different levels.

The word "four," besides counting the little dragons, also has a certain effect of pigeonholing them within a China-centered constellation of language. Especially in the Communist period, numbers have often been used to put things, good and bad, in their proper places: The Gang of Four, The Four Modernizations, and so on.

*Four Basic Principles.* Since the late 1970s, the Deng Xiaoping regime has found it necessary to anchor itself with "Four Basic Principles": *1)* the socialist road, *2)* dictatorship of the proletariat, *3)* leadership of the Communist party, and *4)* Marxism-Leninism-Mao Zedong Thought. To a Westerner this list of four looks redundant. For an ordinary Chinese, the same redundancy, added to the basic irrelevance of the principles to most of daily life, makes it unlikely that a given person on a given day will be able to recite all four. Even among hard-liners in high positions in the Chinese government, the four principles are not analytically distinct and have little daily-life relevance. Their role is to loom hazily overhead as spiritual capital, to invoke, as necessary, in support of conservative crackdowns (such as the massacre of June 4, 1989). What is noteworthy, for our present inquiry, is that the leadership feels it necessary to set down such principles and even to write them into the preambles of the country's post-Mao constitutions. After all, conservatism and brute force are available whether or not such an act of inscription is performed. But without a well-situated text, the claim of a moral basis for action would seem less secure.

*People of Strong Will.* In the United States in 1990, a group of dissident Chinese organized a "Center for the Research of Contemporary China." Their founding manifesto called for "people of strong will" to "offer themselves to the great mission" and "resolutely struggle for Chinese democracy." If a few of the document's key words were replaced with words drawn from the Four Basic Principles, there would be little to distinguish its style from a Communist Party text—or indeed, from a manifesto of the Republican Revolution of 1911. The lofty call to dedication and sacrifice for the sake of a greater China resonates especially with language used by the Communist Party and the Guomindang when they were young. Others among China's contemporary dissidents, both at home and overseas, have worried about the problem of escaping the mind-set of official language. Why, they ask, do we use the guerrilla-war metaphor *xiaomie* (annihilate) when encouraging friends to finish what is left of a few dishes on a dinner table? (Chinese from Taiwan and overseas do not use the term.) Why do we still overuse words that were favorites of Mao, such as *ji* (extreme) and *zuizui* (most, most)? Have decades of accepting Maospeak as China's official, publicly acknowledged, and morally proper language instilled habits that we cannot shed even when we want to do so?

*Qigong.* As Marxism-Leninism-Maoism declined through the 1970s and 1980s as a seat for Chinese identity and pride, a variety of things, many of them popular and originally pre-Communist, appeared as partial alternatives. Rural China has seen a resurgence of *yiguandao*, a moral-religious sect that arose in the early twentieth century and was repressed after the Communist revolution in 1949.

In the cities, there was a dramatic rise through the 1980s of the practice of the physical-spiritual art called *qigong* (breath exercise, but also implying skill with *qi*—a mysterious, and distinctively Chinese, substance and/or force). Stories have arisen about *qigong* masters who can see through walls, make tables levitate, cure disease, and the like. *Qigong's* appeal extends beyond the popular level, to government officials and even elite intellectuals. A distinguished literary critic in Beijing told me in early 1989 that he was skeptical of *qigong* until, one night on a lawn at a conference site outside Beijing, a *qigong* master emitted invisible rays that caused his head to lurch involuntarily to one side and the other. A young physicist, who doubted this story, commented that "*qigong* answers. . . the need for a fortress around our Chinese self-respect, a place that will always be safely Chinese, whatever else happens."

*Backed by a Strong China.* A Chinese scholar who came to the United States in the 1940s, and who had a full academic career in this country, is now living in retirement in New York. Despite his many attachments to his adopted country, he has never felt entirely American or 100 percent accepted as such. He has always had a wish for a "strong China" to be his backing. For many years, McCarthyism and the Cold War prevented him from openly expressing this need. But, instead of killing the need, the Cold War pressures only drove it to a more intensely personal level. In the fall of 1989, in discussing the Tiananmen massacre, he commented that "at least [the party leaders] could make the army obey. That's better than the Chinese government could do in the 1940s." I have no doubt that this statement was sincere and deeply felt. But I am also confident that his siblings and cousins in Beijing, some of whom I know personally, would find such a statement utterly repugnant. For several days in May of 1989, they and most other citizens of Beijing were hoping precisely for the opposite—that the troops on the outskirts of the city would refuse to obey orders to open fire. (I present this example in order to demonstrate that the same China-centered values can sometimes produce extremely different views on current issues. I do not mean to suggest that the professor's view represents the mainstream of overseas Chinese opinion on the massacre, which clearly is not the case.)

The six preceding examples, because they are so disparate, may seem a poor basis for generalization. But their very diversity can also suggest that whatever commonalities do emerge are likely to be fairly deep-seated ones. In such a brief essay, I choose this as a shortcut for making a broader point. My contention is that the historian in Beijing and the professor in New York, for all the differences of their situations, share a deep reverence for China, a concept of its uniqueness, and a wish to be proud of it. Their ideas are rooted in the 1940s, but the 1990s talk of the "Four Little Dragons" implicitly reflects very similar assumptions among the many people in the cities and coastal provinces who use that phrase. The tiny group of senior leaders in Beijing who care about the "Four Basic Principles" also proceed from such assumptions, and add to them China's ancient notion that principles of social morality should be written down in authoritative texts. The political opponents of those senior leaders, while in one sense differing adamantly, embrace the same notions of China-uniqueness, morality, self-sacrifice, and texts. When state-sponsored definitions of Chinese identity fail, popular alternatives such as *yiguandao* and *qigong* arise to fill some of the space where an identifying core should be.

THE INNER VOID

A new or revived identifying core for China, if it can emerge, will probably need to resemble earlier ones. It will need to define what is right in social relations, be accorded widespread assent, be considered universally applicable, and perhaps be inscribed in texts. These are all public features that the Chinese have traditionally wanted in their ideologies. But the public side is only half the picture. For individuals, a sense of emptiness within can be as much of a problem as the lack of external symbols. In the early 1990s, Chinese intellectuals have been discussing the current "thought vacuum." A young Chinese historian, speaking in Beijing in early 1989, said, "I feel a need for something to hold on to, a *zhichidian* (point of purchase); I think many of us feel this way; it may be the special weakness of Chinese intellectuals, but we need this." This young man was unusually articulate; yet, he is undoubtedly correct to guess that his problem is not unique to him. Broadly conceived, it is not unique to intellectuals either. Many kinds of Chinese feel the need for the "point of purchase" he refers to.

The ideological crisis today can be viewed as an exacerbation of a problem that began when the impact of the West began to upset the Chinese world a century and a half ago. A leading Chinese sociologist, also speaking in 1989, put it this way:

> Why do you think China's direction zigs and zags so much? Why are there so many policy reversals? Yes, of course, it is partly because the Communist leadership is continuously torn among factions. But fundamentally the phenomenon is much larger. The whole country is frantically searching for a way out, and has been for many decades, even before the Communists. We're like a big fish that has been pulled from the water and is flopping wildly to find its way back in. In such a condition the fish never asks where the next flip or flop will bring it. It senses only that its present position is intolerable and that *something* else must be tried. We intellectuals complain a lot about the influence of Soviet-style dictatorship in China. But originally, the "Soviet path" was also just one of the flops of the fish, an effort to find a way to save China.[12]

The metaphor of a "path" or "road" (the socialist path, the capitalist road, and so on) has often been used in the Communist period to label alternative policies for development. The problem in the early 1990s is that, other than "make money," no road is clear. Many people, whether looking outside or peering within, come up empty. The Four Basic Principles? Repugnant to many, these seem at best to be a sickly shadow of what an official ideology should be. Democracy? For some the word generates genuine hope, but the concept remains poorly defined, ill-understood, and, because it is an import, raises questions about "Chineseness." *Qigong*? The Chineseness is solid, and the pride of ownership effective, but can something so narrow (and possibly superstitious) take the place of a proper Chinese ideology? A revival of Confucianism? There are advantages here, as the Four Little Dragons seem to demonstrate. But can there be a full return to Confucianism? Is that not "turning the wheels of history backward"? In recent years, Christianity has spread rapidly in China, with the number of believers rising to perhaps as many as thirty million.[13] But a faith of foreign origin, no matter how useful in personal life, would need considerable Sinification before it could play a role that entails definition of unique Chineseness.

A bedrock definition of Chineseness can always rest on ethnic identity. In ordinary usage, the Chinese term *zhongguoren* (Chinese people) normally means the Han people or other ethnicities that physically and culturally resemble the Han.[14] Responsibility to remain worthy of China's glorious past is the boon and burden of today's "descendants of the Yellow Emperor." In recent years, the Communist government, increasingly lacking any other moral capital, has made a noticeable effort to channel popular nationalistic sentiment toward support of itself. The concepts of nation, state, and party have been conflated in official rhetoric; by innuendo, those who disobey the party are unpatriotic and even un-Chinese. Some intellectuals worry that such rhetoric could give shape to popular frustration and lead to a resurgence of nativist xenophobia of the kind that underlay the Boxer movement in the late nineteenth century. But even apart from a danger such as this, a strictly ethnic understanding of Chineseness seems, especially to the intellectuals, uncomfortably narrow. It slights the moral dimensions that traditionally have been essential to China's understanding of itself.

Lacking a sense of "path" today, where can Chinese turn to seek one? By cultural habit, many look to their national leadership for cues. But in 1993, Deng Xiaoping provides only the puzzling slogan, "Develop the Socialist Market Economy." These words, if taken in the senses in which the Communist movement has trained the Chinese people to understand them, are flatly contradictory. Instead of explaining the contradiction, Party Chairman Jiang Zemin and other top leaders avoid the question by vaguely crediting Deng with attaining a new high level of theory.[15] Most people—certainly including those who are most busy "developing the socialist market economy"—give the slogan a perfunctory nod and then ignore it. Those who try to take it more seriously are perplexed. According to reports, Professor Xie Wanying of Beijing University, a Marxist economist, leapt to his death on October 30, 1992 after uttering the words, "Socialist market economy. . . ?!"[16]

As a short-term ideology, "make money" does have some advantages for China. First, no one can gainsay the benefit of more wealth for a poor country. Despite the boom in China's coastal provinces, many in the hinterland still live in dire poverty. Second, the Chinese cultural penchants for family-based enterprise, saving, and investment (which are so obvious in Chinese communities outside the People's Republic) make the get-rich policy both popular and effective. Third, the policy allows the Chinese people at least one kind of freedom. Many who were eager for "democracy" in 1989 are now willing to bide their time on that front while turning to the current opportunity for money-making. This opportunity seems doubly urgent when people recall the history of sudden and unpredictable policy reversals under Communist rule. When might the green light for money-making turn red? Should we not grab what we can until then? It is thinking like this far more than happiness with the current regime that explains the political quiescence in China since 1989.

But as an answer to the problem of an inner core, "make money" can be only a stopgap. It leaves deeper and inevitable questions on hold: To what do the moral implications of the Chinese language, including much of daily-life language, now refer? What is proper behavior? What makes China distinctive?

To look at the rapid modernization in China's "special economic zones" such as Shenzhen, one can wonder whether the traditional problem of a Chinese core might not just erode away in the universal solvent of modern commercial culture. Such a speculation gains plausibility when one looks at Chinese families in the West, where second generations seem rapidly to abandon the China-centered preoccupations of their elders. Some Chinese intellectuals argue that such erosion might be a good thing. Does China really need, in the modern world, another moral-social-political-cosmological core both to set it apart and to hold it together? Do such ideologies do more harm than good? Would it really matter if China drifted apart to some extent? Does the protection of national pride bring benefit or does it waste resources, for example, when the political leadership spends precious funds on the Asian Games and the Olympics—instead of education and health care—or on a huge, world-record-breaking dam in the Yangzi Gorges, when smaller dams would bring more benefit at lower cost?

Yet many, whether explicitly or not, still lean toward preservation of a core. Morality, propriety, and public service seem self-evidently desirable. The fear of "chaos"—which many fear would be the result of a full ideological breakdown—is deep in the modern Chinese mind. And there remains the issue of Chinese pride. Is the twentieth century to mark the end of China's history as a unique and exemplary place? (China has absorbed major outside influences before, such as Buddhism and the Mongol invasion, without dislodging the notion of a core of Chineseness.) If modern international culture does indeed become the first force in history to dissolve China's notion of its moral uniqueness, that process will, at a minimum, take decades or centuries to finish. Before then, the core problem will remain.

ENDNOTES

[1]Jim Rohwer, "China: The Titan Stirs," *The Economist* (28 November 1992): 3 after p. 62. Kang Chen, Gary Jefferson, and Inderjit Singh, "Lessons from China's Economic Reform," *Journal of Comparative Economics* 16 (June 1992).

[2]Nicholas Kristof, "China Builds its Military Muscle, Making Some Neighbors Nervous," *The New York Times*, 11 January 1993.

[3]On trade figures, see PRC State Statistical Bureau, *Zhongguo tongji zhaiyao 1991* (*Chinese Statistical Abstract 1991*) (Beijing: 1991), 3, 5, and General Agreement on Tariffs and Trade, *International Trade 1989–90* (Geneva: GATT, 1980). On foreign exchange reserves, see CIA, *The Chinese Economy in 1991 & 1992*, Booklet EA 92–10029, August 1992, quoted in Roderick MacFarquhar, "Deng's Last Campaign," *The New York Review of Books* XXXIX (21) (17 December 1992): 26.

[4]Sheryl WuDunn, "As China's Economy Thrives, The Public Sector Flounders," *The New York Times*, 16 December 1991.

[5]For example, there have been several reported cases of low-grade—sometimes even poisonous—alcohol substituting for expensive liquor, of artificial milk powder for infants, and of imitation fertilizer that actually damages the soil onto which it is spread.

[6]Loss of arable land because of topsoil erosion, desertification, and urbanization is already a critical problem that is made all the more difficult by a huge and still-expanding population. Air and water pollution are at critical levels as well. In Guangzhou, the water of the Pearl River is not potable even if boiled, because of industrial pollution. In Beijing, on a winter day, the air is an average six times more polluted than on the same day in Los Angeles. For an overview of China's environmental problems, see He Bochuan, *Shan'aoshang de Zhongguo* (*China on the Edge: The Crisis of Ecology and Development*), trans. Jenny Holdaway, Guo Jian-sheng, Susan Brick, Hu Si-gang, and Charles Wong (San Francisco, Calif.: China Books and Periodicals, Inc., 1991).

[7]Václav Havel, *Summer Meditations* (New York: Knopf, 1992), 1.

[8]Craig R. Whitney, "Where Values, as Well as Buildings, Fall into Decay," *The New York Times*, 26 December 1992.

[9]Readers unfamiliar with Chinese history should note that the role of the civil service examinations as summarized here describes an ideal, not the actual record of the system, which suffered various corruptions and discontinuities along with periods of success during its roughly thirteen centuries of existence.

[10]Major examples of the attacks on Confucius came during the May Fourth Movement of 1917–1921 and the Cultural Revolution of 1966–1976. See Chow Tse-tsung, *The May Fourth Movement: Intellectual Revolution in Modern China* (Cambridge, Mass.: Harvard University Press, 1960) and Merle Goldman, *China's Intellectuals: Advise and Dissent* (Cambridge, Mass.: Harvard University Press, 1981), especially chap. 6.

[11]This and other illustrations in this paper are drawn from my book, *Evening Chats in Beijing: Probing China's Predicament* (New York and London: W. W. Norton & Co., 1992).

[12]Taken from an interview with the author. These series of interviews were conducted with the understanding that names would not be revealed.

[13]At the revolution in 1949, when foreign missionaries were expelled from China, the number of Christians in China was about three million. It is an irony worth noting that, in the end, Communist rule has spread Christianity in China much faster than the missionaries could.

[14]Chinese government ideologues would dispute this statement. For them the term *zhongguoren* properly applies to all citizens of China, including Mongols, Uighurs, Tibetans, Uzbeks, and others of the approximately 7 percent of the Chinese population who are not Han. But, although both the Communist government and the Nationalists before them have pushed this understanding of the term, and although the political and academic elite has gone along, the usage has not caught on among most Chinese, who still understand *zhongguoren* to mean a Han or someone who might be taken for a Han. Use of the term *huaqiao* (overseas Chinese or Chinese abroad) is even more illuminating on this point. It goes without saying in China that a Han who emigrates to a place like Vancouver becomes a *huaqiao*. Were a Chinese Uzbek to move to Samarkand, he or she would not merit the term *huaqiao*; even a politically correct Chinese would find such a usage startling. Moreover, just as strong as the concept that overseas Chinese are necessarily Han is the converse notion that overseas Han are necessarily "Chinese"—not, for example, American or Canadian. My wife is an ethnic Han born and raised in Massachusetts. As a girl she once argued with her mother that, "I'm not Chinese, I'm American." Her mother replied: "Go look in the mirror." My mother-in-law, like everyone's, is unique, but in this regard she represents a norm.

[15]See Jiang Zemin's report to the Fourteenth Congress of the Communist Party of China, *Foreign Broadcast Information Service*, Chi-92–196-S, Washington, D.C., 8 October 1992.

[16]*China Forum* (Berkeley, Calif.) 2 (10) (December 1992): 4.

David E. Apter

# Yan'an and the Narrative Reconstruction of Reality

*Death is the sanction of everything that the storyteller*
*can tell. He has borrowed his authority from death.*
                                        —Walter Benjamin
                                        "The Storyteller"

FICTIVE TRUTHS AS SELF-FULFILLING PROPHECIES

PEOPLE MAKE STORIES OUT OF EVENTS. They do so individually and collectively. Recounting individual stories makes for sociability. Collective stories have political consequences when, as myths they purport to be history, as history they are reinterpreted as theories, and as theories they make up stories about events. Theories that become stories create fictive truths. In politics, truthtelling and storytelling are part of the same process by which it becomes possible to interrogate the past in order to transform the future.

Of course, the degree to which this is so varies with time, place, and circumstance. By examining an extreme example of what may be called political storytelling, one can see how fictive truths of the kind we have in mind are generated. Our illustrative case is the Yan'an period (1936–1947) during the Chinese revolution or what will be referred to as "Mao's republic." It demonstrates how stories generate theories and how theories are transformed in the telling, the resultant combination serving as self-fulfilling prophecies (proofs of the cor-

David E. Apter is Henry J. Heinz II Professor of Comparative Political and Social Development at Yale University.

rectness of the theory or line). The same principles are relevant in less remarkable circumstances where discourse leads to power, and power is transformed into hegemonic texts.

A good story in itself, Yan'an was a discourse community. Its formation was a consequence of stories told, theories constructed, and the collectivization of both in a "mytho-logic." It includes a sleight of hand, and the transposition of individual to collective stories and from narration to texts. To make such a transposition requires a storyteller who is able to induce individuals into conveying their personal and recounted experiences to the collective one as an act of conveyance. By such acts it becomes possible to generate what has been called *symbolic capital* as an alternative to more conventional modes of power, the end product of political mytho-logics.[1] In its present usage, symbolic capital represents collective experience as an endowment of meaning from which individuals can draw for their own enhancement. In this sense, collectivization in the form of symbolic capital constitutes a fund of power available to individuals which appears to enlarge their powers. It is less a form of entitlement than "enablement"; it enables the overcoming of the self through participation in a collective project.

Like virtually all great political ideologists, Mao Zedong was a great storyteller, especially during his Yan'an days when he and his associates combined storytelling with truthtelling. They were able to draw from individuals the materials which formed a collective mythology. In turn this mythology was made to yield higher truths, a theory textualized as a dialectical logic. By this means a discourse was constructed which separated "insiders" from "outsiders." It established a boundary around Mao's followers within the Chinese Communist Party (CCP, founded in 1921), and between the CCP and the Guomindang (GMD). Within this boundary, individual self-interest was broken down in favor of "collective individualism."

Collective individualism began to occur when an individual went to Yan'an. "Joining the revolution" was made a conscious and deliberate act in which one yielded part of one's persona to the collectivity. This was the first step in a reeducation process in which a careful reading of prescribed texts, a form of "exegetical bonding," made each person feel that he or she had transcended individual limitations, had "overcome" one's deficiencies, and therefore had gained more from the collectivity than one had given up. Mao's stories and theories offered a powerful sense of insight and interpretative power.[2]

## CONTEXTUALIZING THE STORIES

Mao was no ordinary storyteller. His stories were carefully contrived, and are repeated in various texts. They do not appear as stories, however, but as historical sequences which telescope into the other. There is a long story of the decline and fall of China and the loss of the patrimony; an intermediate one which is the struggle with the GMD; and a short one, the bitter internecine conflicts between lines and factions within the CCP. The shorter the story, the more closed down the optic, the bigger the image, and the smaller the field until Mao virtually fills the entire field of vision.[3]

This condensation and intensification of the image of Mao in Yan'an took place over time, saturating the field with new meaning, which was essential in the process of generating symbolic capital. In Yan'an, three stories were constructed, each representing a different aspect of loss: the displacement of the peasant from land and community; the decentering of China and its replacement by outside forces; and the dismemberment and loss of imperial control. These contributed to an atmosphere of generalized violence, warlordism and banditry, civil and imperialist war, and throughout the country a generalized condition of risk, high uncertainty, randomness, and unpredictability. Simply by connecting loss to remediation, the stories are ordering. They are interpretative devices, the ingredients of which point to a future. Yet as stories they are rooted in the ready-made experiences of daily life. In such narration, time is periodized and sensible sequences are formed, each of which is a surrogate for a modified (sinified) Marxist theory of a marginalized peasantry around which is constructed an inversionary discourse. If the underlying theme is an old one—the last becoming first, the slaves becoming the masters—there is, in Marxist terms, a difference. Peasants cannot be the class of the future. In the end they remain the idiots of rural life. They are a class with radical chains, not the class to universalize itself, as was the designated role of the proletariat under classical Marxism. However, if the peasantry is an insurrectionary class, this defines the role of the party which is to embody the revolutionary idea. The CCP is the product of these stories. It serves as both the agent of history and the surrogate of "truth": A "party of truth" imposes cognitive controls as an agent of history. By joining such a party, one converts his or her own vulnerability into power and control by reducing "the complexity of the encountered environment."[4]

Violence offers ample opportunity for storytelling. It generates despair and yearning. People come to believe that only drastic solutions will work, that any authority is better than none, and that the available ensemble of would-be leaders are wanting. (They succumb to corruption. They kill too many people. They demand too much and deliver too little.) Such conditions are on the whole propitious for totalizing cosmocrats, those who successfully create their own political cosmos, whether political, religious or both, and who in a context of high uncertainty retrieve myths of a golden past and project the logic of a millennial future. When a politics of yearning rapidly goes from despair to redemption, it exorcises cynicism, opening the way for the kind of innocence which favors extremism.

These circumstances prevailed when Mao took command of the CCP, making his extremism sound reasonable. He confronted burdens for which others despaired of finding acceptable solutions. His interpretive logic resulted in the reconstitution of power within a symbolic and redemptive moral order. In Yan'an, Mao's storytelling became an act in itself, an assertion of control over violence by means of a first ordering of mind over circumstance.[5] So considered, storytelling and theory construction were part of the same enterprise. Their raw materials were the negative experiences being transcended. What began as a bricolage ended in a system of ideas, a theory. The combination, formed into a discourse, offered the necessary intersubjectivity for collective individualism, where each person appeared to become or believe him- or herself to be the real or potential beneficiary of another's experiences.[6]

Using this terminology Mao's version of Marxism and the fictive truths and the theories he articulated were assertions of cognitive control. His accounts of the decline and fall of imperial China, the revolution of 1911 against the Qing, and the warlordism and chaos which followed describe a remarkable increase in the complexity of the encountered environment. Sequence, cause and effect—the normal expectations and predictions people make in their daily lives—

were increasingly disrupted. Mao's recounting in narrative form makes sense of the disorder. Each of the stories represents a different overcoming project: violence in society, violence over who will control the state, and violence over who would control the Party. The resulting synthesis is what can be called symbolic capital, the only form of capital accessible to Mao and crucial in the consolidation of his political power.

Along with the deliberate cultivation of such capital, Mao transformed himself from an essentially military figure to a cosmocratic one, from a kind of Odysseus wandering in exile to a Chinese Socrates in full possession of logic and word. The point of transition was the period from 1941 to 1943 during what was called the Rectification Campaign. Twenty-two texts were selected for study, the process beginning at the top of the hierarchy of institutes, schools, universities, and training centers that constituted the core of Yan'an. Under a system of exegetical bonding, Yan'an became a totalizing and tutelary political system.[7] The process involved a deliberate choreographing of narrative and text into a ballet of fictive and logical truths which, one might say, made Yan'an the true model of Maoism (to reappear in monster proportions during the Cultural Revolution).

THE PRECONDITIONS OF STORYTELLING

Rectification was an enforced process of sociation by means of a language to be learned enabling demons to be exorcised. The stories were transformed into a single unified mode of expression in the face of an otherwise randomized universe. A deliberate and highly contrived ordering process, it located particular targets surrogate for or expressions of violence and chaos. Order was collective; it contrasted with conditions where it was each and every person for him- or herself and where that condition could be shown to be counterproductive. Self became a definition of anarchy.

Stories or narratives about such events mythologized experiences, providing validity to explanations which then appeared to be empirical. In such circumstances, myths of collectivized and symbolic capital produce structures of coherence. The universe becomes more predictable through intelligible acts in conjunction with others, i.e., a collective moral strategy. In Yan'an, cause and effect were restored as

interpretation and understanding, and interpretation and understanding generated cause and effect.

How can this jump occur where conflict is persistent and where
central authority appears to have disappeared? If one's starting point
is the individual then the more chaotic one's situation is, the less likely
people are to trust one another and to act in mutual concert. What we
witness in Yan'an is a way out of this dilemma. There, in a particular
refuge, a "republic of the caves," and, indeed, in a condition of what
might be called revolutionary Platonism, an inversionary discourse
was created which enabled each individual to engage in it by
recounting, telling his or her personal story in conversation with
others, and thus making sensible sequences out of fortuitous events in
the temporary sanctuary of what became a mobilization space.

People, however, must want to listen. The conversation needs to be
interesting or one quickly is considered a bore. What Mao did was to
establish the conditions for a compelling conversation, for that form
of dramatic embellishment, which in the act of recounting made for
a recognizable sociability of the human group. But he did not draw
his account out of thin air. He made sure it corresponded to the
stories individuals told each other. Individual and collective storytelling went hand in hand. On an individual level it enabled people to
learn from each other, to recognize typical situations, and to try to
anticipate and head off potentially bad situations. It was the kind of
storytelling, although private, informal, and part of one's persona
that was also public and by its very nature intersubjective for a person
who tells stories only to him- or herself—like an artist whose
paintings are never seen by anyone else. It is a definition of solitude.

Stories became ritualized through repetition both on an individual
and collective level. People established a renditional formula using
exactly the same words, phrases, and expressions. The same events
were repeated in much the same sequence. So too with Mao's
renderings. The richer and more complex the stories, the more
symbolically layered they became, and the greater their capacity to
control.

What kinds of individual stories did people tell each other, and
from which was Mao able to generate collective ones? Here is a
characteristic "tale" recounted in one form or another by many of the
Chinese citizens interviewed from 1986 to 1989 in the People's
Republic. It involves the second or third son or a daughter of a poor

peasant who has been deprived of his or her plot because of death, or indebtedness, or natural catastrophe and the lack of support from the landlord or the community. They describe the circumstances of the decline of the family, the failure of the uncle to help out, and the negative effects of such circumstances on one's own personal situation. The starting point is ground zero in the concrete sense of the term: no land, absolute poverty, minimal opportunity. The story is first about sheer survival: leaving home, being bonded or sold, etc. It personalizes such predicaments—the uncle who steals the widow's small amount of money, and how Landlord Han confiscates the last bit of rice while his own family is provided with luxuries and his eldest daughter is sent away to school. The children of Landlord Han do not work; the children of Widow Li work for nothing and starve.

In Mao's hands such individual tales were made prototypical. Like every good storyteller, the recounting generated both an intimacy and a familiarity of the situation. Everyone knows a version of such a story and many have had similar experiences. Such familiarity adds to its reality. Like music, to know the tune is to enjoy it even more. The Widow Li and the Landlord Han are generalized surrogates for a great many individual experiences while the individual experience endows the surrogate with the flesh and blood of direct knowledge. This endowment is facilitated not only by repetition but by replication in plays, in opera, and in dance. Collectivization in this sense depersonalizes Widow Li and Landlord Han by making them into surrogates of a total history, while the individual versions make the abstracted ones visually and symbolically compelling. Landlord Han may represent the cruelty of China's decline and Widow Li the marginalized peasantry, especially as a helpless woman, but at the same time everyone knows them both as neighbors.

Collectivization begins when a storytelling agent knows that the behavior of Landlord Han is not due to his individual personality but is a consequence of larger forces: the violation of China by outside imperialists—British, French, American, and, of course, the Japanese—who want to colonize China as a whole. Personal insecurity, tenancy, and the spread of violence are seen as necessary properties of compradore capitalism, that is a form of capitalism where an intermediary acts on behalf of a foreign company in his or her native land. In very concrete ways the story opens up the space for a dialectical logic about the systematic nature of imperialism, semifeudalism, and compradore capitalism. The collectivized story is both a symbolic statement and a theoretical *Aufhebung*—a conversion.

All cosmocratic political leaders share the ability to make the individual "give" his or her story to the collective, to its leader. However, since this is also an invitation to lose part of one's mind, teasing this out of individuals requires that something be given in return. To accomplish such a conveyance, individual stories need to reinforce rather than dilute the collective while the collective must add more than it detracts from one's sense of self.[8] Collective storytelling has to convince people that giving over their stories *enlarges* their minds, and by so doing they will better understand, see more, and create collective individualism.

Lifting the burden of storytelling from the shoulders of the individual by enabling that person to share it with others is an act of *communitas*, an act of cognition or an "imagined community" as Benedict Anderson refers to it.[9] Required, however, is an agent who can assume in political terms a role, vis-à-vis the collectivity, between the theocrat acting for divine will and the psychoanalyst who represents agency for the individual. In this sense, storytelling is a catharsis touched with mystery, a cathartic narrative which reduces the need for and the urgency of the individual story as a drive. One might say that by such acts of cognition, the "property" of the story becomes the "property" of the discourse community.

This brings us back to our Yan'an story. The Rectification Campaign established the authority of Mao as the agent. Its object was to induce people to give a piece of themselves by conveying their stories to the collectivity. What they gained was a resignification of the events of their own experience, superior insight, and wisdom—a theory of truth open only to those "inside," but available to all who come inside.

If someone continued to have private doubts, and most people retain such doubts no matter how passionately they affirm the opposite, revealing those doubts in public was a critical factor. The confession of private doubt in a public manner, repeated as often as appears necessary, is a method of exorcism. If Mao's rise to power depended on his ability to set the terms of storytelling, his most intense conflicts were with those among the truest believers who claimed the same exorcising rights/rites. Against these enemies he had to establish himself as the sole authority. Eliminating rivals not only as individuals but as surrogates for a party line with its own story and its own logic was a necessary condition. Only then would party members be able to draw from the collective more than they contributed to it. Good storytelling, therefore, must establish a truth capable of enlarging the individual; the act of conveyance to the agent is in a sense an act of appreciation, even homage. To the extent that exorcising private doubts depends on faith induced by a logic, Yan'an had to represent Mao and Mao represent Yan'an.

Through parables and stories people were taught to make comprehensive inferences from circumstances and shrewd judgments about strategy and tactics. Both individual and collective narration followed a fairly standardized pattern, from situational beginning to identified obstacles, the defining of a negative pole to be transcended, a testing period, a logic of accomplishment, and a positive pole. Intertwined are themes of struggle, defeat, persistence, and arrival at some defined end point. At each point, individuals can insert their individual stories into the collective ones. So doing is an act of "reenactment" which enables the individual to convey and integrate his or her own experience into the more generalized versions. Yan'an represents the field of force for mass conversions with Mao as the agent. We now turn to the question of how Mao became an agent in the first place.[10]

## MAO AND THE STORYTELLING TRADITION

It must be remembered that storytelling is itself an old story in China. Wolfram Eberhard has shown how the Chinese Communists deliberately cultivated the folklore tradition (including overtones of Hunanese banditry from which Mao claimed putative descent):

> Conversely, the popular traditions which portrayed peasant revolts and uprisings, from Huang Ch'ao's insurgence in the T'ang dynasty to the anti-Japanese war, perfectly suited the party's needs, and were encouraged. They were the stuff of reality not fantasy. Cognizant of his rise to power through a people's revolution resembling bandit revolts of the past, Mao gave status to the study of bandit lore. He himself had accepted the support of bandit forces in his uphill struggle with the militarily superior Guomintang armies and pursued bandit practices in marauding the rich landowners and the service corps of the Nationalist forces to feed his own followers. In the epic Long March of 1934 Mao

and his Communist troops retreated from Kiangsi through the vast stretches of western and northwestern China, and swore blood brotherhoods with the wild Yi and Lolo tribes occupying the area. When Mao came to power he stimulated a review and reinterpretation of peasant insurgence from the late Han to the late Ch'ing dynasties.[11]

The model figure is Confucius who based his convictions on the retrieved and shared memory of a golden age of tranquillity in the Chinese kingship of the early Zhou dynasty (1027–256 B.C.). He blended this

> memory with a *conception* of the good socio-politico-cultural order— which he already finds envisioned in the *Book of Documents* and the *Book of Poetry*. When positive memories based on experience are fused with conceptions of an achieved normative order found in the sacred literature, one can readily understand the all-inclusive idealization to which this may lead.[12]

Just as Confucius defines the space for the cosmocratic storyteller, Mao defines this space for himself in Yan'an.[13] His stories were designed to unify a culture otherwise divided between a population which was largely illiterate and powerless and a thin and powerful sliver of teachers, bureaucrats, and literati. In the past, the body of myths, legends, and stories, while representing a common cultural inheritance and an infinite plunderable recourse, were also part of the great divide between illiteracy, orality and storytelling in the classic sense, literacy, and written texts. As performances, activities, and in content, they reinforced as a fault line in society asymmetries of power and political hierarchy. They represented more or less fixed patterns of deference in the ordering of rank, by "ordering" a universe of peasants, landlords, merchants, gentry, the Mandarinate, and the Imperial House. The stories represent the Confucian system of hierarchy, deference, and manner in the home and in society, with honor a function of rank, prestige, and position. In turn, rank was associated with literacy, knowledge of the classics, connoisseurship, and artistic mannerism. As in other societies, class, taste, and distinction went along with power.[14]

Mao drew on both oral tradition and literary narratives. From the vast storehouse of China's myths and folktales carried down by voice through generations or "enscrolled" as literary texts, he selected those with inversionary themes, like the *Romance of the Three*

*Kingdoms* or the *Water Margin*.[15] These stories cut across the hierarchy. He identified previous truthtellers, often in the form of military strategists, or wise emperors, to bridge the gap between the illiterate and the literate. He was simultaneously the wise man of the oral tradition and the sage of the written one. He embellished the oral stories with the force of a scholarly tradition with well established criteria of aesthetic refinement. In his hands, traditional culture now combined the popular and the refined while eliminating them as differentiations of class or as in Max Weber's treatment of Mandarins, of *Stand*.[16] In taking possession of them, like the emperors of preceding dynasties, he rewrote history according to his own needs and interests, fully expecting that his versions would become endowed with a truth value. This tradition was crucial insofar as Chinese "history" was always mythmaking, and not the "historians history" of the professional as the term is understood today.

What then could be culled from that tradition? There were, for example, founding myths which began with the overcoming of chaos and the creation of the world through a series of magical events. There were myths in which a peasant warrior could become an emperor. All were a common property, defining both the boundaries of the Han community and its interior culture. They gave clan names to the insiders, and in every way marked them off from alien tribes (Yi, Tibetans, etc.) and distinguished them from foreigners. The events included dynastic wars, military conquests, peasant rebellions, and Robin Hood-like outlaws performing remarkable deeds.[17]

Mao also created a communist story of the descent of Marxism from Marx and Engels, through Lenin, Bukharin, and Stalin to Mao himself as putative descendent. The finger of communist history thus points to Yan'an as an inheritance bringing down to earth the more rarified reaches of Marxist thought and also the historical struggles of communist parties elsewhere, and not only the Soviet Union but also India and Indonesia and so on. In adapting general principles to local knowledge, he deliberately cultivated the view that he was merely a spokesman and not the founding figure of a myth, nor a moral architect, while in fact he was acting as both, so much so that Yan'an appears to be a center of light and Mao's stories seem luminescent.

Yan'an, in these terms, was the place where an authentically Chinese Communist political culture developed through embellishments of the three stories and their reenactment in plays and

theatrical performances. Mao was extremely sensitive to the importance of culture. He knew the propaganda value of *Protokult* during
the immediate postrevolutionary period in the Soviet Union. He also
knew that to make his stories into more than entertainment would
require the help of intellectuals of all kinds: writers, playwrights,
musicians, artists, translators, and philosophers. For example, Mao
began his Yan'an "talks" on literature and art as follows:

> You have been invited to this forum today to exchange ideas and
> examine the relationship between work in the literary and artistic fields
> and revolutionary work in general. Our aim is to ensure that revolu-
> tionary literature and art follow the correct path of development and
> provide better help to other revolutionary work in facilitating the
> overthrow of our national enemy and the accomplishment of national
> liberation.[18]

His own experience with gifted people had not been terribly successful. Like Stalin he was suspicious of the revolutionary ardor and
purity of intellectuals. Were not intellectuals generally regarded as
inconstant, and, as compared with other party members, too prone
to thinking for themselves? Too difficult to discipline? Though Mao
recognized, of course, that they were important in "broadcasting" the
appropriate cultural formula.

THE EMPIRE OF CLANDESTINITY

Mao began his storytelling in a preliminary way in the late 1920s and
early 1930s when a period of chaos prevailed and there was a
vacancy at the top both in China as a whole and in the CCP in
particular. In this latter instance, one might say that the cosmocratic
pedigree had shifted from Western Marxism to Russian, but had not
yet really arrived in China except in a putative way. This opened a
way for Mao to use the force of his Odysseus role to invent a Socratic
one similar to that of Lenin, but local in style. All previous Party
general secretaries from Chen Diuxiu (the "Herzen" of China) to
Wang Ming were "pupils" of Marxism, insufficiently presumptuous
to tinker with the corpus even though they could be fiercely divided
over how to apply it to China. But for Mao to claim to be a Marxist
theorist, he first had to establish his ascendancy over those better
prepared in the canon than he ever was, and also to innovate in ways

that made the spirit of Marxism stronger than the precision of its application. Mao's storytelling begins in his own wanderings.

Did Mao deliberately set out to tell stories? In general it can be argued that would-be cosmocrats feel themselves touched somehow by the gods, or simply feel a sense of destiny. So it was, for example, with Hong Xiuquan, God's Second Son and the leader of the Taipings, who had a vision, with miracles, precepts, stories, and an earthly prescriptive cosmology, in 1837 about establishing the Heavenly Kingdom on earth. Like any political figure, Mao needed examples and events in order to illustrate and if possible validate his preferred strategies as a "correct line." Mao became a storyteller precisely because of the practical need to establish his hegemony over others who claimed to be better Marxists than he, and an agent because he genuinely believed that he, better than others, saw the principle behind the event.[19]

He was able to address his audiences in such a way as to establish mutual confidence. Mao's audiences became complicit in his way of describing things. He was able to cast a spell in sufficient measure so that people would not only listen, but invest their time and energy into thinking about what he said.

The aspect of confidence in storytelling is of general importance; in China it was critical because of the political conditions prevailing prior to Yan'an. These have been described as a primal condition of chaos. But if they were extraordinarily vicious between the GMD and the CCP, they were even more so within the Party. The factional fighting was so bad, and secrecy and conflict so pervasive that we can call the pre-Yan'an period of the CCP an "empire of clandestinity," using the term "empire" to emphasize the spread of clandestinity as a conspiratorial way of life which reached out in every direction, in part spreading outward from the Soviet Union and penetrating downward from the highest levels of the GMD and the CCP.[20]

In the early period, Mao was not important enough to be involved with the mainstream of Soviet advisors, secret agents, commercial travelers, white Russians working for the Communists, and Communists who were really white Russians. When his influence increased, he reacted as soon as he could to prevent their direct supervision of his activities.[21] Major Party leaders were held on a leash by a Comintern representative: Maring for Sun Yat-sen, Joffe for Chen Duxiu, Borodin for Qu Qiubai, and Voitinsky for Li Lisan. When such a situation threatened Mao during the Long March, Otto Braun, the Comintern representative, was effectively repudiated.

Communist intrigue is only a part of the story. All the major foreign powers in China, not to speak of the Japanese in particular, engaged in a veritable orgy of spying on each other as well as on the different CCP factions, and the left and right wings of the GMD. They worked closely with Chinese secret societies (especially the Green Gang) and with the Shanghai underworld. This involved contacts between Chinese, French, British, American, and Japanese agents at every level. To protect themselves, the Communists required elaborate spying networks of their own operating within the Party as well as outside. Each side, the GMD and the CCP, sought to penetrate the others' organizations, the GMD for a time fairly successfully with their so-called "AB" (Anti-Bolshevik) squads. Investigation, accusation, recrimination, revelation, kidnapping, torture, and murder were commonplaces of politics in China, and to be expected if one became a CCP member.

But in the Party there was an additional problem. Because of continuous shifts in the Party line and fractional disputes of the most intense kind, exacerbated by mutual accusations of Trotskyism, the CCP begin killing its own adherents by the thousands.[22] Although this period is still closely guarded by the CCP, more information about it has become available. Perhaps the most notable event of this kind was the Futian Incident where rival factions, the Left led by Li Lisan (eventually put on trial in Moscow) and the Right by Li Wenlin (killed), clashed with those of Mao. Provincial loyalties (Hunanese against others) exacerbated the conflict in which many died. Not until Yan'an were such fratricidal struggles brought under control and the CCP came out of the underground into the relative openness of Yan'an. There, although not entirely, the killing stopped.[23] In a country so vast that it is difficult to comprehend, the life of a Communist was lived on the run, always with the temporary intimacy of others on whom his or her life depended. Not only a few were betrayed and handed over to the GMD for almost certain torture and death. To be in the Party, especially in the period from its founding until Yan'an, was to inhabit a world of dangers.

To be a vanguard professional revolutionary of the Party meant to belong to an intimate discourse community on a five-person group basis or cell system generating its own interior language. The combination gave the Party many lives. It could be weakened, parts of it destroyed, reduced in number, but no defeat had to be decisive. A good deal of Mao's storytelling glosses over this period except in the fairly stylized terms of key events which add to his credibility. Since the Party depended on the mobilization of a mass movement, especially over the nature of the struggle in urban centers versus agrarian ones and positional versus guerrilla warfare, it determined to a great extent not only the character of the Party, its idea of history, but its military strategy and tactics. Again and again the question was posed of how the Soviet experience was relevant to China. On the one hand, the Comintern kept a heavy hand on the novice Party. On the other, it imposed its own internal factional disputes from within the Soviet Union on China, most particularly over Trotskyism. By the same token, too much admiration for the Soviet model could be dangerous. The task of a would-be storyteller was extremely difficult. In order to be credible, the role requires a party to be both a product of history and a shaper of it. It means overcoming all contenders within the Party, and overcoming all contenders outside it as well. It was in the course of his personal struggle for power on both counts that Mao effectively transformed the Party into his own movement and generalized the movement as a discourse community, both using and redefining the nature of communism as laid down by Lenin and Stalin.

THE STORYTELLER AS AGENT

It is against this background that one needs to see the emergence of Mao. His rise to power is all the more remarkable if one considers that by the time he and his followers arrived in Yan'an, they were just a handful of survivors of the Long March, a small revolutionary band, one of the weaker among the armies of the Red Army as a whole. Joined by other survivors, the local guerrilla forces operated new Yan'an under Liu Zhidan, who had narrowly escaped death at the hands of a factional leader in the Red Army, and Gao Gong, who later committed suicide after being accused of being a traitor. The situation was itself rather miraculous with the Long March quickly becoming a legend. Not only did Mao outwit his arch rival for power, Zhang Guotao, but neither Mao nor his white horse (now stuffed and on view in the museum in Yan'an) were even wounded.[24]

Indeed, for the Yan'anites the Long March was as much a miracle as the crossing of the Red Sea for the Jews. Moreover, it placed Mao on a stage, and once there, he knew just what to do. He was a master of the second order of discourse. In public he rarely put his own ideas first. He preferred to listen, as one informant put it, "allowing others to make the mistakes." He used his position to summarize, integrating the ideas of others in such a way that although the substance was altered, it was done so in a manner agreeable to those who first made the remarks. In effect, the disembodied of voice of agency emerged with the shared experiences of the teacher, the one a spokesman, the other an author. Together they produced, to use Furet's terms, a "dramatization" of historical events and "novelization" of historical processes.[25] In this way he gave the impression that decisions were collective, while the twist he gave them merely expressed better the general sense of the meaning. He gave the impression too of being modest and deferential to the collective leadership. It gave him the advantage of a "theoretically" superior venue for his ideas.

Those interviewed, in fieldwork conducted from 1986 to 1989, who had known or remembered him during the Yan'an period, describe him as "looking the part of the intellectual. He dressed simply and could speak like a peasant, but he was really a teacher. I knew by looking that he was a presence and not a simple teacher."[26] People still comment with amazement at his ability to draw ideas out of the air and then recast them in a manner which made them seem so correct that every sane person would, sooner or later, have come to the same conclusion.

He also gave the impression of availability and accessibility, an impression which was quite false. He worked at night and slept a good part of the day, appearing in the evening at a performance, or at one of his meetings, or giving lectures at the Party school. It has been suggested that he was not a great platform orator with some describing his voice as squeaky and high-pitched. He spoke in an abominable Hunanese accent and much of what he said had to be translated into more understandable Chinese. His less adulating admirers note the flabbiness of his speeches, a lack of precision, and a lack of sureness about the point. All this changes, however, when his speeches were written and rewritten. It is hard to evaluate the relation between speaking and writing. People listening to his oral presentations already knew his writings. One might say that the *writ*-ualization process began early in the very muddiness of his original thoughts. His lack of precision allowed people to interpret his utterances as they preferred or as some inner voice struggling to express some higher truth, causing them to strain in order to hear and understand. He would then rewrite his utterances in ways that were clearer, earthy, and direct. As texts, reworked by himself and others, his remarks had force and pungency.[27] (The written word was broadcast and published with the printing press they carried on their backs during the Long March and installed in the cave of the thousand Buddhas, the highest point in Yan'an.) Some of those interviewed also characterized him as "like the first Ming Emperor" (a peasant who rose high enough to take power), as "basically a peasant," as "an intellectual," and more frequently than not, as a poet, classicist, and calligrapher, one person pointing out that he "could beat both the intellectuals and the gentry at their own games."[28]

When he transcribed events into social texts, con-*textualizing* them in terms of danger, a kind of purity emerged. "Voice" took on a certain ephemeral magic.[29] The relationship of orality to writing was the act of creating texts as *Writ*-uals, requiring listeners to become readers. Doing so put education at the center of the redeeming project—one which made it possible to redeploy people from units where old loyalties had been established into new units, more under the control of Mao. Men and women were made to puzzle over the meanings of those texts as a matter of life and death, a lesson properly learned was a life saved. In this sense, the kind of symbolic intensification that occurred in Yan'an inscribed and made significant the condition, location, space, architecture, and terrain. The sheer physical harshness gave a stark sense of reality to the discourse itself. The difference between Mao as a storyteller and those storytellers who were a featured part of Chinese society as far back and beyond what anyone could remember was that the old storytellers told stories that beguiled and instructed, weaving themes of mystery and charm into the drabness of daily life. Mao's stories stirred one to action, to anger, making people murmur among themselves. They conduced to thought by forcing the story to a logical instruction, one that had to be dialectically understood. If one began to listen, one began to learn.

Despite the difficulties of his accent, it is clear that he knew how to hold the attention of an audience, establishing a bond *between listeners* as well as with the speaker. Virtually every speech of Mao's began with a narrative which defined boundaries of time in terms of the stories themselves, compressing these boundaries into those of space, so much so that, unlike conventional storytelling where when the audience is dispersed the bond breaks, he continued to cast a spell. His storytelling seemed to summarize common knowledge, to establish a tie, a linguistic and experiential basis for a common discourse, punctuated with barnyard humor and classical allusion.

His speeches and writing retrieve and rework time. The past is both a golden age and a patrimony lost, a negative pole leading to a time of chaos and an overcoming project. Retrievals established the point of departure for a redeeming narrative, the platform on which to project and construct a millennial end, in short, a logic.

Mao liked to "authenticate" his stories from "below." Mao "listened" to "proletarian" writers who themselves came from the bottom ranks of society. He knew how to be an audience, an addressee, to act as a listener. In effect his strategy was to "learn" what he knew in the first place, "listening" for the answer he had already placed in the speaker's mouth by the way he posed the question. Well in advance of such conversations he had a clear idea of who would constitute the addressees—the audience. To be effective, listening had to be performative, an engagement of actions through words.

> The cadres of all types, fighters in the army, workers in the factories, and peasants in the villages all want to read books and newspapers once they become literate, and those who are illiterate want to see plays and operas, look at drawings and paintings, sing songs and hear music; they are the audience for our works of literature and art.[30]

This enabled him to prescribe what needed to be done from "above" by intellectuals, artists, and writers. "If you want the masses to understand you, if you want to be one with the masses, you must make up your mind to undergo a long and even painful process of tempering."[31] Knowledge was first to be derived from those on whose behalf it was formed.

### THE LONG, THE MIDDLE, AND THE SHORT OF IT

"All great storytellers have in common the freedom with which they move up and down the rungs of their experience as on a ladder."[32]

The point of departure in all three stories is loss. They recount China's inability to overcome the negative instance until near the end of the short story when the Communist movement changes into a Maoist one. The long story is about the decline and fall of China, the intermediate story is the conflict with the GMD, and the short story is about the internecine Party struggles and Mao's coming to power. In Mao's hands, each failure, military setback, evacuation of a base area, is reinterpreted theoretically. The Nanchang Uprising (1927) was a defeat, but it becomes the bench mark for the founding of the Red Army, that is Mao's army. The Autumn Harvest Uprising (1927) is a failure, but it is the first act of the agrarian rather than the proletarian revolution. In between these events is the Jinggaan Mountain hideout where, as a result of the defeat, Mao formed his peasant and bandit band and gave it substance as a guerrilla army. Later a major base would be established in Jiangxi, a Spartan community where the strictest communism was observed: land was confiscated and redistributed and a rigoristic equality was imposed. The Jiangxi base would later serve as the model for Yan'an.

As epic, drama, and passion play, the three stories deposited their mystique in a common fund. Each offers a different resonance adding layers of symbolic density to Yan'an as a simulacrum. Each is retrieved in speeches, used to illustrate texts. Running through them is a common theme, embodied and embellished by "political yearning."

Through such yearning people acquire political beliefs so powerful that it becomes urgent to discharge that power into political action, political energy seeking an outlet. Sacrifice and martyrdom add to the pleasure of action, the *jouissance*. Out of yearning comes the invented real, the fictive truth, the stories in all their palpable tangibility. All revolutions are in some significant degree phenomena of yearning. To make yearning politically significant is at the heart of the storytelling process. The long story by framing the intermediate one fits the large historic class struggle into a more immediate rivalry between the CCP and the GMD, pitting Mao against Chang Kai-shek. In turn this "frames" the internecine power struggles within the party, and makes conflicts between Mao and his contenders, Li Lisan, Wang Ming, and Zhang Guotao, deadly. Personalization and dramatic impetus build up as a result. Each is also self-contained with its own dramatic impact and force. Each provides a symbolic layer to the next, the short story being the most symbolically dense and therefore the most intensely experienced. Each introduces a set of actors, motivates them, personalizes them with dramatic presence in the story. Each defines a negative pole to be transcended and a positive pole to be realized, the distance between them defining a normative space. Each event takes on a double meaning: one metaphorical, an event interpreted as another, the other metonymical, the same event interpreted as a surrogate for Marxist theory.

Personalities count for a great deal in all of them. In the long story, there is that most remarkable Taiping leader, Hong Xiuquan, with his visions of God and Jesus, his texts which were to be in the hands of everyone and learned by heart, and designed to displace the imperial dispensations. In the intermediate story, the two major figures, Chiang Kai-shek and Mao, tower over the others, each with a coterie, an inner circle of acolytes high priests, and lord high executioners. In the short story, Mao emerges at the center, his party stalwarts steeled in many internal as well as external conflicts, most particularly Zhou Enlai and Zhu De but a host of others as well. As the stories come to an end in the person of Mao, they also come to the end of a great chain of "Beings."

Everything before the Opium Wars belongs to prehistory. The central theme of the long story is China's humiliation at the hands of imperialists.[33] The recounting of the loss of the national patrimony is outlined in a series of episodes which have both time and "seriality" on their side: the Anglo-French war on China (1856–1860), the Sino-French war (1884–1885), the first Sino-Japanese war (1884–1885), the eight-power allied invasion army at the time of the Boxer Rebellion (1900), the Russo-Japanese war in Manchuria (1904–1905), the Japanese Twenty-One Demands (1915), the Japanese invasion of Manchuria (1931), and the Japanese war (1937). The long story represents the fall from grace of the Chinese empire and marks the beginning of the revolution including the decline and fall of the Qing dynasty and the chaos that came after it. Its central event is the Taiping Rebellion, a popular and populist protorevolution. The long story is an epic by no means exclusive to the CCP. It is also the property of the GMD, one of the several mutual and intricate common bonds these enemies shared.

As for the historical dialectic, the episodes do not represent simple cause and effect. The first set are metaphors of violation, expropriation, and pollution. The second are metonymic with each episode signifying a different aspect of Marxist theory.[34] Together they constitute a "mytho-logical" accounting of the causes of the decline of China, its displacement as a national entity by imperialists, the transformation of a feudal society into "an alliance between external imperialism and domestic feudalism," a semicolony of which the Chinese revolution was the natural and dialectical result.[35]

The intermediate story, how to redeem China, is the main theme and in two contexts: imperialism in the form of the war against the Japanese and revolution against the GMD. It begins with the May Fourth Movement of 1919 and includes the founding of the Party as a direct consequence of that movement. Hence the CCP claims a dual pedigree, a sole right to represent the revolutionary heritage, as the only genuinely revolutionary party, and the May Fourth Movement, the movement for modernization in the name of science and freedom. It is thus a story about how the ideals of the movement and Sun Yat-sen, who is the central character at the beginning of the story, are thwarted by the GMD's ideas about how modern China is to be restructured and ruled. In turn, the struggle with the GMD over the inheritance of Sun Yat-sen and his "testament" is over the design for the new China to replace the old.

It includes the bitter break between the GMD and the CCP of April 12, 1927, when the United Front was shattered by the so-called counterrevolutionary coup staged by Chiang Kai-shek in Shanghai and the martyrdom of leading CCP officials, Li Dazhao, Chen Yannian, and other "proletarian" revolutionaries. Other events in the narrative stand out like so many stations of the cross including the Nanchang Uprising, the Autumn Harvest Uprising, the battles in the Jinggaan Mountains, the founding of the Jiangxi base, the forerunner of Yan'an, and the extermination campaigns by the Nationalists, the last of which results in the Long March and the "Xian Incident," in which Chiang Kai-shek is captured and forced to agree to the effective prosecution of the anti-Japanese war as the price of liberation. It is a story of heroics, sacrifices, and betrayals, and the testing of the limits of endurance of the Communists, who by surviving become purified and larger than life. China is thus transformed into a gladiatorial theater in which the two chief wrestlers become Mao and Chang, surrounded by their retinues and retainers. It is a drama full of the intensity of a wrestling match.

The third or short story is a passion play about the CCP. Its center piece is the rise of Mao Zedong to power despite internecine power struggles within the Party. It is a duel between Mao and his contenders. It begins in 1921 in Shanghai with the founding of the Communist Party itself. It is a dirty story, full of secrets, of intrigue and secret Comintern interventions. It includes the vicissitudes of Mao himself, his exile to Hunan, his role in the Jinggaan Mountains, his chairmanship of the Jiangxi base, and above all his coming to power during the Long March. It deals with the factional disputes within the CCP and which theoretical line will prevail. It ends with Mao leading the survivors into the light of the Yan'an.

The official founding of the CCP occurred in late July and early August of 1921. Even the meeting itself was the stuff good stories are made of. Interrupted by a spy, everyone was forced to flee from Shanghai. The last session was held on a hired boat on South Lake (Nan Hu) near Chiahsing where Chen Diuxiu, Zhang Guotao, and Li Da were elected members of the Central Committee, the first becoming Party Secretary, the second in charge of the organization, and the third in charge of propaganda.[36]

Thus the "founding" as an event has a dramatic episode inside it. The Party has a "miraculous birth," floating on the waters in a boat, the dry land around it a hostile sea, swarming with spies and enemies. The Party formed under such circumstances requires long evolution, like the egg of stone under the sea which eventually cracked and produced on land the people of China, "qualifying" the Party to act as the agent of history. Mao was present at the creation. But one comes to realize it showed the "tasks" he had to accomplish in order to win the right to become the agent of the Party.

This episode, the spy, the water, the dangerous terrain, the trials, and tasks are the conditions for Mao's own story of coming to power. It is a tale of overcoming in which not only does he defeat his enemies despite serious setbacks, he overcomes his ignorance of Marxism to triumph over those Russian-trained adepts who represented themselves as the real Marxist intellectuals. His story is also about the evolution of his thoughts.

Triumph includes the successful negotiation of intrigue and power struggles among rival contenders within a party whose clandestine character was established from the start. Like everyone else, Mao operated on two levels, above and below ground. In the first capacity he publicly proclaimed his objectives while in the second he pursued them on his own terms.

Such storytelling enabled the Communists to convert every defeat, retreat, and crisis point into a victory of some sort, a slight of hand, in which disasters become magical occasions, and failures superhuman accomplishments, a kind of magic realism matched by ruthlessness. But in the end, such fictive truths became self-fulfilling prophecies, enabling the Communists to become virtually miraculous in their own eyes.[37] Yet, to call such storytelling *fabrication* in the sense of lying is to trivialize it. Of course there was manipulation and machination. But to work on a collective level, storytelling must do more than tell a story. It must by the same token become an art form utilizing all the opportunities for dramatistic performance and embellishment which by its very nature it embodies. Among these is the significance of space as an identifiable and symbolically significant place for coming together, for the intersubjective communication of shared experiences, a function of orality first and writing later, of speaking first and modifying afterwards, the oracular pronouncement followed by the logical argument, of event as metaphor and theory as praxis. It is in the immediacy of the first that an initial lexigraphic system of dialectical thinking evolves, moving easily between classical references and sinified-Marxism, a praxis of developmental socialism which is textualized and *writ*-ualized.

ACKNOWLEDGMENTS

The research for this essay was done under a grant from the Committee for Scholarly Communication with the People's Republic of China and joint sponsorship of the Marxism-Leninism Mao Zedong Thought Institute of the Chinese Academy of Social Science and the Department of History, Beijing University. I am indebted especially to Professors Su Shaozhi and Luo Rongqu. Fieldwork was undertaken intermittently over a period from 1986–1989, coming to an abrupt end in Tiananmen Square on June 4, 1989. Much of the material here is drawn from interviews with survivors including military people, generals, political commissars, guerrilla commanders, and ordinary soldiers, as well as writers, teachers, artists, filmmakers, dancers, musicians, etc. Interviewing was done mainly in people's homes and by a group-interviewing method in which several people, mainly Chinese, shared in what became a lengthy discussion. Many people were interviewed several times, in which time the entire character and tone of the interview became richer. Much of the information on which this discussion is based is the joint product of Michelle Chua, Zhao Yi, Zhang Meng, and Song Xioping. They are not, of course, responsible for the present discussion.

ENDNOTES

[1]The term symbolic capital is, of course, Bourdieu's. But there are major differences between the way the term is being used here and the way Bourdieu uses it. For Bourdieu, symbolic capital is a highly organized and precisely valued set of nonmonetary exchanges. As with economic capital, value is exchanged for value. The relations of people are defined by the exchanges of symbolic capital, and the values of symbolic capital are realized through exchanges. The model is highly rationalistic and parallels that of a market. In the present usage, symbolic capital is an endowment. It is a fund of power on which to draw. See Pierre Bourdieu, *Outline of a Theory of Practice* (Cambridge: Cambridge University Press, 1977).

[2]See Jerome Bruner, "The Narrative Construction of Reality," *Critical Inquiry* 18 (1) (Autumn 1991): 1–21.

[3]Periodization of history had a particular resonance, oracular in tone. For example, Shang history (sixteenth century to eleventh century, B.C.) was divided into five periods based on oracular divination. See Benjamin I. Schwartz, *The World of Thought in Ancient China* (Cambridge, Mass.: Harvard University Press, 1985), 37.

[4]See Daniel Dennett, "Commandos of the Word," *The Times Higher Education Supplement* (London) (1012) (27 March 1992): 15, 19.

[5]Ibid.

[6]Collective individualism contrasts but is not entirely alternative to what political scientists refer to as methodological individualism as used by Olson, Elster, and others.

[7]There were plenty of precedents, both in the Soviet Union and in the Jiangxi base, in 1934; in the latter instance less to establish conformity than to rid the Party of GMD spies and others who had insinuated themselves into the Party including Chiang Kai-shek's notorious "AB" (Anti-Bolshevik) Squads.

[8]Any shrewd political leader knows that if an individual's private story varies substantially from the collective, it will be a false conveyance. Doubt will lurk underneath conviction.

[9]See Benedict Anderson, *Imagined Communities* (London: Verso, 1983).

[10]Such powers, once achieved, were regularized and made official in the form of organization codes. The continuing support of the Central Committee was absolutely essential for Mao, enabling him to play by the rules of the game while dominating those who made the rules.

[11]See Richard M. Dorson's forward to Wolfram Eberhard, *Folktales of China* (Chicago: University of Chicago Press, 1973), xviii.

[12]See Schwartz, *The World of Thought in Ancient China*, 65.

[13]See Joseph R. Levenson, *Confucian China and its Modern Fate* (Berkeley, Calif.: University of California Press, 1968).

[14]See Max Weber, *The Religion of China* (Glencoe, Ill.: The Free Press, 1951). See also Ibid.

¹⁵See Shi Nai'an and Luo Guanzhong, *Outlaws of the Marsh,* 4 vols. (Beijing: Foreign Languages Press, 1988).

¹⁶Or to put it in Claude Levi-Strauss's terms, "the raw and the cooked."

¹⁷Mao's stories were never freestanding. They were always worked into a more general argument. They served iconographic purposes; they cultivated an already existing visual imagery. Tailored to meet contemporary needs, the old stories were intermingled with the exploits of the party.

¹⁸See Mao Zedong, "Talks at the Yan'an Forum on Literature and Art" (1942), *Selected Works,* vol. 3 (Beijing: Foreign Language Publishers, 1985), 69–98.

¹⁹Repeated questioning on this point rarely produced disagreement. When asked, "Do you think Mao really believed that his own insights were so superior to others that it constituted a unique gift," with only one or two exceptions, people said yes. Some thought he was in this regard simplistic. Others believed that he was much shrewder than some of his associates, who were educated in France or in the USSR, gave him credit for.

²⁰A world of conspiracies, intrigues, murders, retributions, and mesalliances with the GMD, the Party inherited all the factional splits in the USSR: Stalin-Trotsky, Zinoviev, Rykov, Bukharin, the antiparty Rightists and Leftists. In addition to Soviet feuds, which became "sinicized" as swarms of Soviet agents descended on China especially after 1920, it had plenty of its own: Mao against Li Lisan, Mao against Wang Ming, Mao against Chang Guotao, etc. The Comintern agents made things worse. They helped to organize the CCP and the GMD. They permeated both. Following Soviet models of organizations, the structure of both the GMD and the CCP began to look very much alike in formal terms, at least at the top. At its second Party conference, the CCP built into its Party the cell system as the unit principle, making clandestinity a principle of Party organization. This similarity of structures combined with the fact that while the CCP joined the GMD, the latter did not join the CCP, became, especially given the larger prevailing political chaos, an invitation to internal intrigues and factional conflicts, the Soviet Union sometimes urging unity and sometimes playing both sides against the middle, depending on which Soviet line and agent prevailed at what time. So, for example, the Stalin-Trotsky conflict was superimposed on China, not to speak of other internecine struggles between anti-Rightist and anti-Leftist blocs in the Soviet Union. All these brought into the fledgling CCP terror and murder from the start.

²¹Joffe had great influence over Sun Yat-sen before the death of the latter. Both signed the joint Declaration of Association which signalized the beginning of the CCP and the GMD alliance in January of 1923.

²²While, of course, Mao's notion of peasant revolution contrasted strongly with Trotsky's emphasis on the proletariat as both the most functionally significant and enlightened sector of the class spectrum, Mao's notion of continuing revolution looked very much like Trotsky's notion of permanent revolution.

²³For a detailed description and documentation on this period, see C. Martin Wilbur and Julie Lien-ying How, *Documents on Communism, Nationalism, and Soviet Advisers in China 1918–1927* (New York: Columbia University Press, 1956). See

also Tso-liang Hsiao, *Power relations with the Chinese Communist Movement, 1930–1934* (Seattle: University of Washington Press, 1961).

24His wife, however, was severely wounded several times.

25Cited in Hayden White, *The Content of the Form* (Baltimore, Md.: The Johns Hopkins University Press, 1987), 44.

26Interview in Yan'an, 1986.

27As Stuart Schram, the leading expert on Mao's life and work, demonstrates, Mao's least noteworthy essays are those where he makes the greatest claims to theory, as, for example, in his lectures on dialectical materialism which are wooden, labored, and not very interesting, and over which Mao labored mightily, refusing to allow others to lecture on the subject. See Stuart R. Schram, *The Political Thought of Mao Tse-tung* (New York: Frederick Praeger, 1963), 56–70.

28Interview in Changsha, May 1986.

29Several interviewees remarked on Mao's language "musicality," not in sound but as a total performance including gestures: "his hands fluttered like birds."

30Mao Zedong, "Talks at the Yan'an Forum on Art and Literature," *Selected Works,* vol. 3 (Peking: Foreign Languages Press, 1967), 72–73.

31Ibid.

32See Walter Benjamin, "The Storyteller" in *Illuminations* (New York: Schocken Books, 1969), 102.

33Opium stands for poisoning the Chinese body politic, corrupting and destroying the social and moral fabric of society. It is not an accident that Mao's first published writing is on the relationship between physical and mental health and the need for Spartanism to purify and restore the collective health.

34For the analysis of the relations between mythic metaphors and logical metonymies, see David E. Apter and Nagayo Sawa, *Against the State* (Cambridge, Mass.: Harvard University Press, 1984).

35For an early interpretation of Mao as a "historian" and the "events" of which the story is composed, see Howard Boorman, "Mao Tse-tung as Historian" in Albert Feuerwerker, ed., *History in Communist China* (Cambridge, Mass.: MIT Press, 1968), 306–29.

36Prior to the formal founding of the CCP, Party branches had been set up a year earlier in Peking, Canton, Hupeh, Hunan, Shantung, Japan, and Paris.

37Insofar as the Party acts in the name of the people, Party members in Yan'an become agents in the overcoming project and in ways impossible as individuals acting on their own. By the same token, individual or autonomous acts such as terrorism, for example, were ruled out as opportunistic and nontheoretically based.

*Benjamin I. Schwartz*

# Culture, Modernity, and Nationalism— Further Reflections

I
N ALMOST ALL CURRENT DISCUSSIONS OF THE present situation in the East Asian cultural sphere, and of the "non-Western" world in general, there are two terms which seem to be unavoidable: "culture" and "modernity." Both categories are, of course, of modern Western origin, although I would be prepared to argue that in East Asian thought one can find concepts which resemble the modern Western cultural-anthropological concept of culture. The category of modernity, however, remains incorrigibly Western in most of its terms of reference. Any sustained scrutiny of the meaning of these terms will thus inevitably be highly Eurocentric and abstract. Those of us who use these terms—whether Westerners or East Asians—must continue to examine the latent assumptions which govern their use, despite the vast libraries of books which have been written on both terms. The question of where "the heart of the matter" lies remains unresolved.

To what kinds of entities or states of affairs do the terms culture and modernity refer? I discuss them together because, in an odd way, both categories present certain common semantic perplexities. In current discourse, both are often treated as closed totalities or wholes that subsume a wide variety of themes and components. They are often treated as wholes in the strongest possible ontological sense—almost as two physical objects which cannot occupy the same space. Occasionally, the prevailing metaphor is that of the static, unproblematically integrated "sys-

*Benjamin I. Schwartz is Leroy B. Williams Professor Emeritus of History and Political Science at Harvard University.*

tem." Sometimes the underlying metaphor is that of the biological organism. There are obvious differences between culture and modernity. "Primitive" and "traditional" cultures are treated as finished, static structures whose origins are lost in the mists of prehistory, while modernity is a kind of "turn" which emerges in the history of Western civilization in recent centuries. We have thus been able to observe not only its origins but its subsequent ongoing evolution in the "process of modernization"—a process which has been completed even now only in certain societies. Much of the discussion of modernity has in fact centered on the process of modernization. While the debates about the process and models of modernization rage on, modernity itself is nevertheless assumed to represent a final stable structure. It is like a mesa plateau whose ascent has been achieved by few, while others are still involved in the painful process of the ascent. Once achieved and globalized, it will constitute an essentially homogeneous "total state of affairs"—a kind of "end of history."[1] It can thus also be described as a closed, static totality.[2]

If culture and modernity do represent "wholes," they are wholes in a weak, unstable, and indeterminate sense, eminently open both to influences from without and to the effects of an unknown future. Not only may we find deep diachronic and synchronic tensions and conflicts among the components of the "system," but elements of the system—as in chemical compounds—may be quite detachable from the whole. Furthermore, these components, far from being unique and incommensurable, are often easily comparable to the components of other structures.

Without automatically accepting the fashionable authority of Jacques Derrida, it seems that there is much to be learned from some of his remarks on structures which claim to be holistic. He points out that any structure which claims some kind of internal coherence must have some center or underlying principle which governs the structure as a whole. In a highly-articulated rigid system, this central principle acts as an organizing core which tightly governs the play of elements within the system.

When I suggest that categories such as culture and modernity are in some sense wholes, they are so in a precarious and loose sense that is very much open to influences from the outside. In neither case is it easy to achieve any agreement on where the center or the heart of the whole resides. Furthermore, the question of how the parts relate to the whole, and to each other synchronically or diachronically, remains open to constant reexamination.

In this essay, I shall attempt to concretize some of the questions which have arisen in my efforts to struggle with both of these vast and unstable categories.

In dealing with the term "culture" in *The World of Thought in Ancient China*,[3] I chose to refer to what Derrida calls the "center of the structure"[4] as "persistent dominant orientations" of Chinese culture. Many have referred to a kind of "monistic" or "organismic" holism—the predilection for a notion of an all-embracing order which is pervasive in much of Chinese "high cultural" thought, and has even been internalized, up to a point, in the mentalities of the "popular culture." Others more particularly concerned with the sociopolitical aspects of Chinese culture have been deeply impressed by the "fusion of the political and cultural order" (*cheng chiao ho i*) which is not only implicit in most varieties of Chinese political thought but is strikingly apparent in the actual practice of the Chinese polity over centuries. Others have suggested different central principles. I use the word "orientations" in the plural since there is, of course, no agreement concerning which orientation provides the ultimate key or on how they relate to each other. Despite their pervasiveness and persistence, these orientations do not give rise to a static, integrated, and closed system. In their confrontation with the complexities of human experience, they give rise to diverse and even conflicting modes of reflective thought. They produce not an integrated harmony but ongoing *problématiques*. These *problématiques* were not resolved throughout the long history of China, even after "official Confucianism" had presumably won a clear ascendancy on the high cultural level.

I refer to dominant cultural orientations because one can in fact find (even on the level of high culture) the presence of deviant countertendencies which challenge the dominant orientations themselves. In texts such as the *Zhuangzi* and *Mozi*, one can find minority challenges both to the moral-spiritual claims of the political order and to the holistic-organismic bent of Chinese cosmology. On the level of popular culture and religion, one finds over the centuries both an internalization of the dominant orientations and a stubborn resistance to them.

I would also suggest that neither the dominant orientations nor the *problématiques* to which they gave rise are incommunicably unique or incommensurably "other." However different they may be, they relate to universally shared areas of human concern. Confucius' observations concerning the family and its function may be refracted through the medium of shared Chinese cultural orientations and Aristotle's observations through the shared ancient Greek cultural orientations. Yet, with all due respect for the formidable problems of translatability, they do in fact discuss communicable issues.

There may be some areas of experience within which different cultures are indeed irreducibly unique, particularly the sensual-aesthetic sphere. Chinese architecture, ancient bronze vessels, ceramics, painting, food, and dress may be unique, but they are hardly incommunicable. There are Westerners who may find East Asian landscape painting incommunicable, but the same individuals may find John Cage's music even more incommunicable.

If neither the dominant orientations nor the *problématiques* of East Asian culture are unique and "other," they are also not in principle hermetically sealed off against influences from outside the cultural orbit. I am referring not only to the diffusion of separate technologies and the borrowing of artistic motifs and forms, but even of fundamental ideas, despite the inertial resistance of long established cultural ideas and practices. Buddhism, as we know, was to have a profound impact on Chinese culture on the level of both high and popular cultural life. It made its impact during a period of internal crisis by relating to problem areas which were already present within the Chinese world. Again, I am not asserting that the total *problématique* of Theravada and Mahayana Buddhism as it had developed in India and Central Asia up until the second and third centuries corresponded to a totalistic *problématique* of Chinese thought. To many Chinese, however, it appeared that various aspects of Buddhism seemed to offer fresh and even novel approaches to concerns which had already been addressed within the culture. In its novel aspects it may have turned attention to other concerns which had not, in the perceptions of many, been adequately addressed in the dominant orientations of Chinese culture.[5] I am here, of course, positing the possibility of universal human concerns transcending the different cultural responses to such concerns. There are indeed vast problems of translatability in the broad meaning of the term. Yet the assertion that the Chinese could not possibly understand what was different in Buddhist texts is in my mind an unproven dogma. Also, it is quite clear that Buddhism in its various forms inevitably underwent adjustments to the environment of Chinese culture as a whole which had by no means been displaced by a total Buddhist culture. Yet, modern Chinese cultural nationalists, who lean very heavily on the Western metaphor of the notion of culture as a biological organism, will insist that China finally "digested" whatever was consumable by the Chinese organism, rejecting the foreign "Indian" elements. Others skeptical of this image might say that the absorption of Buddhism may have changed and complicated the very nature of the "organism" as a whole.

It need hardly be pointed out that certain extremely strong versions of cultural holism—particularly those concerned with "primitive" societies—have in the past devalued the significance of historic change. Claude Levi-Strauss, whose view of culture exalted the clear and invariant structures of primitive cultures both from an intellectual and a moral point of view, seemed reluctant to apply the very concept of culture to the large higher civilizations which have not escaped the vast disorganizing effects of historic change.

In the modest version of cultural holism which I am advocating, there is no necessary contradiction between the presence of persistent cultural orientations and the fact that China has had a long and significant history. Even if we ignore the undoubted effects of external forces, the fact is that the persistent orientations discussed above give rise not to closed, totally integrated structures but to unresolved *problématiques,* sharp historic changes, and even convulsive crises in intellectual, social, and political life. In the sphere of aesthetic and art history, the changes and innovations are indeed palpable and undeniable.

To many, this history is not significant since it does not lead to some of the crucial outcomes which we call modern. It is nevertheless interesting to note that within Chinese—particularly

Confucian—culture, one actually finds a deep concern with historic process even though this concern is not necessarily linked to a theory of inevitable progress.[6] Much of this historic concern involves an inquiry into why and how the actual course of history does or does not actualize the highest norms of the culture (often called the *Tao*) either in individual, familial, or social life. Often, to the extent that the history becomes a kind of intellectual history (as in Huang Zong-xi's history of schools of thought in the Ming dynasty, the "Ming-Ju xue-an"), we are also made aware of far-ranging controversies concerning the nature of the *Tao* itself, thus vividly illustrating the problematic nature of basic cultural orientations.

This acute awareness of the gap between culture as normative ideal and culture as it works itself out in historic actuality is in sharp contrast to the views of some cultural anthropologists who are not inclined to dwell on the discrepancy between "norm" and "actuality," as this is perceived even within the literature of the culture in question. In the case of "primitive" cultures where literary texts do not exist, it is generally assumed that the gap between the two is nonexistent. We, as outsiders, may find the norms totally unacceptable or even revolting, but there seems to be a widely accepted assumption that, whether good or bad, the norms are basically actualized—except perhaps for those individuals who are constitutionally incapable of fulfilling the requirements of the norms.

In fact, in the case of the higher civilizations, we find that during the ages in which these norms prevailed, both the cultural elites and the masses were often acutely aware of the gaps between professed norms and actual behavior. Indeed, my own unfashionable respect for some of the great books of the high cultural canon rests on the realization that what makes them great is not that they are rapturous enunciations of the inherited norms but that they often relate themselves in profound ways to the question of why the ideals are not fully or even partially realized. One may, of course, question both the norms of these great books and the analyses and diagnoses provided by the texts, but at least in such texts one is always aware of the gap between norms and actualities.

When we turn, however, to the apologetic defense of the culture of the past which we often find among modern cultural nationalists, we tend to see an overwhelming tendency both to minimize the synchronic and diachronic tensions and conflicts among norms within the culture and to avoid an account of the gaps (often clearly perceived within the culture of the past) between the norms and the actualities. Their need to assert their "national identity," whether in the mood of victims or victors, seems to require a basically unrelieved "happy story" in which the richness and complexity of the past is sacrificed for the image of the happily integrated whole.

When we turn to the totalistic conception of modernity we confront other problems. As already mentioned, modernity conceived of as a total structure is seen as a major turn in Western civilization over the last few centuries. The question of the relationship of this turn to the Western culture of the past remains a matter of ongoing dispute. One view is that modernity as a total state of affairs represents a qualitative break with the traditional Western society of the past—a break which is in essence so radical that it amounts to nothing less than a Cartesian "beginning from scratch." To others, the turn would have been inconceivable without the presence of certain powerful predispositions already present in the Western past. To those who stress the radical qualitative break with the past, the basic antithesis is not between Western culture and other cultures but between traditional society and modern society. Here, the basic metaphor is that of the growth of the biological organism. Presumably all the civilizational cultures of mankind, like all "normal" biological individuals, traverse a certain unilinear path of growth and development. On the whole, many intellectuals in non-Western cultures who have come to accept the universal validity of modernity tend to prefer the unilinear tradition/modernity dichotomy to the notion of essential cultural difference—a notion which seems to imply innate cultural superiority. Premodern Western society was after all no less "traditional" than any other. The fact remains that this view hardly mitigates the problem of cultural arrogance. If the West was the first society to achieve the full breakthrough to modernity, one must ask why this is so. If one does not have the problem of cultural superiority, one does have the problem of arrested (or retarded) development.

The weaker and more problematic versions of both culture and modernity here proposed may make it possible to avoid these stark alternatives. The modern turn in the West may indeed draw on certain predispositions which were most strongly developed in the premodern West. It thus may indeed be true that the scientific revolution of the sixteenth and seventeenth centuries drew heavily on both the pre-Socratic and the Platonic strains of ancient Greek thought. Yet, the same scholars who would support this contention would emphasize the fact that Aristotelian rationalism was not particularly favorable to the perspectives of the scientific revolution. Within the larger *problématique* of premodern Western culture, there existed tendencies both favorable and unfavorable to the emergence of the total configuration of the scientific revolution.

By the same token, it is by no means impossible that many of the predispositions which were to play a role in the modern turn in the West were also present in greater or lesser degrees in other cultures. Thus, there is no reason to deny that the slow premodern economic growth from a basically natural agrarian economy to a more commercialized, more monetarized, and more urban economy did take place in China without, as both Marx and Weber have suggested, *necessarily* leading to the total configuration of a modern industrial economy. The same can be said of the premodern progress of mechanical invention, of bureaucratic "rationalism," and even of certain modes of "individualism." It now appears that many social and cultural habits and predispositions often associated with Confucianism have proved in actuality to be favorable to the project of economic modernization in East Asia in the twentieth century. The question remains whether the major orientations of Chinese culture would themselves have led to the modern Western overwhelming obsession with economic and technological rationalization.

This, however, still leaves us with a question: What is the center or the heart of that whole which we call modernity? To many, the heart of the matter is, in fact, the scientific revolution and/or the economic/technological rationalization. However, there are others more oriented to questions of social ethics for whom the liberation of the individual from all authority both human and supernatural is central. Some see the equalization of all human conditions as the ultimate promise of modernity. Others may point to the dominant role which modern secular nationalism has played and continues to play within the mix of factors which we call modern. On the level of philosophic and religious thought, there are those who stress that science has totally reincorporated the human into the reductionist universe of Darwinian biology or of particle physics, while others see a radical disjuncture between the human and nonhuman realms. Whether the essence of the human lies in the human subject, in culture, in the social system, in language, or in the historic process, the human's total being is primarily shaped by forces operative within an anthropocentric realm. It is a curious fact that both of these utterly contradictory visions can be derived from the paradoxical dualism of Cartesian thought.

The effort to comprehend the interrelations of these factors has been undertaken by a variety of ideologies ever since the eighteenth century. "Individualism" itself assumes a multitude of forms ranging from Immanuel Kant's conception of moral autonomy, to the romantic individualism of the nineteenth century, to the economic individualism of the classical economists. The relations of individual liberty to equality remains a matter of continuous debate. The relationship of economic and technological growth to what might be called the social-ethical dimensions of modernity has been fiercely debated in a host of divergent ideologies from conflicts between Rousseau and the philosophes until the present.

At the moment, with the seeming retreat of the radical antiliberal outlooks of communism and fascism which had won such a position of prominence for much of this century, there has been the resurgence in the West of the older liberal (in the broadest sense) conviction that the heart of modernity is to be found in the combination of constitutional democracy and market capitalism, although the question of the relationship between the two has by no means been resolved.

The notion that at the heart of modernity lies an absolutist dichotomy between "individualism and collectivism" has made it plausible to describe the entire antiliberal wave of the mid-twentieth century as a throwback to premodernity. Yet, there are excellent reasons to doubt whether the individualism/collectivism antithesis is the central shared orientation of modernity. To Max Weber, the heart of modernity lay in the processes of rationalization which involved not only the economic but the political, military, and legal orders as well. It is true that in his account of the origins of capitalism in *The Protestant Ethic,*[7] Weber concentrates on the inner life of individuals. Yet, in his more general discussion of rationalization in the fields of politics, and the economics of "capitalism" as an ongoing concern, the emphasis tends to fall very much on the rationalization of large collective organizations, and on what he unenthusiastically called the bureaucratization of modern society. The absolute states of the early modern period were thus not simply extensions of premodern feudalism but had in many ways prepared the groundwork of rationalization in many areas of social life.

In the 1930s and 1940s, there were many brilliant people in the West who saw the very culmination of economic rationality in the Stalinist leadership of the Soviet Union. Rationality was not to be found in the immanent forces of the market system but in the minds of rational social engineers who would not only create a more dynamic economy but also realize the eminently modern ideals of social and economic equality. Fascism and Nazism had elevated the modern phenomenon of nationalism to the level of a kind of modern religion of societal solidarity. To the extent that both were in their ascendancy, both found support in the modern historicist notion of the inevitable "wave of the future."

The basic suggestion here is that the radically antiliberal ideologies and movements of the twentieth century were not a throwback to premodernity despite the Nazi appeals to the mythical past of the German *Volk* and despite Mussolini's invocation of the glories of ancient Rome. Marxist-Leninist communism was in its professed doctrine resolutely modern and future-oriented.

If one can speak here of a culture of modernity, we find that, as in the traditional cultures, its central orientations, whatever they may be, have given rise to a vast and by no means completely resolved *problématique*. One crucial aspect of this *problématique* is the fact that the nation-state societies which have emerged within the precincts of modernity, such as France, Germany, and the United States, have produced highly diverse subcultures of their own. We also find that it is by no means easier to define the term "modernity" in wholly normative terms of good and evil than it is to define traditional cultures in such terms. If fascism and communism were indeed modern phenomena, we cannot allow ourselves to be detached completely from the evils of these modern societies, including the enormities of both fascism and Marxist-Leninist communism, anymore than we can accept the entirely "happy stories" of tradition-oriented cultural nationalists.

I shall not venture here to provide an answer to the question of where the heart of modernity lies. Certainly, the scientific revolution and Max Weber's notion of the unlimited "rationalization" of every sphere of social, economic, and political life immediately come to mind. Yet, what I would point to here is not so much the direct effects of these developments but the philosophic perspectives with which they are associated—particularly, the radical post-Cartesian disjuncture between the human realm conceived of as totally encapsulated within itself and a nonhuman realm to which we relate only in theoretical, scientific, and technological terms. It seems that it is this perspective which has made possible the entire Faustian thrust of the modern world and which has deeply affected every other aspect of modern culture. How this perspective relates to the more purely socioethical aspects and nationalist aspects of modernity remains a question of unresolved complexity.

At this moment, it may indeed be appropriate to focus attention more closely on that particularly problematic strand of modernity which has been called nationalism. While the presumption is now widespread that market economy and democracy have gained a decisive victory over communism, we are acutely aware of the resurgence of nationalism in many parts of the world. Indeed, despite all the talk of globalization, it is by no means dead in the very heart of the "industrial democracies" themselves.

If nationalism is a strand of modernity, it remains one of the most problematic and elusive strands. Among many of those who tend to define modernity in terms of a total break with the reactionary culture and histories of the past, the tendency among many cultural nationalists to exalt the national culture and history is often regarded as a simple manifestation of an antimodern traditionalism. Yet some of the most recent books on nationalism such as Ernest Gellner's *Nations and Nationalism*[8] and Benedict Anderson's *Imagined Communities*[9] emphasize the modernity of nationalism. As in the past, however, there is little agreement on where the heart of its modernity lies.

Perhaps one of the more positive aspects of the entire postmodern development is that we are now no longer so inclined to dismiss an entire area of discourse because of the absence of an exhaustive definition which demands total consensus. While my own perception of where the heart of the matter lies may be no more accurate than many others, I would agree with those who accept the reality of nationalism. I would also agree that it belongs to the complex of modernity. Again, however, as in the case of the other strands which enter into the complex of modernity, I see no need to posit a total rupture between the modern and the premodern. Nationalism may in fact draw on many factors and predispositions which can be found in the Western past as well as in the history of other cultures.

Because of the incorporation of the word "nation" in the term nationalism, there are many who believe that the definition of nationalism is very much dependent on the preexistence of entities defined as nations. Some also insist that the nation itself is a peculiarly modern creation. I would nevertheless suggest that entities which in many ways resemble what we now call nations or even nationalities or ethnic groups are to be found in many times and places. They are not exclusively modern. In the Hebrew Bible we find reference to groups such as Edomites, Moabites, and Midianites who are often referred to as *goyim,* a word which has frequently been translated as "nations." Is this translation justified? In fact, they do share many of the attributes which we often ascribe to nations. There is often the shared assumption of common kinship origins, of a shared intelligibility of language. They frequently occupied given territories and were governed by their own polities. They may have shared cultural traits with their neighbor but were also often marked by their own subcultural traits, and often had their own patron deities. They probably perceived themselves as belonging to a kind of multinational world made up of comparable entities with which they were involved in competitive and agonic relationships.

It would appear that such rudimentary nations also existed at various times in ancient and medieval India and in China during the "Warring States" period. It may be argued that such regional, sociopolitical entities were basically states rather than nations in any full-bodied sense of the term, yet in rough ways they often related to regional, cultural, and linguistic differences. Such regional states were perhaps more like the dynastic monarchies of late medieval and early modern Europe. If we bear in mind Ernest Barker's somewhat extreme and unqualified statement that "historically the state precedes the nation; it is not the nations which make states; it is states which create nations,"[10] it may not be fanciful to think of the states of Lu, Chu, and Qin in "Warring States" China as in some sense nations. It nevertheless remains a fact that neither in India nor in China did such rudimentary nation-state formations become "terminal communities." While they operated within a kind of de facto competitive multistate order, such an order never became institutionalized as a normative order. In the Near East as well, we find that many of the nations mentioned in the Bible disappeared without a trace into the Assyrian, Persian, and Hellenistic universal empires.

This fact forcibly reminds us that even if something resembling nations existed in the premodern world, in many parts of that world they confronted the more formidable model of the "universal" empire conceived of as continuous with the ecumene of a universally conceived higher civilization. The polity of such empires is often envisioned as a unique polity of civilization culminating in a universal state and incommensurable with any "barbarian" polity. The relationship between the universal civilization and the polity differed markedly in all these empires. Indeed, in the case of ancient Greek civilization one would have to say that during the classical age of the city-state, there was a complete disjuncture between the Panhellenic civilization and the plural nature of the local polities. It is only in Alexander's empire that polity and civilization become united. Yet, however different, they all seem to share a profound consciousness of the crucial nature of the divide between the realm of civilization and the realm of the barbarian. It was a way of conceiving the "other" which probably differed markedly from the way in which the Moabite regarded the otherness of the Midianite.

It should nevertheless be noted at this point that in a most stimulating essay recently written by Prasenjit Duara, professor of modern Chinese history at the University of Chicago,[11] we find a striking challenge both to the view that premodern China was not a nation and even to the view that the term nationalism cannot be applied, at least to some extent, to premodern China.

In making these assertions, Duara raises some very pertinent questions about the formula "from culturalism to nationalism" which has often been used to describe at least one salient aspect of modern China's evolution. While the word nationalism seems to imply the notion of a nation as the social bearer of nationalism, the word culturalism almost seems to imply that China was maintained only by the disembodied essence of a culture. The Chinese themselves, as Duara asserts, remain convinced that Chinese culture was always maintained by a tangible politicosocial bearer clearly marked off from other politicosocial entities. In choosing to call this entity a nation, Duara refuses to accept the theories of Gellner and Anderson who insist on the modernity not only of nationalism but even of the nation. In Duara's words, they insist that "national identity is a radical novel form of consciousness."[12] In their view, it is only in the modern nation "that people from various locales could imagine themselves as part of a single community."[13] Both Gellner and Anderson attribute this either to the rise of industrial economy as such or to what Anderson calls the rise of a "print capitalism" which created the horizontal, densely interconnected communities of the national society.[14] In contrast, we are led to believe that in premodern societies the illiterate masses were barely conscious of the larger cultural and political structures with which they were involved. Duara is quite right when he attacks this overdrawn contrast. In China there were complex relations between the political, cultural, and economic networks and "the widespread presence of common cultural ideas which linked the state to communities and sustained the polity." What he says concerning China may be equally true of the Roman Empire, of India, and even of medieval Europe. My main objection lies in his insistence that any political community thus constituted must be called a nation. The nonliterate inhabitants of the Roman Empire were, on the whole, quite aware that they were part of the Roman imperial political order and of what they regarded as high civilization. In the parlance of the average premodern Chinese, the phrase *tian-xia* (under Heaven) as a way of referring to the ecumene of civilization to which he belonged was much more common than any term which might be called ethnic. The same was true for the religiously based Islamic civilization despite the early collapse of its universal polity.

Duara, however, not only asserts that premodern China was a "self-conscious political community" (and thus in his view a nation) but in some of its aspects might be called nationalistic. Some Chinese have over the centuries defined their differences from others not simply in terms of a superior universal culture which might conceivably be internalized by others but in terms of something like a built-in "racial" superiority based on irreducible geographic, climatic, and even biological factors. In later centuries, it became common among some to refer to Chinese culture as the culture of the "Han" people. It thus sees the culture as the outgrowth of a natural ethnicity.[15] This is indeed a theme which can be linked to Johann Gottfried von Herder's concept of the nation as a kind of primordial natural growth which engenders its own national culture.[16] In the West, this theme could be linked to the benign version of nationalism which accepts the essential equality of all national cultures. In the case of the Chinese "protonationalist" Wang Fu-zhih, however, it by no means shook his profound convictions concerning the objective and unique superiority of Chinese civilization over barbarian cultures. In sum, while accepting Duara's critique of the concept of "culturalism" and his focus on protonationalist themes in premodern China, I believe that nationalism nevertheless represents a fundamental "turn" in modern Chinese culture.

Finally, in seeking anticipations of modern nationalism in premodern societies, something must be said concerning the ancient Greek city-state, which bequeathed to later ages a most vivid and tangible embodiment of the idea of patriotism as a sentiment binding individuals to the city envisioned as an almost palpable organism. Here, we find the image of the city as a kind of terminal community and supreme focus of loyalty as well as the fact that, in effect, these polities were conceived of as competitive actors in a multistate arena. In the West, this model exercised its fascination for many centuries. The effort to apply this model of what might be called the city-state protonationalism of ancient Greece to the large territorial state of modern Europe produced its own dilemmas.

In surveying some of these premodern anticipations of nationalism, we have not yet answered the question: What is modern about nationalism? If we assume that a truly modern nationalism came into being sometime during the late eighteenth and early nineteenth centuries, it may be highly relevant to examine the rise of the territorial states of early modern Europe. While it may be true that something like nations, nationalities, or ethnic groups existed long before modern times, it is a fact that these states, which witnessed the rise of many other aspects of modernity, also created the most vividly articulated and full-bodied image of the nation which has ever existed. They strongly promoted the official vernacular language, fostered the notion of a national high culture, affirmed the idea of the supreme sovereignty of the secular nation-state, and played a crucial role to the extent that they could in promoting the kind of early industrial development so much stressed by Ernest Gellner. It was also in this period that the multistate system became more or less institutionalized as a normative legal state of affairs. While it may be true that most of these states were ruled by dynastic monarchies whose concepts of dynastic interests may not have always coincided with what might be regarded as national interests, it was the nation which became their fundamental base of operation. Again, while they may have based their legitimacy on the divine right of kings, in the vast controversies over the jurisdiction of the sacred and secular power which marked late medieval Europe, the kings represented the secular even when, in the theories of Marsiglio and Bodin, they claimed their power directly from God. It may also be true, as Isaiah Berlin insists, that Herder's decidedly nonpolitical eighteenth-century version of the nation as the embodiment of *Volksgeist* was to become a crucial aspect of later nationalism. It was, however, combined in the early nineteenth century with a decidedly political German nationalism. One reason why the French Revolution is often cited as the birthplace of modern nationalism is because it (and also the American Revolution) shed a clear light on the ambiguities of the words *Volk* and people. The people as the collectivity of the oppressed in confrontation with the oppressing ruling classes speedily becomes the people as a collective subject or collective organism regarded as the bearer of such clearly national attributes as common national language and national culture. It was only natural that "people" in this sense should achieve their own political expression and independence. We thus find that in the era of nationalism, almost all nations, whatever the nature of their polity, tend to claim to derive their sovereignty from the people.

It is in the light of such consideration that I find that my own tentative view on the question of where the modernity of nationalism lies tends to be somewhat close to that of Anderson in *Imagined Communities* (despite my disagreements with many aspects of his book). Anderson maintains that in an age in which cosmically rooted religion has declined, nationalism has provided a quasi-religious center of meaning for vast multitudes. Its primary significance does not lie in its supposedly instrumental, functional role. The nation is not only a collective subject realizing its collective destiny over the course of history. It is a kind of immanent deity emerging wholly out of the human realm which is able to provide present meanings to those who participate in its radiant sphere. To many, it provides the sense of grandeur, glory, honor, and feeling of connectedness with some more ultimate state of affairs—feelings of transcendent loyalty and gratitude otherwise absent in their lives. Whatever Marxists may say about "false consciousness," to the members of great successful nations it provided the sense of participation (on however humble a level) in the glory and power of one's country. To those who consider themselves members of victim nations or ethnicities, it lends a transcendent dimension to their fears, hatreds, and desires for revenge.

As many recent writers on nationalism have pointed out, nationalism as the religion of the nation does not really require the long historic preexistence of ready-made nations. Once the nationalist model of the nation is posited, the model of nationhood can come to be adopted by a variety of collective actors. The administered territories arbitrarily created by colonial powers in Africa can become the focus of nationalisms built up around the state structures left by colonial administrators. This again, however, reminds us of Barker's view that even in Europe "states created nations." In the case of Japan, the premodern polity and even culture easily adapted to the religion of nationalism. In China and India, there have been major efforts to convert universal communities into nations. Nations controlling multiethnic empires have both attempted to absorb subject communities into the national religion and also attempted to keep them out. As we can see, the question of what kind of community will or will not constitute a nation still remains unresolved. For a time it seemed that the Soviet Union, although it was a multiethnic empire, was nevertheless eminently a nation in the full nationalist sense which could draw on a large reservoir of "Soviet patriotism." The same was true of Yugoslavia. We thus find that within the nationalist dispensation, it is most difficult to predict the history of what groups will or will not come to provide the nucleus of nationhood.

In focusing here on nationalism, it has not been my intention to maintain that it is a strand which can be considered in isolation from the entire complex of modernity. On the contrary, it has, of course, from the outset been intimately entangled in complex and even paradoxical ways with all the other aspects of modernity as well as with the premodern cultures of the past.

We have spoken of nationalism as a quasi-religion not necessarily instrumental to other goals. Yet, there can be no doubt that what attracted the eye of many in the non-Western world to the powerful nation-states of the West was the entirely unprecedented growth in the wealth and power of these states. Indeed, the fact that they were all more or less equivalent entities striving with each other in a battle for ascendancy as well as the more ominous fact of the inability of others to compete with them in this Darwinian agon led to a concentrated attention on the power of nationalism as an organizing and mobilizing force.

The relationship of nationalism to the more universalistic ideologies and values of the modern West—to all the varieties of liberalism, socialism, scientific humanism, and romanticism—has been most complex and entangled from the very start. In the abstract, the quasi-religion of the love of one's nation can be conceived of as a highly particularistic love requiring no transcendental claims to the possession of universal truths or values. In fact, of course, modern nations have claimed to be the bearers of universal truths and values such as the American way of life, or the Soviet model of socialism, or the civilizing mission of French culture. Again, there is the Janus-like aspect of nationalism which leads some to believe that the flourishing and power of the nation requires a radical rupture with the premodern past and others to feel that a high sense of national identity requires a devotion to and pride in the culture of the past. This does not necessarily mean that all commitments to either the culture of the past or to modern universal values always tend to serve the national interest or reinforce the sense of national identity. Many Americans genuinely believe that aspects of the American political experience may be of universal relevance. There are also Chinese who deeply believe that aspects of the Chinese cultural tradition may be of universal human value. To the integral nationalist, however, the universalistic cultural claims, whether modern or traditional, are clearly functional to the promotion of the national communal interest or the enhancement of national pride. His view tends to be indiscriminately holistic and celebratory.

Despite the recent resurgence of nationalism in large parts of the world, the question of its long-term fate as an aspect of modernity remains an open question. We are aware of the predictions of those who maintain that it will soon be overwhelmed by the leveling effect of economic and technological globalization. Yet, we are also aware that the notion that nationalism is an anachronism within the world of modernity was already widely held among the classical economists of the early nineteenth century.

The point to be reemphasized is that modernity does not represent an end of history in either the West or the non-West. In the course of its transactions with other cultures, many separate aspects of the modern "turn" have indeed been globalized even though the *problématiques* internal to modernity have not yet been resolved either in the West or in other culture areas. Nor have we yet seen any conclusion of the transactions between modernity and all the cultural experiences of the past.

ENDNOTES

¹There is, to be sure, the entire "postmodern" movement in the West which claims to have gone beyond the boundaries of modernity. Much depends here on how one defines the "central principles" of modernity. In my view, the postmodern movement still operates within the boundaries of modernity.

²It may seem strange to speak of modernity as a fixed, stable structure, since some aspects of modernity such as the notion of unlimited technological and economic growth suggest constant change. It is often implied, however, that such change represents quantitative growth within a stable culture of modernity.

³Benjamin Schwartz, *The World of Thought in Ancient China* (Cambridge, Mass.: The Belknap Press of Harvard University Press, 1985).

⁴Some of Jacques Derrida's reflections on the nature of closed structures are extraordinarily illuminating. See Jacques Derrida, "Structure, Sign and Play," in Jacques Derrida, *Writing and Difference* (Chicago, Ill.: University of Chicago Press, 1978), 278–80.

⁵While the impact of Buddhism is often thought of as affecting mainly the conscious level of Chinese life, the totally novel institution of the monastery was to have a profound effect on the sociopolitical history of later centuries.

⁶Here again one may find some strains of historic thought which suggest some notion of progress and even "Buddhist-Taoist" views which suggest an ultimate eschatology.

⁷Max Weber, *The Protestant Ethic and the Spirit of Capitalism*, trans. Talcott Parsons (London: Unwin Hyman, 1989).

⁸Ernest Gellner, *Nations and Nationalism* (Ithaca, N.Y.: Cornell University Press, 1983).

⁹Benedict Anderson, *Imagined Communities, Reflections on the Origins and Spread of Nationalism* (London: Verso, 1983).

¹⁰Ernest Barker, *National Character and the Factors in its Formation* (London: Methuen, 1927), 15.

¹¹Prasenjit Duara, "De-constructing the Chinese Nation," *Australian Journal of Chinese Affairs* (30) (July 1993).

¹²Ibid., 6.

¹³Ibid.

[14]Anderson, *Imagined Communities,* chap. 3.

[15]Ironically, the word "Han" refers not to an ethnicity but to an identification with the glories of the Han dynasty which provided the model of the later imperial state.

[16]See Isaiah Berlin, *Vico and Herder: Two Studies in the History of Ideas* (New York: Viking Press, 1976), 145–216.